# The Urban Prospect

# BOOKS BY LEWIS MUMFORD

# THE
# URBAN
# PROSPECT

# Lewis Mumford

A Harvest/HBJ Book
Harcourt Brace Jovanovich
New York and London

Library of Congress Catalog Card Number: 68-20631
Printed in the United States of America

HIJ

ISBN  0-15-693201-6

'Quarters for an Aging Population' was first printed
as 'For Older People—Not Segregation but Integration' and
'Landscape and Townscape' as 'The Social Function of Open Spaces.'
The article 'Home Remedies for Urban Cancer'
appeared originally in *The New Yorker* as 'Mother
Jacobs' Home Remedies for Urban Cancer.'

During the last thirty years there has been a dramatic eruption of books about cities—their nature, their forms, their planning, their deterioration and renewal, their probable future. Despite this growing interest, our cities have been going steadily from bad to worse; and many of the achievements in urban renewal that officialdom is wont to boast about—from urban expressways to governmentally subsidized high-rise housing—have only hastened the pace of metropolitan disintegration, random suburban dispersal, regional spoilage. Since most of the essays and papers in this book were written during the last half-dozen years, they focus on the contemporary city; and their main purpose was not to expose defects and failures, but to open up happier prospects for urban development. Today everyone at last realizes that our cities are in trouble. This has impelled me to make a fresh diagnosis of that trouble in the three final chapters. So it is important to realize that this diagnosis was first published, in all essentials, more than forty years ago. That is my passport to the future.—L. M.

Amenia, New York
Spring, 1968

# Contents

# Preface:

# The Fourth Migration

In a period of flow, men have the opportunity to remold themselves and their institutions. The great migrations that swept over Europe in the past; the migrations that surged past the water-boundaries of Europe and crawled through the formidable American wilderness—these great tides of population, which unloosed all the old bonds, have presented such an opportunity. To some of us it seems that in America we are in the midst of another such tidal movement of population—and for convenience, we have called it the Fourth Migration.

Historically, there are two Americas: the America of the settlement and the America of the migrations. The first America consists of the communities that were planted on the seaboard and up the river valleys during the seventeenth and eighteenth centuries. By 1850 these communities had achieved their maximum development; they had worked out a well-rounded industrial and agricultural life, based upon the fullest use of their regional resources through the water-wheel, mill, and farm, and they had created that fine provincial culture, humbly represented in the schools, universities, lyceums, and churches, which came to a full efflorescence in the scholarship of Motley, Prescott, Parkman and

Marsh, and in the literature of Emerson, Thoreau, Melville, Whitman and Poe.

The second America is the America of the internal migrations; the first migration that cleared the land west of the Alleghenies and opened the continent, the work of the land pioneer; the second migration, that worked over this fabric a new pattern of factories, railroads, and dingy industrial towns, the bequest of the industrial pioneer; and finally— and this brings us down to the present period—there is the America of the third migration, the flow of men and materials into our financial centers, the cities where buildings and profits leap upward in riotous pyramids. These three migrations have covered the continent and knitted together its present framework; and our efforts to promote social welfare, to 'make crooked cities straight,' and to conduct industries efficiently are based for the most part on the notion that this framework is complete and satisfactory—and final.

But the mold of America has not been set: we are again in another period of flow, caused like the flows of the past by new industrial methods, new wants and necessities, and new ideals of life, and we have before us the great adventure of working out a new pattern so that the fourth migration will give to the whole continent that stable, well-balanced, settled, cultivated life which grew out of its provincial settlement. We can hinder this tidal change and rob ourselves of its potential benefits by adjusting our plans to the forces that were dominant in the recent past; or we can remold our plans and guide our actions in terms of a more desirable future. This alternative goes down to the very roots of social philosophy. John Dewey has implicitly warned us of the fallacy of the first attitude; for in dealing with social facts that lie in the future, our hypothesis and our working plan are among the elements that determine the outcome. The articles that follow uncover a new set of facts and present a fresh set of alternatives, which seek not to create the fourth migration—that is already under way—but to guide it into positive and fruitful channels.

In order to put the fourth migration in perspective, let us consider briefly the three great movements of population which every civilization in Europe has experienced at some time in its history. In America this experience was crowded into the short space of a little more than a century; and these three movements had certain peculiar characteristics which left their mark on our landscape and our life.

The first migration was the clearing of the continent; and its symbol was the covered wagon. Before the Revolutionary War America was in reality a fringe of Europe: here was a Biblical 'city of refuge,' there a penal colony, and in another place an experimental society. From the close of the war the colonists found themselves bound by an unprecedented urge to take possession of the continent; and the history of the pioneers is the history of restless men who burned the forests of the Mohawk Valley in order to plant farms, who shifted into the soft glacial deposits of Ohio in order to cleave their plows through its rich soil; men who grabbed wheat land and skinned it, who grabbed urban sites and 'turned them over'; who staked out railway lines, sometimes strategically, like the Lehigh, and sometimes stupidly, like the Erie, in a mad scramble to cover the continent.

During the period from 1790 to 1890, when almost the last good free lands were disposed of, the farmers and loggers and miners of the country lived symbolically, if not actually, in the covered wagon. The little communities that clustered about the mine or the railway station were towns and villages only by courtesy of the census taker: they lacked the traditional resources of a common life—their games, their religious revivals, their intellectual stimuli, were all of the crudest. Pleasure never interfered with the 'business' of the early pioneer; because business *was* his pleasure. The gospel of work needed no Carlyle for preacher in pioneer America.

It is conceivable that the first migration might have been made soberly; that there might have been a consistent prospecting for good sites, an attempt to sort out the newcomers by directing them to the type of land and community they needed, and an effort to secure stable farming and a sound exploitation of resources. The 'necessity' for opening the continent swiftly was largely mythical: it was, in all probability, a rationalization of the land-hungry European. All these better methods were, perhaps, conceivable; but as things stood, they didn't come to pass; and ever since 1890 we have been feeling the effects of the disorderly first migration: the butchered forests; farms gone to ruin or into a ruinous system of tenantry; villages so sterile that they drive all their ambitious or sensitive young people to the big towns. The conservation movement is a belated attempt to repair the evils of the first migration, and to use the land and its resources with some respect for their permanent productive capacity. Its chief weakness is that, in protest against our misuse of the remaining resources, it tends to be negative, and is only beginning to develop a consistent regional program for their proper social use and development. As conservation passes out of this negative state, it tends to find common cause with the rural side of regional planning. But this is to anticipate.

The second great flow of population in America was from the countryside and from foreign countries into the factory town; the covered wagon gave way to the iron horse. Up to 1820 the chief concentration of people had been in the trading centers of the seaboard and the river junctures. With the introduction of steam power, factories were erected in places where power, as in the mill towns of Pennsylvania, or factory hands, as in the seaports, seemed most available. Cleveland in 1820, Columbus in 1830, and Chicago in 1840, with the rapid growth of all the industrial towns in the industrial expansion of the Civil War, tell a graphic tale of the westward march of men and manufactures.

The conditions that determined this flow of population were narrowly industrial: a city was considered solely as a place of work and business opportunity. That children need a chance to play and grow, that families need decent shelter and privacy and a few amenities, that learning and culture are worth encouraging for their own sake—these things were too often forgotten and ignored by the men who fostered the new industrialism. The result is familiar, and there is scarcely a town with more than ten thousand people and a working population which will not serve for example. Homes blocked and crowded by factories; rivers polluted; factories and railway yards seizing sites that should have been preserved for recreation; inadequate homes, thrown together anyhow, for sale anyhow, inhabited anyhow. The result was called prosperity in the census reports, but that was because no one tried to strike a balance between the private gains and the social losses.

To offset the depletions and dilapidations of the second migration, a special kind of 'conservation' was instituted. The housing movement began in New York when a group of public-spirited citizens discovered that vice, crime, and disease were largely by-products of an impoverished and congested environment. City planning came later. Meanwhile in every industrial center remedial agencies from soup kitchens to building and loan associations, from social settlements to employment bureaus, have been endeavoring to supply, partly from private means, the necessary civic facilities for living and enjoyment that were left out in the growth and expansion of the industrial town.

On certain sides the deficit has been terrific; scarcely any large town founded before 1880 has attempted to house the whole community with a respectable minimum of light, air, garden space, and playgrounds, to say nothing of parks and access to open country; and although a great part of mechanical industry is burdened with overproductivity—which it recovers from by periodic shutdowns at the expense of the workers—it waited the suggestion of Peter Kropotkin, and the technical innovations of Henry Ford, actually to hold out the prospect of an environment in which industrial idleness might be bridged over by a certain sustaining minimum of agricultural labor. In short, if the first migration denuded the country of its natural resources, the second migration ruthlessly cut down and ignored its human resources. This, too, is the history of a wasted opportunity. With every chance to begin afresh, the industrial revolution in America reproduced—if we ignore a few isolated villages—all the bad characteristics of industrialism in Europe. Dickens' Coketown duplicated itself in Pittsburgh, Chicago, St. Louis, Newark, Bridgeport, or where you please.

The magnet of the third migration was the financial center. As the industrial system developed in America productive effort came to take second place to financial direction, and in the great consolidations of industry that began in the eighties, in the growth of banking and insurance facilities in the nineties, and in the development of advertising for the purpose of securing a national market, which got under way in the present century, the sales and promotion departments have absorbed, directly or indirectly, a large part of the population.

The greatest concentration in all these departments took place, of course, in New York, whose overseas connections put it into a peculiarly strategic position; but within the past generation a similar development has taken place in the regional sub-metropolises, that is to say, in the twelve cities which now have a nominal population of over five hundred thousand and in most cases an actual population, when suburban areas are considered, of over a million. With the

exception of New York, which controls very largely the jour-
nalism, banking, insurance, and advertising of the whole
country, and of Chicago, which operates similarly in the
Middle West, these sub-metropolises—as a glance at their
position will show—are really regional centers whose natural
growth has received an additional stimulus from these peculiar financial opportunities.

The third migration has resulted in a steady drain of goods,
people, and pecuniary resources from the industrial towns
and villages of the earlier migrations, and along with it the
new sub-metropolises have acquired cultural resources which
the rest of the country has lacked, or has achieved only
tardily. The art museums, libraries, universities, research institutions, and theaters were at first monopolized by the
older cities of the seaboard; and it has been only with great
effort that the sub-metropolises, with their original industrial
base, have begun to equalize the financial advantages of
New York. As it is, no one can do first-rate scholarly research
in many lines without going to New York or Boston, Philadelphia or Chicago; and by the same token, it is New York
that monopolizes the theaters and sends out road companies
to the rest of the country, as Dives might scatter the crumbs
from his table.

When we speak of the disadvantages of the third migration,
it is important that we should distinguish between the economic basis of that migration and its cultural by-product.
So far from looking for the growth of regional centers of
culture to cease, we should perhaps count upon its increasing
as soon as the social and economic disadvantages of excessive
concentration are done away with.

There are two things that should be noticed about the
first three migrations. The first is that the movement of population is not from farm-village, to industrial town, to financial
metropolis: the migrations, rather, come as successive waves,
and while one wave recedes as the next comes foaming in, the

first nevertheless persists and mingles with the second as an undertow. The present migration to the fruit farming and dry farming areas, or the new migration to the reclaimed swamps, marks the continuance of the first migration. Each migration represents a particular type of economic and social effort: the life that Daniel Boone sought is a different life from that a Wall Street broker or advertising man thinks desirable. The first migration sought land; the second, industrial production; the third, financial direction and culture; but as a matter of fact, each of these types of effort and occupation is needed for a stable, all-round community. Only here and there have we even fitfully attempted to utilize the land intelligently, relate industry to power, resources, and market, and provide an adequate 'human plant' for the community at large. To effect this union is the task of the fourth migration.

What, then, is the basis of the fourth migration? Its basis is the technological revolution that has taken place during the last thirty years—a revolution which has made the existing layout of cities and the existing distribution of population out of square with our new opportunities. The first change is that which has taken place in transportation: the railroad line is no longer the sole means of rapid transportation. The automobile has brought goods and markets together, not linearly, as the railroads tend to do, but areally; so that a great deal of ground untouched by the railroad has been made accessible to the automobile. Chain stores have been quick to grasp the advantages of covering territory in this fashion, and the truck that makes its rounds through the small villages and towns receives the current surplus of eggs and butter, for distribution beyond the local market area.

Similarly, the automobile has increased the radius of the school and the library service, and it has likewise provided a basis for a system of direct marketing which now exists, unfortunately, only for summer communities, but which could, were summer communities made permanent, be made the basis for a year-round supply of milk, eggs, butter, poultry, and garden produce. In many parts of the United States the summer community has assured the farmer of a stable income which his remoter metropolitan markets did not assure him. The railroad, moreover, tends to concentrate population near its lines; and there are city planners who, thinking in terms of the railway era, look forward to a complete consolidation of population in the seaboard and lake areas, along these lines. The railroads themselves have done what they could to promote this concentration by subsidizing a large commuting population, in order to increase the amount of non-commuting traffic.

Mark the contrasting type of development brought in by the automobile. The motor road does not depend upon concentration of population for its upkeep; indeed, instead of concentrating on main highways or trunk lines, the motor highway system is best kept up, without heavy wear and tear on one hand or practical disuse on the other, by spreading the load of traffic and taxes. The tendency of the automobile, in other words, is within limits to disperse population rather than to concentrate it; and any projects which may be put forward for concentrating people in Greater-City areas blindly run against the opportunities the automobile opens out. Whether the airplane will work centrifugally or centripetally it is hard at the moment to tell: at present, with the volume of traffic slight, aviation has tended to develop air lanes; but if the volume increases an aerial network, less bound to linear movements than even the automobile, seems at least a likelihood.

The second factor which bears upon the new layout of population is our new means of communication. The set toward urban concentration in industry and social life dates before the days of the telephone, when all personal contacts had to be made on the spot. Today the spot can be any point in a large area—in theory, the whole United States; in practice, the ten-cent call zone—and still the contact can be effective and personal. In certain lines, where the bargaining between buyer and seller is still intimate, face-to-face meeting is a necessity; but this concerns the business end of production more than the factory end, and a great many factories, which are now on the periphery of Chicago, St. Louis, or Philadelphia, might with equal success be conducted at any point in a much wider region, even if the eventual market for the product were concentrated. The telegraph symbolically follows the railroad; the telephone, with kindred symbolism, follows the motor highway. So much for the business end of communication.

Socially, the popularization of the radio has made concentration even more obsolete, for today the songs, the news, the gossip, and the speeches, which were once available only by taking a journey and sitting in a hall, are now increasingly the property of anyone who possesses a radio set; and the remote countryman is just as near the events and amusements which many people regard as the indispensable benefits of the big city as the flat-dwellers of the Bronx or the rabbit-hutch dwellers of Philadelphia. In other words, the radio is potentially a distributive and decentralizing agency. Again, the parcel post has placed the rural dweller who has the postman collect the mail from his door even nearer to his market or his neighbor than the city dweller, who must walk to the post office to mail a package. Our modern methods of transportation, in fact, have reduced many of our boasted metropolitan advantages to nil.

Finally, electric transmission, in its recent phase, can send energy over a wide area without undue loss, and here again, instead of being tethered to the railroad and its coal shipments, industry can move out of the railroad zone without moving out of the power zone. Where electric power is available, the location of the factory need have no relation at all to the older technology. Moreover, for the economic distribution of power, engineers have found it advisable to have a balanced load, that is to say, a day-consumption (industrial) and a night-consumption (home) within the same local area; for when these two types are separated, the equipment that serves the daytime city lies largely idle at night.

All this, it goes without saying, means that our modern power facilities are favored by, and favor, a wide distribution of population. The three-hundred-mile transmission belt, plus the motor highway, has made the coal railway center an antiquated industrial site. Industry under modern technology has a much wider choice of site than ever before. If it does not exercise this choice it tends to lose in efficiency of operation and personnel. As yet, it has scarcely begun to exercise it, partly because the inertia of custom and business enterprise has bound it to the old centers, and partly because its attention has not been directed to the advantages that would accrue to it; and, finally, because it can make no move which does not involve the housing of its workers and the provision of municipal services. An occasional factory or steel plant has made the attempt; but industry as a whole has not. It remains for regional planning to develop all these factors *at once,* as part of the technique of the fourth migration.

Now the third migration has not produced a good environment: it has sacrificed home, health, and happiness to the pursuit of business enterprise designed to produce maximum profits. Those centers which have concentrated most feverishly upon business efficiency are farthest away from having adequate homes and all the accessory institutions that round out a well-developed community. The forces that are concerned solely with business enterprise lose no opportunity for stressing the necessity of continuing the third migration; and city planners who fall in line with it plan for the agglomeration of ever-greater urban regions. This method and this attitude take altogether too much for granted, and if they have the great advantage of following the line of least resistance they too easily ignore the significance of new methods and new procedures which shift the direction of that line.

It is evident that each great movement of population, in sum, presents a new opportunity and a new task, and wisdom consists in taking advantage of the movement while it is still fluid. Fortunately for us, the fourth migration is only beginning: we may either permit it to crystallize in a formation quite as bad as those of our earlier migrations, or we may turn it to better account by leading it into new channels. To suggest what these new channels are, to show how necessary it is for us to trench them open, and to indicate how much the future may hold for us if we are ready to seize our destiny and shape it freshly—that was the purpose of the articles that originally followed this introduction, and it is still the purpose of the chapters that follow. Even if there were no fourth migration on the horizon it would be necessary to invent one. It is at least a fruitful hypothesis and it offers a more humane goal than any of those we are now blindly following!

Note: This 'Preface' first appeared as an introduction to the Regional Planning number of the *Survey Graphic*, May 1925.

# The Urban Prospect

# 1

# California
# and the Human Horizon

The human prospect today is both brighter and darker
than it has ever been in the historic ages. For the first time,
mankind exists as a self-conscious collective entity, bound together by communication at the speed of light, and by transportation at the speed of sound; we command physical
powers that were once locked in the depths of nature, and
knowledge enough in every department of thought, if we
had the good will and the social imagination to use it, not
merely to free the race from the old threats of starvation
and destitution, but to give to every human being on the
planet the cultural resources for personal development and
enjoyment that only a minority ever participated in on any
scale in the past.

But at present these happy prospects are heavily overcast
by well-justified fear and dismay. The method of thinking
that has made these advances possible, and the very technology that has brought them to the point of realization, are
at the same time working in precisely the opposite direction.
As our machines become more automatic, more intelligent,
more self-governing, the life that they make possible in our
communities becomes humanly less interesting, partly because we have transferred so many of our activities, even

3

thought itself, to these mechanical agents. What is just as bad, the whole apparatus of power on which we necessarily depend has gotten out of control and is running away with us. As a result we have only replaced the old slavery of production with the new servitudes and compulsions of consumption; and in comparison with the power and resources now at our disposal, the net human gain has been dismally small.

At any moment all our boasts of scientific proficiency and progress may be nullified by a man-made nuclear catastrophe, brought on by minds that have ceased to be able to deal with political realities because they themselves are encased in a system of abstractions and measurements useful only for the control of machines. Thus our power threatens to collapse into impotence—our creativity into total destruction.

I shall not end on this negative note; but it is necessary to begin here; for unless we take the full measure of the dangers that confront us, with open eyes, we shall not summon forth the human energies that will be necessary to overcome them. The threat of wholesale nuclear extermination, on a scale that might permanently mutilate even that part of the human race which escaped immediate destruction, is only the most spectacular example of the negative results produced by science and technics when they are divorced from any other human purpose than their own propensity to increase knowledge and power, and expand the use of their own special products in a fashion profitable to the producer.

But we are in the midst of other explosions, other forms of destruction, actual, not just threatened, that will be just as fatal as long as they go in the present fashion: the population explosion, the freeway explosion, the recreation explosion, the suburban explosion (or should one say the 'slurban' explosion?) are all working toward the same blank goal—that of creating more and more featureless landscapes, populated by more and more featureless people. Never before has any country possessed such a surplus of wealth, energy, food, and natural resources as the United States, and in particular, the state of California. But in addressing ourselves solely to the increase of power, profit, and prestige, we have failed to develop a varied, many-sided culture, a culture based on the realities of life itself, on human growth in a biologically sound and socially stimulating environment, on sexual maturation and a good family life, on disciplined emotional expression in the arts and in daily practice, on constant citizen participation in the public affairs of the community, for the sake of human association as well as for the practical and cultural ends. Rather, all our dominant forces today now tend to cramp and dwarf our life, to automatize and increasingly dehumanize our activities, when they might be hugely increasing our actual wealth and our real enjoyment.

Now, where the machine takes precedence of the man, and where all activities and values that sustain the human spirit are subordinated to making money and privately devouring only such goods as money will buy, even the physical environment tends to become degraded and inefficient. To say that we have not made the most of our opportunities is putting the case mildly: disorder, blight, dingy mediocrity, screaming neon-lighted vulgarity are spreading everywhere, producing, as I said, an empty life, filled with false vitality expressed in occasional outbreaks of violence and lust, either in brutal action or in more frequent fantasy.

Ever since I visited the ancient Italian town of Pompeii, buried under the ashes of Vesuvius in A.D. 79, I have found myself comparing the dead city that has been brought to life there with the seemingly live cities that we are living in—or more often trying to get away from—in America. This comparison continues to haunt me. The landscape around Pompeii is not too different from that of many parts of California; the vineyards and the olive groves and wheat fields in Roman times were no more productive. Yet this little provincial town, of some twenty-five thousand inhabitants, produced such an orderly and coherent and esthetically animated life that even in its ruined state it gives a less ruinous impression than the central areas of most American cities of ten times that population. The Pompeian frescoes and mosaics are famous in the museums of Europe, and when one compares the noble Forum of Pompeii with the jumbled junk-edged surroundings of San Francisco's own Civic Center, when one considers the amount of space and fine building given to Pompeii's temples, its markets, its law courts, its public baths, its stadium, its handsome theater, all conceived and built on the human scale, with great nobility of form, one realizes that American towns far more wealthy and populous than Pompeii do not, except in very rare cases, have anything like this kind of civic equipment, even in makeshift form.

Closer comparisons make our own achievements seem even more destitute and fraudulent: the neighborhood bakeries of Pompeii still made real bread, with flour ground on the premises just before baking—not the kind of devitalized foam-rubber loaf, laden with additives and substitutes, mechanically sliced for built-in staleness, that boasts of never being touched by human hand, though if we were not so enamored of large-scale enterprise and long-distance transportation, we could all have fresh local bread, with flour ground on the spot by small, efficient, electrically driven mills, bread fully the equal of Pompeii's, without the slave labor that probably turned the Pompeian baker's mill.

Every part of Pompeii was within walking distance, just as if its inhabitants enjoyed each other and wished to profit by each other's company. And the thousands of people who gathered to watch the games, or attend the theater, could leave their seats and reach home on foot before a similar American crowd could begin to get their cars out of a parking lot. In terms of biological vitality, in terms of social life, there is no question as to which kind of community could offer the best facilities and enjoyments for its inhabitants. Now, mind you, Pompeii was not a showpiece or an ideal community; far from it: it was just an ordinary Roman provincial town, so well designed that were it not for Vesuvius it might still be doing business on the same spot, within the same general pattern of life, as is so largely true today in the old Roman colonization towns, like Piacenza and Pavia.

The moral I draw from Pompeii is that we Americans must be spending our money on the wrong things if our towns are so poverty-stricken in civic facilities, so confused, and so ugly by contrast, in spite of all their boasted wealth and energy. What Pompeii spent on the vital contents of life, we spend on wasteful processing and meretricious packaging and phony publicity. Our trouble, then, is not merely that we have fallen in love with the machine, and have treated it as a god, to be flattered with prayers and propitiated by human sacrifices—more than forty thousand dead by motor accidents every year: a million injured, many of them maimed for life. Our trouble is that equally we have ceased to respect ourselves, just as we have ceased to love our neighbors and want to be near them; we have ceased to cherish our own history and to enlarge our own prospects, by promoting character and variety and beauty wherever we find it, whether in landscapes or in people. Because the machine, if left to its own devices, goes in for standardization, mass production, automation, quantitative excesses, we have let our lives be governed by these same mechanical factors, forgetting that all these capacities are beneficial only when they are at the disposal of a purposeful life that is itself more rich, complex, varied, individualized, stimulating, and humanly valuable: something different from a machine's existence.

In their worship of the machine, many Americans have settled for something less than a full life, something that is hardly even a tenth of a life, or a hundredth of a life. They have confused progress with mechanization, and, lacking any will or purpose of their own, having lost any real religious faith or personal pride, they have let mechanization take command. Even where choice is possible, they prefer an air-conditioning unit to the more subtle and satisfactory method of controlling insulation and temperature by proper orientation, and by using trees and gardens more copiously. They respect the steam shovel that levels down a hill more than they value the view that their houses would command if they kept the hill and used its contours. The speculative builder prides himself on the bulldozer that gouges out a stand of trees while he rejects opportunity for a more organic type of plan that would group the houses in a more adroit irregular pattern. These bad habits make it seem as if our countrymen were hostile to all manifestations of life, including their own, except in so far as they enhanced the power and glory of machines.

Some of this attitude is doubtless left over from the pioneer days, when the individual settler had to carve a place for himself barehanded in a sometimes difficult, if not inimical, environment. Under these conditions a certain ruthlessness was sometimes unavoidable in self-defense. At all events the pioneer never had to live with the damage he did, as we do now: he could always cancel out his sins, or at least forget them, by moving on to another virgin spot. Even when the pioneer didn't rape Nature, he divorced her a little too easily: he missed the great lesson that both ecology and medicine teach—that man's great mission is not to conquer Nature by main force but to cooperate with her intelligently and lovingly for his own purposes. Yet for all our careless habits, we Americans once loved the wilderness, for the free mode of life and the self-reliant men and women it bred: whatever is left of adventurous initiative and self-government in this country owes a debt to those days.

Since in our hearts we don't altogether like the kind of mechanically sterilized and spiritually stupefying existence we now live, we have begun to tell ourselves fairy stories about our present state: fooling ourselves into believing we are recovering the old pioneer spirit with barbecue grills in the backyard, just as we call the most compulsive and tension-producing avenues of locomotion our 'freeways'—and even boast of the freedom of going at sixty miles an hour for hundreds of miles and never having to stop for a red light, completely forgetting how often we are stalled for ten minutes at a bottleneck, as we creep into the city. So again in attempting to fill up the empty hours of leisure that our mechanical achievements have brought about, we tend to turn every great recreation area into a congested metropolitan slum, pretending to find solace in the beauties of nature, at Yosemite or Lake Tahoe, in an actual environment that strangely resembles a parking lot around a· hamburger joint. *If the places where we live and work were really fit for permanent human habitation, why should we spend so much of our time getting away from them?*

Let us face the truth. The real life of a large part of the population, even those who live in agricultural areas, is one long retreat from the vitalities and creativities of a self-sustaining environment and a stimulating and balanced communal life. We have accepted an assembly line existence, in which all human functions take place in an increasingly sterilized and uniform environment, cut off from every reality except that which serves the machine. Whether he wears a white collar or a blue collar, the typical American now serves as a baby-sitter to a machine, or is geared into a collective organization that is itself a more formidable and all-embracing machine—a machine that can be run effectively only by bureaucratic personalities, punched and coded to perform a limited set of operations. The factory or the office,

with its thousand identical windows, its uniform air conditioning, its uniform fluorescent lighting, its equally bare and
uniform parking lot, has the typical features of this age:
faceless anonymity. As far as it is mechanically feasible, this
environment has insulated its occupants from every form of
reality except the machine process itself: heat and cold, day
and night, the earth and the stars, woodland, crop land,
vineland, garden land—all forms of organic partnership between the millions of species that add to the vitality and
wealth of the earth—are either suppressed entirely from the
mind or homogenized into a uniform mixture which can
be fed into the machine.

Look at the life we lead. At the end of a day our countrymen leave this humanly insulated collective environment for
an equally cribbed and cabined mechanism on wheels, for a
journey that may take anywhere from half an hour to two
hours, depending upon how filled the parking lot is and
how clogged the freeway. This piece of defective rolling
stock, with its lethal, health-vitiating exhaust, provides the
fading illusion of freedom along with the reality of constant
tension and constraint: its utility decreases in direct proportion to its mass use, and in taking over the burden of public
and private transportation, both passengers and freight, the
motorcar has, with the aid of extravagant public subsidies,
under pretext of 'national defense,' wrecked the balanced
transportation system that existed a generation ago, and crippled the functions that the motorcar and the freeway, if part
of a more complex and flexible network of transportation,
would actually—and admirably—serve.

Physiologically the worse for wear, our American finally
reaches his dwelling, where he finds a house and a wife in the
midst of what is usually called ideal suburban surroundings:
a green ghetto, half natural, half plastic, also cut off from
human contact, where his wife has for her chief daily companions in her solitude the radio set, the soap opera, the

refrigerator, the automatic mixer, the blender, the vacuum cleaner, the automatic washing machine, the dishwasher, and, if she is lucky, the second car. They and their children finally, together or by turns, immobilize themselves before a television screen, where all that has been left out of the actual world, all their unlived life, flickers before their eyes, in images that give a faked sense of the realities they have turned their backs to, and the impulses that they have been forced to repress. Even here, the machine-conditioned American has no proper life of his own: for what he sees and hears and interprets contains only so much of the real world as the great corporate organizations, military, commercial, political, which control this medium, will permit for the furtherance of their own machine-expanding, power-buttressing, or money-making ends. Freedom of selection is chiefly the freedom of choosing more of the same from another channel.

I have of course intentionally, and doubtless grossly, caricatured the life of the representative American today; and I am as well aware as you are of the many happy qualifications and modifications that make much of it bearable, and some of it positively rewarding. There are still real cities in America, like the core of San Francisco, and some of your smaller towns, which, like Palo Alto, with the benefit of Olmsted's great original plan for the campus of Stanford itself, have so far held their own against the bulldozing highway engineers and have even, by the orderly addition of industrial parks and shopping centers, taken on the more complex and varied and vivid life of a city, without eroding the landscape.

For all this, that caricature is too near reality to let one feel altogether comfortable about the human prospect: especially since it is fast becoming the universal life of mankind, alike in other countries that still call themselves free, and in countries that are under a Communist Party dictatorship. In the latter countries, indeed, people are resentfully aware of the official pressures and external compulsions, and therefore, if one may judge by recent short stories and motion pictures coming out of Soviet Russia, they have reacted against their oppressive political regimentation by cultivating a warmer sense of the eternal human decencies and moralities, as between family and family, person and person. Few of our own Hollywood or Radio City productions show anything like the same human tenderness as the recent Russian *Ballad of a Soldier*.

At all events, the ultimate pattern of gracious American living, if we continue our rigid and unqualified commitment to the machine, is already in sight. Six hours for automatic production and forced consumption in order to maintain the expanding economy: three hours for transportation as we get farther and farther away from the place where we don't want to work, to the place where we no longer have much opportunity to sleep: six hours for mechanized togetherness, sometimes called family life and recreation: and finally, at least nine hours of sleep, partly to forget that we have not been living, partly to provide for the increasing sale of sleeping pills, hypnotics, and tranquillizers, those indispensable adjuncts of the kind of life we offer to our highly mechanized and urbanized population. The only element I have left out of the day's schedule is mating: but plainly, with artificial insemination from a bank of frozen sperm cells, in accordance with Dr. Herman Muller's formula for human improvement, this injection can be combined with an influenza shot or an X-ray checkup. So much for the nightmare of our Brave New World: we are lucky if what we see when we move about and what we do in our day's work turns out to be sufficiently different to reassure us that we are awake.

Isn't it about time that we took a hard second look at this life of ours and faced the fact that if we go on acting this way, the human prospect will be increasingly dismal? Are we creating the kind of life that anyone in his senses would bargain for, still less regard as the sufficient consummation and justification of civilization? Sinclair Lewis took such a look at Zenith and Main Street a generation or more ago; but what he found there was relatively healthy, sweet, decent, and sane compared with the kind of life that has been thrust upon us by the automatic proliferation of scientific invention and mechanical organization during the last twenty years. The human prospect, in California or anywhere else, does not hold much promise as long as these conditions are unrecognized for what they are, not real signs of progress, but symptoms of human disturbance and social disintegration; or, even when they are recognized, if they are looked upon as outside human control, and are allowed to go on uncorrected. The time has come to understand that mechanization without a corresponding humanization is monstrous: just as passive consumption, without selectivity and without any ensuing creativity in other departments than science and technics, is empty; and power without purpose—the kind of power we now have in such abundance, power enough to exterminate the human race—is immediately destructive and suicidal, and ultimately impotent.

If you ask me how California or any other region can be improved without altering our prevailing view of life, without changing our routines, without attaching ourselves to more public purposes and higher human ends than those we now respect, I must answer with a sad smile that no serious improvements are possible on those old terms. If we want to improve the regional environment, we must also improve ourselves, that is, we must change our minds and alter our objectives, advancing from a money economy to a life economy: in many matters we must acquire new values, new sensitivities, new interests, new goals that will ensure a self-sustaining, many-sided life. That life must not depend

as it so largely does now upon our constantly dancing attendance upon the machine, and pursuing only such activities
as will give the makers of machines and machine products the
maximum market for their goods.

In short, it is the whole pattern of our life that must
change; and the pattern of our local life will not alter
significantly until the over-all pattern for a much wider area
does. As long as our country spends astronomical sums for
weapons of extermination, weapons which endanger our
own lives—sixty million dead on the first day of a nuclear
attack—and indeed the lives of all mankind, quite as much
as they threaten any enemy's, we shall not have the funds
needed for more rational public purposes: for our schools
and hospitals, for our theaters and churches, for our recreation areas, for the old and the young who need public help.

Part of our local planning, then, must be deliberately ad-
dressed to bring the local community into relations with
larger associations of peoples, if only in order to safeguard
the very life we are building here; and one of the most
ominous items that appeared in the paper the other day was
the report that a chapter on the United Nations was being
excluded from an official textbook on civics in California.
I hope that report was unfounded, for if California is still
populated a hundred years hence, it will be because the universal forces for cooperation and mutual understanding embodied in the United Nations, not least in UNESCO, have
prevailed over egoistic, nationalistic presumptions and nuclear delusions of absolute power. If the world overcomes the
irrational forces that are now undermining human culture
everywhere, forces long embodied in the dangerously obsolete
institution of war, it will be because people everywhere realize
that all the goods of life are the joint product of the human
race as a whole, and that we are bound to all our neighbors
by all the facts of history and by the hopes of the future,
as they are bound to us.

The kind of cooperation that still exists between all nations in the world of science and scholarship—at least that part of science and scholarship that is not under the control of totalitarian military agencies operating in secret—sets a pattern for the future relations of regions and countries: so much so that the core institution in every vital city today is no longer the palace or the temple or the market, but the university, and it is to the honor of the university that such an open discussion as is going on here today is possible in contrast to the death-oriented doctrines and isolationist nonsense taken as a prescription for 'national survival.'

In discussing the role of planning we all too easily get lost, however, in details of political organization, economic support, population movements, transportation facilities, metropolitan or regional government; and we neglect the factor that is central to all of these things: the dimensions of the human personality. The answer to the problems of human organization and human control will not come from computers; the answers will come from men. And it will not come from the sort of men whom we have indoctrinated with the myth of the machine—the disoriented experts and specialists whose uncoordinated and lopsided efforts, uncorrected by the more humane wisdom of their peers, and untutored by historic experience, have produced the overmechanized, standardized, homogenized, bureaucratized life that now surrounds us increasingly on every side.

Our first job in controlling the forces that are now working such destruction and havoc in every regional community is to cultivate men who are capable of exercising this control: proud, confident, self-respecting, cooperative men. Not men for sale, men tailored and trimmed to fit the machine, but men capable of using all their powers, taking back to themselves the functions they too easily resigned to the machine, and projecting human goals, in the full trajectory of life, goals which they often disregarded in their eagerness to exploit some immediate opportunity. If our mode of life or our education had produced such men in sufficient numbers, we should not now be living in an increasingly denuded and life-hostile environment; and if we are ever to give to this region, or any other region, the life-sustaining richness and variety that are possible, even in areas where natural conditions are unduly uniform or climatically difficult, we will have to begin all over again at the very beginning, with the infant in its crib. That is where education starts.

Let us consider the most limited environment. If we look at it carefully, we shall perhaps have a key to what must be done in every other area. Consider the newborn baby of the last generation, the generation of my own and immediately after my own. Our mechanized civilization, in the interest of a speedy delivery, at the convenience, even at the timed participation of the physician, often endangered mother and child with impatient interference in the natural process, and too often compounded this mistake by anesthetizing the mother completely. All too soon, as a result of scientific pride over inventing a formula for feeding independent of the natural source of milk, the child was parted from its mother and deprived not only of mother's milk, but of the experience of a warm, loving, commensal relationship with her, the kind we must have also with Mother Earth.

In other words, both mother and child were cut off from a basic physical and spiritual experience, an experience which is a vital model for all remoter forms of cooperation and association. When behaviorist doctrines were at their height the next point in the child's development consisted in a systematic effort to make clockwork habits take the place of organic responses timed to the organism's own needs, especially in bowel training. Thus, as one of our most able child psychologists, Erik Erikson, has pointed out, before an American child was three—this held with his patients at least up to 1950—he had been conditioned to accept an external mechanical order as absolute, and to believe that there was nothing he could do to change it, particularly if he wanted to win the approval of those who stood in authority over him. Such a training made bad citizens for a democracy; but it fitted admirably, with its mechanical punctuality and regularity, with its human docility and conformity, into larger bureaucratic and totalitarian systems.

While many of the present generation of young people are, happily, beginning to reject every part of this process, beginning with the young mothers and enlightened physicians who accept childbirth as a normal organic process—it can take place in a home, though nowadays it too often takes place in a taxicab or a car on the way to a distant hospital!—not as a surgical ordeal like a major operation. In justified reaction against the mechanical regimen that prevailed a generation ago, some of the young have even reacted to the opposite extreme, quite naturally, an extreme of heedless permissiveness and irresponsibility, thus abdicating the parental role and turning the infant itself into a tyrannous monster, subject to all the psychological disorders that befall every creature that has delusions of absolute power, devoid of purpose but endowed with every attribute of freedom except the ability to select a path and follow it. If you look closely at these two patterns of child training—one too rigorous, too machine-dominated, too overstrained, the other too feckless and reckless to pay attention even to the natural rhythms of the body and natural hierarchies of power and responsibility—you will perhaps have a clue to the characteristic weaknesses of planning today.

On one hand we have the compulsiveness and arbitrariness of our highway planning, our urban renewal projects, our centralized recreational facilities, in which the demands of the administrator, the investor, the engineer ruthlessly override the human needs to be served and deform the final product, making it really unfit for human use. But against this you have the unlimited permissiveness of suburban sprawl; and along with both tendencies an attitude of hopeless passivity, based on the curious assumption that although all these mischievous and maladroit activities are the result of human actions and human plans, they are beyond human control, once they are in existence, and are doomed to get worse and worse. This is nonsense. I would challenge that assumption, even were it necessary to wait for a whole generation of new young people to emerge—a generation who have come into the world without having to submit to an over-mechanized, oversterilized, deliberately anti-organic regimen that has no faith in either life or love.

We shall never succeed in dealing effectively with the complex problems of large units and differentiated groups, unless at the same time we rebuild and revitalize the small unit. We must begin at the beginning; it is here that all life, even the life of big communities and organizations, starts. The home and the neighborhood are an integral part of the region, and some of the most pressing problems in adequate land use cannot be solved, with the big population that is flooding into California, unless we handle the whole pattern of settlement, including the layout of the individual houses and apartment units. The child has a right to live in an orderly, intelligibly patterned world, scaled to his size and his capacity for movement, and designed for encouraging his activities, and for making him feel at home with his fellows and neighbors, even when he leaves his domestic nest.

If we are to recapture the initiative from our machine-centered civilization, we must establish a life-centered environment from the moment of birth. Who can pretend that a fifteen-story, high-rise apartment in an urban renewal project is such a family environment? But neither—let us not fool ourselves—is an insulated single family house, entirely cut off from its neighbors, or lined up, side by side, for the convenience of the builder and the deed of sale, on a long uniform street, one uniformed unit after another. Neither of these environments serves as a surrogate for the mother or as a proper sample of a bigger community.

Every housing development should have the virtues of both a village and a kindergarten; the houses themselves should form a protective enclosure, so that the child can move about freely, among other children, and still be under the eye of his mother, or, rather, a whole group of mothers, safe from moving traffic, not having to share his play space with a motorcar or be toted a mile or two by car to find it. Real human communities must preserve social as well as visual variety; hence the fact that we no longer attempt to house a three-generation family within a single dwelling makes it all the more imperative to restore this combination to the neighborhood. Age segregation is just as bad as income segregation or racial segregation: we need mixed age groups to sustain life even at the simplest levels. A child needs grand-parents, or substitute grandparents, as well as parents; he needs to live in a normal human community with the companionship of other children—of different ages, too—as well as those of his own peer groups and family.

None of these things happen automatically nowadays on any scale: automatic processes tend to produce isolation and segregation, or a congestion which is just as bad as the mass production of single unrelated units, not the complex pattern produced by integrating in appropriate structures and forms a whole variety of human needs and functions. Nor can the benefits of such an integrated social design be produced by private individuals, no matter how great their financial means. Public authorities must take the lead in experimenting with new urban patterns, new layouts: they must seek to establish a tradition that the individual developers—perhaps with public assistance—can themselves carry out, instead of, as now, following the line of least resistance, which always is a mechanical repeating pattern.

I have taken this simple illustration to show how many-sided the organic planning process is, even at the smallest scale, when you understand and attempt to do justice to human needs. What I have said of housing alone applies in equal degree to the neighborhood, which must be built again into an active political unit, if our democracy is to become active and invigorated once more, as it was two centuries ago in the New England Village, for that was a superior political unit. The same principles apply again to the city and the interrelationship of cities in a unified urban and regional network or grid. But I have used this illustration of how to give order, variety, and protection to the growing child for still another reason; and that is because it offers a model of the chain of relations that bind the small unit to seemingly remote parts of the environment and to problems which seemingly have nothing to do with it.

Already you have let the pressure of population and of private real estate development destroy some of your best agricultural land. Even here in the broad Central Valley, you are threatened with this evil, no less than in the Santa Clara Valley and the San Bernardino Valley, valleys whose orchards and vineyards not merely gave character to their little towns, but had positive recreational value for the bigger cities like Pasadena, Los Angeles, and San Francisco. That soil was precious; that combination of agricultural production and recreative beauty were essential to the vitality of the whole urban community; and by packing these valleys with a disorganized overload of people and vehicles you have even been lowering the health levels with smog and carbon monoxide, as recent official reports show. This random scattering of population has spoiled both the urban and the rural potentialities of these valleys: whereas if you had thought of housing in direct communal terms, to begin with, the care of the child and provision for the child's healthy growth in his family and neighborhood, you might have built two- or three-story houses instead of the low sprawling ones of a single story, a type that is now eating up land all over the country, and you might have doubled, and in many cases quadrupled, the number of people per acre, with an enormous improvement in their social and domestic environment.

By proper planning alone, you could have preserved from fifty to seventy-five per cent of the land now misused and wasted. Indeed, by means of proper planning you may still save much precious land, which is now about to be misused, from such a fate. At a residential density of from fifteen to thirty families per acre—fifteen to twenty families is the usual density in the spacious, perhaps even too spacious English New Towns—you could have provided better gardens, better playgrounds, safe green walkways to school, more accessible schools for the children, and a far better life for the parents as well: a life designed deliberately to favor the neighborly interchange of services that must become, as once it was in pioneer days, our communal substitute for menial helpers that hardly anyone can now afford to hire. Not the least advantage of such organic communal and neighborhood designs is that they would release the individual housewife and mother from the slavery of her present twenty-four-hour tour of duty.

This illustration has many ramifications; but its chief use today is to indicate that respect for human conditions and for development and growth will help improve every part of the regional landscape, and will make possible a complex interlacing of functions, in a pattern of mutual aid, not mechanical regularity, that will be superior to any one-sided solutions, based on single-factor analysis and compartmental thinking devoted mainly to the exploitation and profitable use of the machine.

But before the kind of thought and design I have indicated becomes popular, we shall have to overthrow the myth of the machine and replace it with a new myth of life, a myth based upon a richer understanding of all organic processes, a sharper insight into man's positive role in changing the face of the earth, and a passionate religious faith in man's own capacity to transform and perfect his own self and his own institutions in cooperative relation with all the forces of nature, and, above all, with his fellow men. To put all our hope in the improvement of machines is the characteristic inversion and perversion of values of the present age; and that is the reason that our machines threaten us with extinction, since they are now in the hands of deplorably unimproved men. This is no moment to fight a rear-guard action, a mere delaying action, against the forces that are denuding the landscape and dehumanizing the capacities of men. The time has come for bold counterattack—and we may not have long to wait.

During the last three years I, like many of my colleagues, have noted a new generation coming into the colleges: a generation trained perhaps more lovingly than their rigid and passive predecessors. They are no longer cagey conformists, no longer bent on dodging all the adventurous possibilities of life by an overemphasis on security, measured in income, or in status, measured only by the things money will buy. These young people, sometimes at great sacrifice, put babies ahead of careers; and they find, in themselves and their family life, resources that are not found in machines and are often deplorably lacking in the bigger community itself, lacking especially in the big cities. Though they have grown up in an age of violence and totalitarian conformity, they now challenge its brutalities and reject its compulsions; and their respect for themselves is greater than their respect for anything the machine, with or without their help, has created. They are still in all probability a minority; but the seed of life has

ripened in them: if their elders do not betray them by sur-
rendering even more abjectly than they have already done to
the forces of disintegration and extermination, this generation
will assume responsibility that too many of us still shrink
from. They will overcome our passivities, overthrow our regi-
mentations, and place the guardians of life once more in command. This is still an uncertain promise: but at least—and at
last—it opens up a human prospect.

Address before the Institute on Planning for the North Central Valley, at
Davis, California, January 12, 1962.

# 2

# Planning for the Phases
# of Life

Almost a generation ago Dr. Joseph K. Hart, in the Regional
Planning number of the 'Survey Graphic' (May 1925),
pointed out that city planning was mainly conceived in terms
of a single phase of life: that of adults without family responsibilities. He noted the significance of the old saying that
the crowd on the boulevards never grows old: namely, that the
boulevard, by reason of its purpose and design, draws to it
the same age groups, following the same interests, pursuing
the same ends.

In spite of that timely reminder, the city planner has not
yet come to realize the full nature of his task: the provision
of an environment suited to every phase of life and growth,
from infancy to senescence. Too much of our recent planning
up to now, certainly in the United States, has been concentrated on adult life: indeed, on the adult life of mainly the
masculine half of the population, and on only so much of this
life as is concerned with business, industry, administration,
traffic, transportation. Even in handling adults, the city planner has omitted important areas of activity.

The purpose of this paper is to make a preliminary exploration of the territory Dr. Hart's original question opened up.
In its brief compass, it seeks to suggest how a consciousness of

the phases of life may perhaps alter the planner's attitude toward both the methods and the ends of planning; and even lead to a reconsideration of the design of certain units, like playgrounds, where administrative convenience has caused us, at least in America, to concentrate upon forms whose outward order reflects mainly their inner sterility. If a consciousness of the human life cycle does nothing else, it may at least serve as a check list of requirements: enabling one to spot the weak places in a seemingly admirable design.

*First Phase: Infancy.* Let us begin with the newborn infant and inquire what planning does for him, till the time he is ready for school. This is partly, to begin with, a matter of housing from the very hour of birth onward; and whereas in every country, during the last generation, there has been a steady movement to provide for childbirth in hospitals, we now begin to suspect that these are not the best conditions for a normal delivery and for the earliest days of an infant's life. The experience of the Peckham Health Center, and else- where, seems to show that there is a balance of advantages, very strong on the psychological side, in favor of home con- finement: yet even where housing conditions are as good as they are in a British housing estate of pre-1940 standards, childbirth itself tends to disrupt the household and cause temporary overcrowding.

At this point the planner might well consider if there is not, in terms of planning, an intermediate solution: midway between the expensive, heavily equipped hospital, ready for every emergency, and the normal household, capable of han- dling minor illnesses, but without the space or equipment for handling childbirth. Such a solution would be in the nature of a small nursing home: established as an integral part of a unit of, say, two hundred and fifty to five hundred families: attached perhaps to a local medical clinic, which needs so many of the same facilities. Confined in such a place, a mother would have access to her other children, could be visited easily by her husband, and could be looked after by relatives or neighbors, except where special care was required: an important economy. Such a solution would restore the missing human element, an element lost through what Dr. Richardson, the Victorian hygienist, once mordantly described as the 'warehousing of disease.' I shall return to this matter of scale, simplicity, and intimacy, when I come to old age.

In planning further for the infant's life the first care must be to give the mother peace and respite from the too constant pressure of household duties: absence of tension in her is one of the conditions for a happy and affectionate relation between the two. At no period can even the most limited household be wholly a self-contained unit: people need their neighbors, in the emergencies of life, certainly, but also in their daily routine; and that need should not be confined, by inept planning, to those dire moments when an air raid brings people compulsively together in a common shelter, or causes them to queue up for their daily food. Even in housing estates that are laid out at twelve families to the acre—perhaps one should say especially there—there is often a lack of common meeting places for the mothers, where, on a good day, they might come together under a big tree, or a pergola, to sew or gossip, while their infants slept in a pram or their runabout children grubbed around in a play pit. Perhaps the best part of Sir Charles Reilly's plans for village greens was that they provided for such common activities: as the planners of Sunnyside, Long Island, Messrs. Stein and Wright, had done as early as 1924.

There should be something snug, intimate, protective about this order of planning, if it is to correspond to the needs of the very young, who have perhaps not altogether forgotten the environment from which they originally emerged. Little children—perhaps even up to the age of ten—need hiding places and cubby-holes: walls and bushes, if not caves and pits, perform their function in the open. Above all, the little ones, especially those under six, must get the feel of their environment: they need sand, gravel, stones, boards, branches, billets, for their play activities; and to prevent these materials from being put to destructive uses, the most elemental type of playground might well be placed in a shallow, well-drained sand pit, surrounded by a stone or brick walk, around which their mothers could sit: this area, in turn, should be walled off from the rest of the precinct, and reached through a gate whose latch would be well above a child's reach. Such an area might have a great stone or concrete animal in the middle, which children could climb upon: even an abstract shape, such as the sculptor Noguchi has designed for older play groups, might be used, particularly if it provided little caves, hiding places. Once built, the chief administrative problem arising from such play areas is that of policing them at night against their misappropriation by cats: but a charged wire on the wall would probably handle that difficulty. People who love gardens and haven't too much space for them tend to begrudge a child the freedom he needs in digging and grubbing; so that a collective way of handling the early play of children, solitary though it so often is, would, at the very moment it brought the mothers together and prepared them for other forms of cooperation, also give more liberty to the child.

*Second Phase: The School Child.* The transition from home to school is a critical one for the child; and we perhaps have minimized too glibly the shock and inner disorder that comes, not only from leaving the protective oversight of the mother, but also from the change of physical scale from the single dwelling to what is often, from the child's point of view, a gigantic complex building: awful in its impersonal immensity. There are places, like California, where even in big cities like San Francisco the elementary school has been kept relatively small, and where the unit, in the newer schools, is the classroom with its own play area, not wholly absorbed into the bigger structure. But perhaps the best way to effect the transition is through a nursery group in the neighborhood unit; and to make this possible, I for one would willingly forego wholly professional care in exchange for the more amateurish part-time treatment by partly trained mothers, working for a nominal reward. Planning cannot, of course, anticipate too many new social arrangements: but it may occasionally suggest them and point to the appropriate social solution. There are housing developments in Zurich where, if my memory serves, this has long been done.

With the child's walk to school comes a new problem in planning: that of making his walk an amusing and—in an unconscious way—an educative one. Among the many things that damn the habits of suburban segregation and class zoning we have practiced so widely in the United States, not least, perhaps, is the blank dullness of the ride to school. Walking, a child will often pick unsuspected treasures out of a rubbish heap: a puddle, left by a poor drainage system, will become a lake, and a branch, twisted off in a storm, will become a war club; but there is nothing like a trim, orderly, defensively respectable suburban environment to discourage a child's imagination—or, for that matter, an adult's. When I lived on the campus of Stanford University, I had for choice, in my walks to the university, either the sight of the trimly tailored front lawns of the prosperous houses, or the rear service lanes that ran parallel, with their outbuildings and occasional clutter, their unexpected glimpses of carpenter sheds and garden tools, of a motorcar being repaired or a heap of plant clippings waiting to be carted away; and more often than not, I would prefer the rear alley, precisely for all these little hints of life, activity, transition, which the placid visual arts of suburbia did their best to suppress or politely disguise. Animation, though at the price of a little disorder, is more exhilarating, even esthetically, than frozen respectability.

For a child to get a true sense of the world that he lives in, he should at least have a glimpse, on his walk to school, either of nature plain, as at Radburn, or of man's work, in the form of workshops, minor industrial operations, markets. The activities that serve a neighborhood's life should not be too severely segregated: they should be at least within a school child's walking distance; and running errands and fetching should be part of his experience of life. This is an injunction perhaps less needed in Europe than in America, where middle-class canons of respectability and the reliance on motorcars have effected a fantastic separation of commercial areas from residential areas. But if a quarter or a third of a mile is the normal radius of play—so that a play field beyond will, till adolescence, not be frequently used, distances of the same order will hold for other activities.

In our efforts to provide space for the formalized play of children in cities, we have forgotten, especially in new communities, the role of spontaneous play. The endeavor to take children off the dangerous street, in crowded urban areas, has made us too easily content with creating equivalent asphalted areas that lend themselves only to a limited round of activities: slides, swings, or—in America—jungle-gyms, apparatus for danger-free climbing, safe, easily kept up, but, from the child's standpoint, often inhibiting. Meanwhile, in the bombed-out areas in London, we have discovered a new kind of playground, more to the fancy of children above the age of six: old foundations, opened-up cellars, rock and rubble for clambering over, sometimes a pool of undrained water for dabbling in or sailing an impromptu boat.

Such playgrounds have a fascination for the child that never becomes dulled. Growing up in New York, almost half a century ago, I still had the run of open lots, with rocky uneven surfaces, where the boys of my street roasted apples and potatoes; and where we played games impossible on pavement or street. Bushes and parapets may be used to separate such informal play areas, visually, from the rest of the community; but a certain untidy plentitude of facilities—old boards, stones, boxes—may increase their value for play. They are the urban equivalent for the more primeval type of wilderness which so delights the heart of children. Such areas would afford a channel where destructive impulses could innocently run off and lose their force: countered, often in the same area, by the urge to build and construct. Perhaps the only special contribution to such areas would be to design them in depth: grading down some of the hazards, or, by digging and quarrying, creating artful opportunities for adventure.

*Third Phase: Adolescence.* With adolescence, the neighborhood unit no longer is the sole focus of a child's activities. Going to a secondary school, even in a relatively small community, he meets children from other neighborhoods: in the organized games of adolescence, he needs broad playing fields for cricket or baseball, football or soccer: he not merely visits back and forth within the city, but begins to go on hikes and picnics and outings in the surrounding region. At some point in the development of our civilization the idea that has long been brewing in the minds of philosophers and educators, of Fourier and Goethe, of Schreber and William James and Rosenstock-Huessy, the idea of work armies, will finally become implanted in our educational systems. Just as there is no better way of making a male parent feel the responsibilities of parenthood than by giving him the active care of a child for a whole day, so there is no better way of making citizens than by turning some of the care of the community over to the young: in such fields, an hour of practice is worth a week of book-learning.

Now perhaps the best place to begin with the constructive tasks of work armies is in the care and upkeep of our common environment. The initiative of the Civilian Conservation Corps, instituted by the Roosevelt administration during the depression, need not be limited to tree planting and fire-protection activities in rural or wilderness areas. Actually, if we are to afford the parks and park-strips and gardens we envisage for the new type of open planning, we shall find the cost of their upkeep prohibitive unless we can make it a service of citizenship: voluntary if possible, compulsory if necessary. Otherwise, the eventual unkemptness of the great public spaces that are being laid out in the New Towns of England, for example, may cause a swing back to more constricted and petrified open areas, which have some prospects of remaining comely and decent, if not actively pleasant. The planting and gardening and policing of open areas might well be the task of the next generation of adolescents: one of many moral equivalents of war that a peace-minded generation will have to devise.

In some ways, this task would be a preparatory one; for its chief beneficiaries would be the youths themselves, at their next phase of growth: that marked by courtship. The period of late adolescence, when sexual energies run high and direct outlets are relatively few, is a trying and difficult one for both boys and girls. Often it is a period of inner disruption, whose very turmoil should be counterbalanced by the wonder and beauty of the environment. If prolongation of infancy was the first mark of Man's ascent, the prolongation of courtship, with all its rich by-products in art, literature, music, and religion, represents a further stage. This elaboration of the erotic impulse also intensified it, adding meaning and emotional color to purely instinctual manifestations. In the open country, lovers have little difficulty in finding places of seclusion that match their mood, but the lack of such walks and retreats in our cities, even in our parks, makes courtship too often either brief or furtive, harassed or embarrassed to the point of desperation.

Helen Thomas, the wife of the poet, left a memorable picture in 'As It Was' of urban courting, at the end of the last century, in a common that had some of the romantic attributes of concealment; but much of the planning that has been done since, certainly in America, has been conceived as if openness and publicity were the sole qualities to be embodied in design. What lovers need are accessible places where they can easily lose themselves and get away from the visible presence of others. The maze, that favorite device of Baroque planners, certainly served that purpose; and Frederick Law Olmsted, in designing Central Park in New York, deliberately made The Ramble, with its irregular topography, a place to get lost in; with the admirable result that it is perhaps the one place well adapted to love-making in the whole city of New York. If planners were conscious of the phases of life, they would not be so blank about the need of late adolescence for places of secluded beauty, accentuating and expanding, and yet tempering, their erotic needs; and enriching, with happy visual images, their erotic rewards.*

*Maturity: Work Phase.* Along with the increasing division of labor, in modern times, has gone another process: the intensification and segregation of work. Both the farm worker and the manual worker, in an earlier day, worked for longer hours than their modern counterparts; but work itself went on in an environment which had many other aspects and uses, within sight of the family, for example, and often with the

---

* I do not overlook the fact that 'the Pill' and a permissive code of sexual relations have lessened some of these tensions. But the personal results of indiscriminate sexuality—'Instant Sex'—have still to be appraised. Lack of tension, lack of meaningfulness, may curb sexual ardor and restrict sexual fulfillment as much as rigid abstention. Even animals and birds have prolonged courting rituals.

cooperation, in different degrees, of all its members. There were no walls, visual or functional, between business, domesticity, education. The age of specialization, concentrating on mechanical efficiency alone, has robbed working life of some of its esthetic and human dimensions. Here as elsewhere in modern cities a deliberate attempt must be made to reunite these severed aspects of life, which create, almost automatically, radical divisions and disharmonies in the personality; but the way to achieve this is not to go back to an earlier primitive form, but to create a new form, as different from the workshop-household as from the grimly isolated business or factory district of Victorian pride.

Seeking some such integration, the authors of 'Communitas' have suggested that houses and factories should be united around 'city squares.' As Messrs. Paul and Percival Goodman have described it, this would seem to restore a willfully archaic pattern of close association; whereas the problem is to create a modern equivalent. The equivalent, I suggest, is to introduce into the industrial zones of our towns, either by renovation or by new design, the domestic and social functions appropriate to the working day: accessible playgrounds, for example, for physical recreation during the lunch hour and at other intervals; a diversity of dining halls to replace the canteen; meeting halls and committee rooms, usable not by a single plant but by the whole area, for conducting the political affairs of both the management and the worker; school buildings and museums, so that vocational preparation and part-time study of a non-vocational nature might be encompassed with a minimum waste of time and effort. There are single industrial plants, like the Cadbury complex at Bournville, where these functions—and medical services as well—have been incorporated in the working structure: what we need now is to organize a whole industrial quarter on the same principles, with further functional and visual clarification.

The same principle holds, of course, for business quarters. Everyone knows the immense recreational value of even a small patch of ground such as St. Paul's Churchyard or the happy social effect of Princes Street in Edinburgh, with the shopping area thrown on one side and the park on the other: but for all that, too few business districts are planned with any recognition of the need for recreation space near at hand; in fact, one of the first marks of 'progress,' in America at least, is the cutting down of trees on the main shopping street. The great contribution of Haussmann's new boulevards in Paris was their unification of business and recreation and social entertainment: perhaps nowhere else have the functions of an adult been kept so fully unified as in the heart of Paris. The mechanical segregation of functions, practiced in the interest of purely mechanical efficiency, does not produce an interesting social life or fully animated personality. That is why so many of the desirable things in a community usually occur only through a breakdown or a lapse in its normal functions.*

*Maturity: Domestic Phase.* When our society provides a young couple with a dwelling house and a garden, placed among a thousand other dwelling houses, we feel that we have accomplished much for family life, and we have. When such homes can be achieved, without absorbing too much of the annual family income, a long step is taken toward rehabilitating family life; for who can doubt that Victorian domesticity, among the upper half of the middle classes, was encouraged by all the comforts and conveniences, the sense of internal space and peace, that brought the Victorian

---

* The classic example of this was the spontaneous organization of traffic control and rescue operations in the great electricity breakdown and blackout in the northeastern United States in 1965, along with a revival of neighborly intercourse.

father back nightly to his snug household; with the reading circle, the games, the sentimental and amatory singing, that attended, so often, the family gathering. But mere domestic closeness is not enough: the ingrown family tends to become self-absorbed, isolationist, exclusive, hostile to the further development of its members. Something more, therefore, is required for the success of family life: companionship and common interests outside the home, first on the part of husband and wife, then such companionship as may take in, directly or indirectly, the younger members of the family. Here is a place where the city planner must invent public ways of performing economically what the old, three-generation bourgeois family once privately encompassed.

Not the least contribution of the Peckham Health Center is, beyond doubt, the opportunity that it gives a family for having a common meeting place, outside the confines of its home, where the varied age groups, now so often thrust apart by the variety and intensity of individual interests, can become united again, or at least go about their work or play within view of the other members. This business of being 'within view,' though not necessarily in active association, is one of the community-binding attributes that we have too often neglected in modern planning: it is what enhances, for many of us, the value of musical performance in a concert hall, as opposed to its reception by radio in an individual home, though technically the second performance may be as perfect as the first. This visible being together, again, is one of the attractions of a crowded street. Perhaps the most elementary definition of a community is that it is a collection of people who live within sight of each other: in a country hamlet, even to see a neighbor's light at night is to have a special sense of security and sociability. For parents and children to be constant companions is far from advisable; but there are much more likely to be good family relations if each has some idea of what the other is doing—instead of having their activities so separated that they live in different worlds.

In reaction against formidable conditions of overcrowding and physical disorganization, modern planners are naturally tempted into a uniformity of openness which may undermine the social sense as much as brutal congestion. Here Winston Churchill's wise words about the new House of Parliament building, that it should not be big enough to hold all its members at one time, apply to many other activities. One of the things to be said in favor of a compact shopping center, like the medieval market place or like one of the new markets in Los Angeles,* as opposed to the interminable old-fashioned shopping avenue, is that it concentrates and so multiplies the occasions for informal meeting and greeting: minimal social activities which, like the formal calls of an older day and order, tend to renew neighborly and friendly relationships. It is better to risk occasional overcrowding in such compact areas than to plan them so spaciously that they will hold the maximum conceivable load without discomfort—which means that they will be physically time-wasting and socially bleak on normal occasions.

The Settlement House, the Community Center, and the Health Center are all worthy attempts to find some point of focus for special activities outside the home. In America, the tendency is to place most of the functions served in such centers into the neighborhood school or the secondary school; for most adult activities occupy parts of the day when the school is not used by children, and auditoriums, swimming pools, gymnasiums, and workshops need not be kept inviolate

* This reference is to an older (pre-1945) type of covered market, abounding in fresh fruit, vegetables, and meat brought in daily from nearby farms—not to the sterile automated supermarkets of today, whose local sources of fresh food have been wiped out by the spread of Megalopolis.

PLANNING FOR THE PHASES OF LIFE

for scholastic use, provided they are restored to working order before the children arrive next morning.

But the adult life needs, to begin with, an even simpler form of meeting place: as simple as a room capable of holding fifty people seated, where neighborhood discussions may take place, and where occasional social festivities—on a scale too populous for the home—may take place. One of Patrick Geddes' happiest suggestions, in his report on Dunfermline, was for the setting apart of a handsome historic house to be rented at a nominal fee by any family in town, where a big party might be held. (Even a single large room with appropriate kitchen facilities would meet this need.) In Brooklyn, such houses, run by commercial caterers, used to be available and filled an important function in the domestic life of the middle class in that very home-minded borough. In a community of five thousand people, I had rather see five of these rooms functioning in each precinct than have the same facilities concentrated in a single community center. In England, where the pub has a solid place in the community, there is no reason why such community rooms sometimes should not, for simplicity of administration and service, be attached to—though perhaps not fully incorporated into —the pub itself.

*Maturity: Phase of Social Interaction.* The phase I would deal with under this head could be more properly called citizenship, if we meant by that term the art of living together in a city. The city, when it fully performs its functions, is a representative of the world at large: containing a diversity of products, people, organizations, associations, customs, and beliefs not ordinarily found in any single environment of a more specialized order. Whereas a village, properly, emphasizes likenesses and kinships—and the city in its neighborhood aspect does likewise—the city as a developed form must

emphasize—and reconcile—varieties, differences, even antag-
onisms. A good plan will multiply the spontaneous occasions
for mingling and mixing.

In our time, two forces have broken down the capacity of
the city to foster the maximum interplay of capacities and
functions among its members: that interplay which is necessary to personal growth, and without which men become
more solitary, brutish, and ungovernable. One of these forces
is the tendency of our mechanical inventions, from the railroad to modern radio and television, to disperse the members of the community over a wider and wider area: a large
part of their activities consists in doing business with people they never meet, listening to voices they never see, participating as members of an invisible audience in activities
that were once inconceivable in isolation. Actually, these instruments bring into working partnership thousands and even
millions of men: multiplying the fact of sociality. But at
the same time the sense of sociality becomes dim—until it
is restored temporarily, in a gross form, for example, in the
crowds in a football stadium.

The other force that has attenuated the social functions
of the city, particularly in great conurbations, is the tendency
toward segregation: a tendency accentuated by the seemingly
progressive function of zoning, which, in the United States,
often segregates classes and income groups as well as races,
into identifiable quarters, whose members have relatively little
to do with those of higher or lower status. As a result, each
group, each class, each social caste lives in a world which,
in both its architectural and its social arrangements, denies
the manifold cooperations of all human communities. In
the United States, a good deal of our technically most progressive planning, like the great parkways and viaducts
that tempt to further suburban expansion, merely break
down what traces still remain of a common life at the
center; while the suburban pattern of loose open planning

in turn increases, even in a country teeming with motorcars, the difficulties of getting together. As a result social isolationism tends to increase directly with area and population.

Now, from the standpoint of citizenship, the office of planning must be to maximize the instruments of positive and negative cooperation. The planner must provide visual aids for the realization of the true nature of the common life today: reminders that must be made dramatically effective precisely because, without the intervention of planner and architect, they would in such a large degree remain invisible. Further, a good plan will multiply the occasions of an accidental and unpremeditated character, such as those that take place in compact market areas and in public eating places. Though the department store at Welwyn Garden City was originally, no doubt, out of scale with the community itself, it has, in combination with its great dining room, provided an indispensable point of focus for the common life, otherwise neglected in the original plan for the community. Thinking in these terms, the planner will multiply the internal spaces of the city, where people may meet for diverse purposes—marketing, eating, drinking, talking, debating—instead of merely multiplying the occasions for escaping from sight and contact with other people or of massing together to perform a single function. A plan that does not further a daily intermixture of people, classes, activities, works against the best interests of maturity. In our efforts to do away with the unseemly congestion and disorder of the overgrown city, we must beware of swinging so far in the other direction that we loosen the social bond.

*Maturity: Personal Phase.* Throughout this analysis, I have been indicating the necessity for developing public forms for activities which, among people of imagination and means, have hitherto been performed privately: activities which one now seeks to distribute throughout the whole community. Emerson stated the case for the public assumption of household duties long ago, when he pointed out that he needed books, but did not want to become a librarian, that he valued pictures, but he did not want to be a curator of paintings. Even the relatively wealthy members of the community today cannot content themselves with having only a moiety of the real wealth that is available to them as members of a community.

This rule holds true, not only for those functions which must be socialized, but for those that must be de-socialized: solitude for example. One of the marks of maturity is the need for solitude: a city should not merely draw men together in many varied activities, but should permit each person to find, near at hand, moments of seclusion and peace. The function of withdrawal, so far from being segregated as in the medieval cloister, must be recognized as a daily human need. One of the great attractions of a crowded center, like Westminster, is the ease with which a solitary walker may lose himself in the maze of little streets that twist and dodge behind the main thoroughfares. In new communities, smaller in scale, with lower density, one must use art to accomplish the same results. In the parks that bound neighborhood units, for example, one might leave wider graded paths on the outside, to tempt the sociable, while any footpaths would thread through the inner area. It should not be necessary to pass beyond the boundaries of a community in order to find, for a few minutes or a few hours, an adequate retreat. Too much of our thinking, both in modern architecture, with its open plan, and in modern city design, has been of an entirely extrovert order: admirable for public and social occasions, but life-defeating for those introverted moments when withdrawal, brooding, innerness require some special sustenance from the physical environment. Just to the extent that we break down the privacy of the traditional wall and the hedge in domestic planning, when we exchange the free-standing upper-class suburban villa for the worker's terrace house, must we replenish the opportunity for privacy and solitude in the collective plan of the city.

*Final Phase: Senescence.* Perhaps no part of life has been so neglected by our civilization—and so by the planner himself—as old age. In the course of the last half century, throughout the Western world, the old three-generation family has been reduced to the two-generation family: indeed, sometimes, in an effort to maintain spurious standards of youth on the part of the parents, afraid to acknowledge their years, to a one-generation family. The sign of this change has been the increase in the number of separate households, even at a time when the birth rate was drastically falling off. But while the number of old people has increased in every progressive country, thanks to the improvements in hygiene and medical care, no commensurate effort has been made either to build new old peoples' homes, on the old pattern, or to find some new and better means of providing for their care. Old-age pensions are no compensation for their increasing social destitution. Unwanted in the small home, even when they are loved, and too often unloved because they are unwanted, the aged find their lives progressively curtailed and meaningless, while their days are ironically lengthened.

In the general replenishment of family life, which is one of the objectives of good planning, the restoration of the aged to a position of dignity and use becomes one of our principal aims. How shall it be brought about? The first thing to realize is that, if we cannot, and probably should not, try to restore the three-generation family in its more patriarchal form, we can and should restore the three-generation community: this mixture of age groups is as essential to good life as the mixture of economic and social classes. Now there are many important social functions that the aged, so long as their mental faculties are not impaired, may perform to everyone's benefit: the women are capable of participating in the household arts, sewing, mending, knitting, crocheting; old men, though sometimes too slow in pace to earn a full day's wages, can nevertheless remain effective gardeners, doers of odd jobs and repairs, caretakers and overseers. No community can get along without such minor but important services. Moreover, the aged have a natural affiliation with the young, which often works out reciprocally: as experienced baby-tenders and patient 'sitters' they would relieve the parents of the awful confinement of twenty-four-hour attendance upon the young.

Because the old can be so immensely useful here, no community should be considered well laid out, and no housing adequate, unless it provides special accommodation for them. A small one-story unit, of from five to ten couples, or a score of individuals, not segregated in any way from the rest of the housing development, is a far more adequate provision for the aged till they need continuous professional care in a nursing home. Such units should be placed, preferably, near playgrounds or schools or neighborhood markets, for the old want most of all the reassuring presence of life, to overcome the loneliness and the growing sense of alienation or frustration that age itself brings with it. Like the admirable home for the aged at Wythenshawe, the quarters for the aged should be on ground level and minimize the efforts and dangers of climbing steps; but unlike that home, the aged, instead of facing inward upon themselves, should be diverted by the bustle and activity of the life outside.

Housed under such conditions the aged could be near their families, near enough at hand for affectionate supervision or occasional nursing; best of all, capable of participating, without a sense of being burdensome, in the lives of their children or their neighbors; useful, blessed with a purpose in life, even as their days narrow, as is possible under no other condition. The important part about the adequate design of accommodations for the old—whether run publicly or privately, whether for the hale or for the crippled and the infirm, in need of special nursing service—is that they should avoid segregation and institutionalization: even the ministrations of a visiting nurse should not diminish the friendly, intimate scale of these arrangements. Here again, the principle of being 'within view' is an important one to re-establish, as the basis of a score of little intimacies, adventures, stimuli, that even the magnificent housing quarters, if too segregated or too grandiose in scale, do not provide.

All this suggests that an organic conception of city planning, dealing with all the phases of life as well as all the functions of a community, may devise many solutions that have heretofore been ignored in a more specialized approach. In restoring balance within the urban community, one must think of establishing balance in time through interrelationship between the phases of life, for each plateau of life has its own special requirements, which can be well served only when the coordinate needs of other age groups are taken into account. What perhaps is most needed, as a canon of such design, is the return to the human scale: to units of manageable size, to an order visible at once to the naked eye, to a conception of community less as a maze of organization to be treated by wholesale provisions than as a constantly varying combination of a multitude of associative activities, varying in intensity and duration, and progressing through the life-cycle, from birth to death.

*Town Planning Review* (Liverpool), April 1949.

# 3

# Quarters
# for an Aging Population

Probably at no period and in no culture have the old ever been so completely rejected as in our own country, during the last generation. As their numbers have increased, their position has worsened. The breakup of the three-generation family coincided here with the curtailment of living space in the individual household; and from this physical constriction has come social destitution as well.

Now the problem of housing the aged is only one part of the larger problem of restoring old people to a position of dignity and use, giving them opportunities to form new social ties to replace those that family dispersal and death have broken, and giving them functions and duties that draw on their precious life experience and put it to new uses. "Old age hath yet his honor and his toil," as Tennyson's Ulysses put it. The first step toward framing a sound program is, I believe, to examine the human situation as a whole, not to center attention solely upon the problems of destitution, chronic diseases, and hospital care. We shall not, perhaps, be able to care for the aged, on the scale their needs and our national wealth demand, until we are ready to put into the rebuilding of human communities something like the zeal, the energy, the skill, the dedication we give to the monomaniac production of motorcars and superhighways.

As things are now, the process of aging seems to go through three stages. The first, which begins around the age of forty-five, but may not be final for another twenty years, brings liberation from biological reproduction and increasing detachment from the active nurture of children within the family. For the sake of their own growth and independence, young people start at the earliest possible moment to live by themselves. Poverty or a housing shortage may prolong the two-generation family or even restore, in shaky desperation, the three-generation family. But in general, early marriages and early child-bearing hasten the hiving off of the next generation.

Some time during this period of transition, those who have maintained a household big enough for a large family find their quarters empty but burdensome: for they are too expensive for their incomes, and even too large to keep clean, except at an extravagant cost in menial service. In cities, this leads either to a remaking of the single-family house, if owned, into multiple dwellings, or to removal to a small apartment. This shrinkage of space is often accompanied by other losses, such as the breaking of neighborhood ties, the abandonment of a garden and a workshop; and that in turn brings about a further contraction of opportunities and interests. Mark the result: well before senescence has set in, even people in the upper-income groups, in robust health, may find the orbit of their lives uncomfortably narrowing, in a way not adequately compensated by increased local mobility in the motorcar and increased opportunities for general travel.

The second stage in senescence is that of economic retirement: withdrawal at the age of sixty-five, often enforced by benign pension provisions, from the active working life. Unfortunately, our wide practice of automatic retirement often brings on a severe psychological crisis: but even if we showed greater flexibility in imposing retirement, still at some moment, early or late, this blow would fall. In addition to removing a worker from the main sphere of his life-interest and competence, it often halves his income or—as the recent Twentieth Century Fund report shows—cuts it down to a starvation level. At the same time, for those who have invested their energies too exclusively in their work, retirement tends to make their whole life seem meaningless. If at this moment the community sharpens the crisis by weakening other social connections, too, it may aggravate the psychosomatic disabilities that begin to dog this period.

The final stage, that of physiological deterioration, is more variable than the cessation of reproduction or work. Whether the old are happy or bitter, active or frustrated, depends partly upon how long the period of health and vigor is in relation to that covered by the lapse of biological functions that leads to death. But also it depends partly upon how well the community's efforts are directed toward preventing minor impairments from turning, through lack of prompt and adequate care, into major disasters. In any event, senescence proper brings about a gradual slowing down of the vital processes, the deterioration of bodily functions, eyesight, hearing, locomotion, fine coordinations, memory. With this goes a loss of self-help and, with that, self-confidence. In the end this loss may necessitate institutional care, in a nursing home or a hospital. Since the cost of such institutional care, if prolonged over any considerable period, taxes heavily even the upper ten per cent of our income groups, every effort must be made, not merely to lengthen the period of active health, but to restore, through neighborly cooperation and friendly oversight, the kind of voluntary care that the three-generation family once made possible.

If we carry our analysis far enough, we shall find, I think, that the three phases of old age—liberation from reproduc-

tion, economic retirement, and physiological breakdown—
demand a common solution. We shall also find that no
present institution, certainly no simple architectural scheme,
and no mere extensions of existing services, will supply that
solution.

The main point I would make is that the transition from
middle-aged maturity to old age is a long process; and if
we meet it imaginatively at the earliest period possible,
instead of waiting till the last desperate moment, we can
make the transition without a jar, and in some degree turn
a crisis, full of cruel decisions and bitter acceptances, into
a positive and fruitful phase of life. Even more, by extending
active life on the upgrade we can perhaps shorten the period,
now so burdensome, when it is on the downgrade. By contrast, the worst possible attitude toward old age is to regard
the aged as a segregated group, who are to be removed, at
a fixed point in their life course, from the presence of their
families, their neighbors, and their friends, from their familiar quarters and their familiar neighborhoods, from their
normal interests and responsibilities, to live in desolate idleness, relieved only by the presence of others in a similar
plight. Let us ask, rather, by what means we can restore to
the aged the love and respect that they once enjoyed in the
three-generation family at its best.
Unfortunately for any such aim, specialization, mechanization, institutionalization, in a word, segregation, are the order
of the present day: a meaningless, effortless, parasitic, push-
button existence is now put forward as the beautiful promise
of an advanced technology—indeed, the ultimate goal of our
whole civilization. If those terms were actually final ones,
I, for one, should hardly be concerned with the fate of the
aged; for it should be plain that a whole society that can
conjure up no better goals is already moving swiftly toward
early euthanasia, or at least toward mass suicide. If we wish

something better for ourselves, we must be prepared to put forward a program, at every phase of life, that challenges many of the dominant habits and customs of our society and moves boldly in a contrary direction.

At some point in conceiving a good habitat for the aged, we must of course come to an architectural solution; but we must not for a moment imagine that the architect himself, even when backed by ample financial resources, can provide the answers that are needed, or that beauty and order and convenience alone are sufficient. One of the most generous quarters for the aged I have seen is the old Fuggerei in Augsburg, built in the sixteenth century, composed of one-story row dwellings, giving privacy to each old couple, with a handsome fountain and a chapel. But this 'city for the aged and poor' is set apart from the rest of the town; though it has beauty and order, it lacks animation; at best it is only a handsome ghetto. The objection against this solution was indignantly put to me by an old man in another comely quadrangle for the aged at Wythenshawe near Manchester: a modern building set in ample grounds looking inward on a spacious grassy close: also with a little chapel where the dead rested before burial. At first glance, the peace and beauty of this spot seemed 'ideal'—but the inmates knew better. They now had, alas! only one occupation: remaining alive. When the bell tolled, it tolled not only for the departed: it ominously summoned those who were left. "All we do here," said my bitter informant, "is to wait for each other to die. And each time we ask ourselves: 'Who will be next?' What we want is a touch of life. I wish we were near the shops and the bus station, where we could see things."

To normalize old age, we must restore the old to the community. In order to make clear what this means, let me assume that we have a free hand and can plan a whole neighborhood community, as one does in an urban re- development area in the United States or a New Town in Britain. If we establish the right relationships under such ideal conditions, we shall have a clearer view of what to aim for in situations where only a piecemeal solution is possible. We cannot have even a good half-loaf unless we know what ingredients should go into a whole loaf.

The first thing to be determined is the number of aged people to be accommodated in a neighborhood unit; and the answer to this, I submit, is that the normal age distribution in the community as a whole should be maintained. This means that there should be from five to eight people over sixty-five in every hundred people; so that in a neighborhood unit of, say, six hundred people there would be between thirty and forty old people. Any large-scale organization of habitations for the aged which upsets this proportion should be avoided. And this brings us to the second requirement. For both companionship and easier nursing care, the aged should not be scattered in single rooms or apartments through the whole community; but neither should they be thrown together in one large barracks labelled by the architecture, if not the sign- board, Old Peoples' Home. They should rather be grouped in small units of from six to perhaps a dozen apartments. The old monastic rule, that one needs a dozen members to form a community, has had long enough trial to give one confidence in it as a rough measure: when there are less than a dozen, a single cantankerous individual may have a disruptive effect. When there are too many together, they bring on institutional regulations. As an old Navy man once pertinently remarked: There is freedom on a destroyer but not on a battleship.

But once a reasonable degree of closeness is established between small groups of the aged, there is much to be gained by giving them apartments on the lower floors of two- or three-story houses whose upper floors will be occupied by childless people in other age groups: there is likewise reason for providing a covered way or arcade, to make visiting back and forth easier in inclement weather, and to serve as a sheltered place for chatting and sunning at other times. This mixing of age groups within a housing unit primarily designed for the accommodation of the aged would make it possible for those past sixty-five, who found stairs difficult, or who wanted to be more accessible, to adapt themselves to their infirmities with no greater hiatus than moving downstairs.

Now it happens that the number of people over sixty-five in a community is roughly the equivalent of the number of children under six or seven; and in meeting the needs of both extremes pretty much the same conditions hold. Young children need special protection and bodily care; they must be guarded from wheeled vehicles; their difficulties in locomotion and coordination when under three make it desirable to avoid unnecessary obstacles and long flights of stairs. Even psychologically, there are parallels between the self-absorption of the young child and the tendency to withdrawal and inner concentration that mark the last phase of senescence. In a well-designed neighborhood unit, the aged should be able to go to any part of it, including the shopping area, the library, the church, the community center, without crossing a traffic artery; indeed, without, if possible, climbing a step. Someday, when our motorcar production is designed to fill varied human needs, rather than the requirements of the assembly line, we will produce electrically-powered rolling chairs for the aged, which can go safely anywhere a pedestrian can go. That will lessen one of the serious handicaps of old age, if medical remedies for arthritis and feeble limbs remain ineffective. But until then, the ambit of the five-year-old child and the seventy-five-year-old senescent is their normal walking distance. Once these conditions are fulfilled in a neighborhood unit, a larger life would begin to open before the aged.

Now we are ready to rebuild, in our ideal scheme, the other facilities and activities and services that were once performed, more or less effectively, by the three-generation family. And just as the young proceed with their growth through multiplying their contacts with the environment and enlarging their encounters with people other than their families, so the aged may slow down the processes of deterioration, overcoming their loneliness and their sense of not being wanted, by finding within their neighborhood a fresh field for their activities.

But before such an environment can be created, we must challenge the whole theory of segregation upon which so many American communities, not least those that call themselves 'progressive,' have been zoned: zoned so that one-family houses and apartment houses, or row houses and free-standing houses, cannot be built side by side; zoned so strictly for residence that in many suburban communities one cannot buy a loaf of bread or a tin of tobacco without going a mile or two by car or bus to the shops. The pernicious effect of this kind of zoning was first adequately characterized by the Committee on Community Planning of the American Institute of Architects as far back as 1924, and time has abundantly proved all its contentions. Under our zoning ordinances, it is impossible to give either the young or the old the kind of occupational and environmental variety that both a superblock and a neighborhood unit should have.*

In a mixed community, however, many opportunities for service, both voluntary and paid, would open to the aged. Gardening is an occupation that can be carried on at odd

* See Roy Lubove, 'The Urban Community: Housing and Planning in the Progressive Era.' Englewood Cliffs, N.J.: Prentice-Hall, Inc., 1967.

hours, and that can be adapted to the strength and staying power of the old: when a community is well planned, with sufficient amount of parked and gardened open space, it makes greater demands for collective care than it can now often afford. Certainly old people with a turn for gardening should have a little garden plot of their own, too, to look after. Similarly, other opportunities for handicraft should be met by the provision of workshop facilities; making toys, repairing mechanical fixtures, binding books, painting furniture would not merely provide older people with new forms of work: they would, even more importantly, give them the human contacts that a more restricted life fails to offer. Such little shops would have a further educational value for the younger members of the community: indeed, they might be incorporated, with a separate entrance from outside, in a modern school, with great advantage to both the old and the young, who now too often miss the precious experience of intercourse with their grandparents' generation. I know a small town where the carpenter's shop, situated in the old residential area, is the place where school children come to get little repair jobs done; and their contact with the carpenter himself is an affectionate and rewarding one. Such a program would be far more efficacious, psychologically speaking, than merely putting the aged to work on some monotonous specialized task, producing in quantity for the market, under factory conditions.

In addition, there are other services that the aged can perform only in a mixed community, beginning with their most obvious service as baby-sitters. This again, at a dollar an hour, has become a prohibitive luxury even in middle-class communities; and the hazards of leaving the young to the sometimes irresponsible care, if not criminal levity, of inexperienced adolescents only underline the desirability of enlisting the old in the same fashion as they would have been used in the three-generation family. Further, there are many experienced old women, proud of their skill at baking a cake, or even cooking a whole dinner, who would think better of themselves and their life if they might cook and bake occasionally for pay. By having such opportunities, old-age pensions and annuities might be made to go, a little farther, with greater happiness for both the server and the served. To cause the aged to spend all their time glued to a television set is to damn them prematurely to a second childhood. Though these passive amusements have their place in the life of the aged, especially for the crippled and bedridden, there is little reason for reducing their lives as a whole to such a soporific routine. What the aged need is activities: not just hobbies and distractions, but normal participation in the activities of a mixed community.

No single institution, however amply financed and humanely planned, could provide anything like the range of interests that a mixed neighborhood community would do, once age ceases to be regarded as a disease, best treated in an isolation ward. Still, there usually comes a time in everyone's life sooner or later when he requires specialized nursing and medical care. The skillful organization of such care is the duty of the community as a whole; but some fatal inertia has kept our hospital services in an antiquated centralized pattern, and has prevented the creation of small nursing homes, close at hand for family and neighborly visitors, who could, if the hospital were conveniently at hand, take over no small part of the otherwise prohibitively expensive nursing service.

Even before active hospitalization there is need for a public organization of visiting nurses and visiting houseworkers, such as are now provided for on a national scale in England and likewise in certain individual American cities. Here again, by drawing upon all the resources of the community, a much more favorable situation can be created than the most elaborately equipped central institution can provide. I look forward to a day when a small nursing home, for illness and for maternity cases, will be part of the normal requirement of a neighborhood: perhaps as a direct adjunct to a medical clinic and a visiting nurse service. Only when these normal functions of the family are drawn back into the circle of the neighborhood community is there any prospect of our catching up with our needs without raising to a prohibitive height the present cost of highly professionalized large-scale institutional care.

Now we can put together these requirements for the aged. They should, first of all, be part of a normal mixed community, whether they become members of it at twenty-five or at seventy-five. Their quarters should be undistinguishable outwardly from those of other age groups; but they should be sited, as far as possible, where there is a constant play of diverting activity, near a shopping area or a school, so that their chance of being visited, casually and effortlessly, will be increased. Frequent visits, though short, are more refreshing than formal visits, tediously prolonged, that leave desolate intervals of loneliness between them. Many people would find their own family life replenished if the grandparents, though not under their feet, were near at hand; and above all, the young would be the gainers from this; for there are special bonds of sympathy between them and their grandparents' generation, through its very detachment, which often makes them far more ready to heed their advice than that of their own parents. Who can say how much delinquency and brutalized mischief in our American towns may not be due to the very absence of a warm, loving, reciprocal intercourse between the three generations?

Through their nearness to each other, in small units, personal contacts within their own group may easily pass beyond the pleasantries of daily intercourse, the hospitalities of a cup of coffee in the afternoon, or a friendly game of cards or checkers or chess at night; it would also involve visiting each other when ill and performing little services for each other. Everything that makes the aged more independent, yet more confident of the fact that their presence is welcome, increases their capacity to love and be loved; and it is only, in the end, by providing an environment in which the gifts of love may be more easily interchanged, that old age can be kept from shrinking and drying till what is left of life is only a dismal husk. But to say this is also to say that there is no easy shortcut to improved care of the aged: to do well by them, we must give a new direction to the life of the whole community. If we fail here, we shall, in prolonging life, only prolong the possibilities of alienation, futility, and misery.

*Architectural Record,* May 1956.

# 4

# Neighborhood
# and Neighborhood Unit

During the last two decades the idea of planning by neighborhoods has been widely accepted. But this has taken place more in principle than in actual practice, except in the British New Towns. At the same time, a counter-movement has come into existence; the critics of neighborhood planning identify it with many practices that have nothing whatever to do with the neighborhood principle, such as segregation by race or caste or income; and they would treat the city as a whole as the only unit for effective planning. This drawing up for battle is somewhat premature, for there has been little opportunity to experiment with neighborhood units and less time to observe results. Strangely, the arguments for and against neighborhood planning have drawn together the most unlike kinds of people. Thus F. J. Osborn, a staunch advocate of garden cities of limited size, does not favor the physical definition of neighborhoods; while the planners of Amsterdam, though committed to increase the size of their city up to the million mark, have carried out their new developments on the same basic lines as those of an earlier generation: namely, neighborhood by neighborhood, and up to a point they have equipped these neighborhoods as social units.

Much of the argument on this subject has served only to confuse the issues that should be defined; and my purpose in this paper is to clarify some of those issues and make it possible to take a more rational position on one or the other side. By accident, I began this paper in Paris and revised it in Venice. Within these two urban environments the recently posed question of whether neighborhoods actually exist, particularly within great cities, seems a singularly academic one, indeed, downright absurd in their suggestion that neighborhoods are the willful mental creations of romantic sociologists. Paris, for all its formal Cartesian unity, is a city of neighborhoods, often with a well-defined architectural character as well as an identifiable social face. The Parisian neighborhood is not just a postal district or a political unit, but an historic growth; and the sense of belonging to a particular *arrondissement* or *quartier* is just as strong in the shopkeeper, the *bistro* customer, or the petty craftsman as the sense of being a Parisian. Indeed, in Paris the neighborhood attachment is so close, so intense, so narrow that it would have satisfied the soul of Adam Wayne, Chesterton's Napoleon of Notting Hill.

This is not a subjective judgment or a hasty tourist's generalization; M. Chombart de Lauwe and his associates have just begun to publish the results of a careful survey of the movements of Parisians about their city, and have discovered that whereas professional people may move over a good part of it from one day's end to the other, the working people keep close to their own districts, where most of the facilities for life, the café, the dance hall, the church, the school, and, not least, the workshop or factory, are found.* What is exceptional about Paris, I suspect, is not the facts themselves but the way in which the builders of the city, despite their efforts to achieve an over-all unity, have never-

* P.-H. Chombart de Lauwe, 'Paris et l'Agglomération Parisienne.' 2 vols. Paris, 1952.

theless consolidated most of the daily activities of no small part of the population within a limited local area. As for Venice, it is a city of neighborhoods, established as parishes in relation to a dominant church or square; and by its very constitution it reminds us that the medieval city was composed on the neighborhood principle, with the church serving as community center and the market place adjacent to it as 'shopping center,' both within easy walking distance of all the inhabitants. The very word 'quarter' reminds us that, typically, the medieval city, up to the sixteenth century, though it usually contained fewer than twenty-five thousand inhabitants, was divided into quarters: each quarter had its own section of the walls to defend, along with its own churches, workshops, and minor markets. In Florence, for example, each of the six 'quarters' elected two consuls; so under a democratic regime the neighborhood even had a political aspect. These facts did not prevent the city from functioning as a whole, when some great feast or celebration sent the inhabitants into the central area, to worship at the Cathedral or to perform plays from its porch. The common size of these quarters must have been from about fifteen hundred to six thousand persons, except in cities of abnormal growth, like Florence, Milan, or Paris.

Whether it is possible for a city, be it planned or not, to escape some sort of definition or at least local coloring by neighborhoods is problematic. Even in the undifferentiated rectangular plan of Manhattan, a plan contrived as if for the purpose of preventing neighborhoods from coming into existence, distinctive entities, like Yorkville, Chelsea, and Greenwich Village, nevertheless have developed, though they lack any architectural character, except that conditioned by the successive dates of their building. In a rudimentary form neighborhoods exist, as a fact of nature, whether or not we recognize them or provide for their particular functions.

For neighbors are simply people who live near one another. To share the same place is perhaps the most primitive of social bonds, and to be within view of one's neighbors is the simplest form of association. Neighborhoods are composed of people who enter by the very fact of birth or chosen residence into a common life. Neighbors are people united primarily not by common origins or common purposes but by the proximity of their dwellings in space. This closeness makes them conscious of each other by sight, and known to each other by direct communication, by intermediate links of association, or by rumor. In times of crisis, a fire, a funeral, a festival, neighbors may even become vividly conscious of each other and capable of greater cooperation; but in origin, neighborliness rests solely on the fact of local cohabitation. There is nothing forced in this relationship and to be real it need not be deep: a nod, a friendly word, a recognized face, an uttered name—this is all that is needed to establish and preserve in some fashion the sense of belonging together. Neither friendship nor occupational affiliation is implied in the give and take of neighborhood life, though in time such relationships may take form, along with intermarriage. Long-established residence, or the ownership of real property, cements this elementary bond.

At all events, neighborhoods, in some primitive, inchoate fashion, exist wherever human beings congregate, in permanent family dwellings; and many of the functions of the city tend to be distributed naturally—that is, without any theoretical preoccupation or political direction—into neighborhoods. Marked topographic divisions, as in Pittsburgh, or old historic divisions, as in London, with characteristic modes of building, buttress this neighborhood consciousness. Neighborhood grouping, around certain common domestic and civic facilities, is complementary to another form of grouping, likewise ancient, in occupational association or zones, by means of which professions or industries of the same sort tend to form well-defined precincts, sometimes grouped along a single street, like Harley Street, sometimes forming an 'island,' like the Inns of Court in London.

In defining the neighborhood unit, it is important to distinguish it from the occupational precinct or the caste quarter. In the latter, all the members of a trade or corporation are grouped together. In Indian cities, the quarter is composed of people of the same caste and occupation, and in American cities, during the last generation, caste quarters, based on race and income, have been created by zoning or deed restrictions, which equally narrow the basis of human association. In his well-founded distrust of this manner of organization, so hostile to the principles of democracy, Reginald Isaacs, one of the chief American critics of neighborhood planning, has attributed to the neighborhood principle the very vice of specialization and segregation that the modern concept of the 'neighborhood unit' in fact attempts to break down. But the selective nature of these specialized zones should prevent a trained observer from characterizing them as 'neighborhood units,' even though the fact of cohabitation engenders neighborly relations.

How was it that spontaneous neighborhood grouping, so well defined before the seventeenth century, tended to disappear in systematic new Plans, like those of seventeenth-century Amsterdam and nineteenth-century New York, though never entirely disrupted in the more organic growth of a great city like London? One of the answers to this is the segregation of income groups under capitalism, with a sharp spatial separation of the quarters of the rich and the poor; the other was a technical factor, the increase of wheeled vehicles and the domination of the avenue in planning.

The development of transportation caused the traffic avenue to become the dominant component in nineteenth-century design: the emphasis changed from facilities for settlement to facilities for movement. By means of the traffic avenue, often ruthlessly cutting through urban tissue that had once been organically related to neighborhood life, the city as a whole became more united perhaps; but at the cost of destroying, or at least of seriously undermining, neighborhood life. Where, as in the big American metropolises, the grid-iron plan forestalled or overrode neighborhood development, the subordinate parts of the city came more and more to lack any character of their own. Though the successive times of building and the diversity of human purposes might still give a certain residual color to the growing urban extensions, in general, the traffic avenue, abetted by other means of mechanical transportation, tended to break up, not just the rituals of local attachment, but the very sense, conveyed by street plans and architecture, of being part of an identifiable and often lovable whole. Even when the neighborhoods of the nineteenth-century city were identifiable, they were usually not esthetically attractive or lovable; so that, in a sense, it was only in the older quarters of the city or in the better suburbs that the neighborhood, as a cluster of visible and conscious domestic relationships, survived. Otherwise, the long uniform avenue, the random placing of public buildings, created a nightmare of the indefinable. It was easier to lose oneself in the city as a whole than to find oneself in the neighborhood.

Thus things stood with the neighborhood at the beginning of the twentieth century; and so completely had the concept of the neighborhood disappeared that in the first attempt to design a complete, self-contained city, at Letchworth, Messrs. Raymond Unwin and Barry Parker, the town planners, made no effort to define or even suggest the neighborhood. The emphasis still lay on the city as a whole, treated as a single unit. But about this time a movement appeared in America that was to challenge this whole order of planning; and it came from two directions. On the scientific side, it stemmed from Charles Horton Cooley, who was to describe, in a series of books on social organization and social process, the part played by the intimate, face-to-face community, one based on the family, the commonplace, and general shared interests, rather than on specialized vocations and conscious affiliations. What the German sociologists called *Gemeinschaft,* as opposed to *Gesellschaft,* had its basis, Cooley pointed out, in this primary group, with its spontaneous, instinctual, largely 'given' relationships. No matter how differentiated and directed the life of a great metropolis finally became, there remained, at the core of its activities, the same processes and loyalties one discovers in the village.

But the discovery of the neighborhood as an important organ of urban life had two other points of origin. One was due to social impoverishment; the other, to an attempt at social integration. In the East End of London, Canon Barnett and his associates discovered, there was a vast urban wilderness that lacked even the bare elements of social life and had sunk into a state of barbarism. In creating the social settlement, at Toynbee Hall, Barnett provided a common building and meeting place where the residents of the neighborhood could come together for the purposes of play, education, or sociability. This social settlement (sometimes called Neighborhood House in America) answered so many of the needs of the great city, particularly those that grew out of its anonymity and loneliness, that it is hardly surprising that a parallel middle-class movement started in Rochester, New York, about two decades after Toynbee Hall, and became known as the Community Center movement. The advocates of the community center sought to animate civic life by providing a common local meeting place to provide a forum for discussion and to serve as basis for community activities that otherwise had no local habitation. One of the leaders of this movement, Clarence Perry, was led by his analysis of the local community's needs to give back to the neighborhood the functions that had been allowed to lapse, or had become unduly centralized, since the decay of the medieval city. That path led him from the neighborhood to the neighborhood unit: from a mere cohabitation to the creation of a new form and new institutions for a modern urban community. In planning, the result of this was to change the basic unit of planning from the city-block or the avenue to the more complex unit of the neighborhood, a change that demanded a reapportionment of space for avenues and access streets, for public buildings and open areas and domestic dwellings: in short, a new generalized urban pattern.

The other movement that stimulated the consciousness of the neighborhood was the growth of the suburb, especially the suburb planned in a unified way by a development company. In the better suburbs, like Bedford Park and Hampstead Garden Suburb in London, Roland Park and Guilford in Baltimore, Riverside, Chicago, or Kew Gardens, New York, the flowing street plan, the fuller use of tree-lined streets and public open spaces, and the new romantic architecture, made people conscious of the neighborhood as an esthetic unit. Did not the first experiments in concentrated and planned shopping centers, usually adjacent to the railroad, take place in the suburb? Few suburbs were indeed mixed neighborhoods: segregation by income and social class characterized all of them, except, perhaps, those that had grown slowly out of an original country village; but in creating domestic quarters of a more ample nature than the city afforded, the suburb also prompted the beginnings of a civic consciousness, on a neighborhood scale. Though E. L. Thorndyke's rating for cities is not perhaps an infallible guide, the fact that suburbs stand high in the list is not altogether the result of accident or class bias. At least as identifiable neighborhoods they often have facilities that the disorganized and blighted metropolis, whatever its financial and cultural resources, lacks. (When the history of recent Town

Planning comes to be written, it will be clear that most of the fresh initiatives in urban design—the open plan, the superblock, the differentiation of pedestrian and wheeled traffic, the parkway, the shopping center, and, finally, the neighborhood unit—were first tried out in the suburb.) From the suburb, as well as from historic quarters of the city, came the notion that the neighborhood should have a certain coherence of architectural expression, both through the general plan and through the individual design of buildings.

The community center movement seemed to collapse around 1920, along with another more ambitious effort, the Social Unit movement in Cincinnati, which likewise sought to rehabilitate democratic institutions at the neighborhood level. Yet both movements left their mark; for they brought forth a few simple concepts, long neglected, that have had, at least in America, a wide effect upon the minds of planners. The first is the recognition of the need for a definite building to serve as a meeting place for the local community; and the second, following from this, is the simple practical suggestion that the elementary school, the most ubiquitous of local institutions, need only be provided with suitable halls, offices, and committee rooms to serve both children and adults, and to function both by day and by night.

As a result, the minimum requirements for a community center have now become a standard basis for school design in almost every part of the United States; and in such buildings, even in cities otherwise as backward in civic design as New York, an endless round of neighborhood activities goes on. As an historic fact, then, the core of the neighborhood unit, its central nucleus, was projected and actually embodied before the idea of the neighborhood unit as such was defined, or a rational means of determining its boundaries suggested. That final act of clarification took place when Clarence Perry published his work on the subject, as a contribution to the Russell Sage Foundation's 'Regional Survey of New York and Its Environs.'

Meanwhile, however, the notion of redefining and replanning the city on the basis of neighborhoods had been broached in two other quarters. Perry himself was perhaps aided in his inquiry by the publication of the results of a now almost forgotten competition, held by the Chicago City Club, for the planning of a quarter section—six hundred and forty acres—of Chicago. This is a much larger area than most students today would take as a neighborhood; but it brought forth, nonetheless, a remarkable group of designs; remarkable, at least for their time, and not without occasional hints and suggestions even to designers today. Published in the midst of the First World War, it has long been a forgotten item; but it focussed attention on the process of integrating the domestic areas of the city and relating their housing to markets, schools, churches, and other institutions that serve the local area rather than the city as a whole.

Shortly after the publication of this report, Raymond Unwin, surely the most fertile urban innovator in his generation, published a paper on Distribution in the Town Planning Institute 'Journal' (1920–1921) in which he asked: "How far is it possible for the growing city to secure an end so desirable as the greater localisation of life?" And he answered: "I believe that the proper distribution of the parts of the city and the clear definition of its various areas would do much to secure this. Each area in which it is intended to develop a localized life must of course be provided with every facility for all the different branches of life that it is practicable to localize. There should be local work and occupation for as many as possible of the people living there; there should be local markets and shopping centers to provide for their daily needs; there should be educational and recreational facilities. It will not be practicable to have a university in every such locality but at least there should be high schools. You cannot expect to have your Albert Hall for great concerts or your Kennington Oval for international matches in each locality, but at least there should be the Hall of Music, the theater, and such ample provision of playing fields that no one need journey from the locality in order to enjoy the ordinary recreations." In this article Unwin even anticipated the new uses of the greenbelt, which he had already foreshadowed in his Hampstead Garden Suburb, for he observed: "It will be found that the proposed distribution will largely depend on the proper apportionment of open space around each area, and that this open space will serve two main purposes. It will provide all the opportunities for recreation, gardening, and so forth, and it will give a degree of definition to the area and separation from other areas which will emphasize the locality as a defined unit. Referring to the importance of defining areas, I may perhaps quote what I wrote in 1919 that 'these belts might well define our parishes or our wards and by doing so might help to foster the feeling of local unity in the area.' "

When one is describing a movement as complex as this one, one is perhaps tempted to ascribe to one or two leading figures what was really the outcome of many minds, converging from different directions. But though Perry no more discovered the neighborhood principle alone than Le Corbusier discovered modern architecture, the work of each of them has had a dramatic value in crystallizing many diffuse efforts. In his thinking Perry certainly went no further than Unwin, except in so far as he filled in the sketch with concrete details and proposals. What Perry did was to take the fact of the neighborhood; and show how, through deliberate design, it could be transformed into what he called a neighborhood unit, the modern equivalent of the medieval quarter or parish: a unit that would now exist, not merely on a spontaneous or instinctual basis, but through the deliberate decentralization of institutions that had, in their overcentralization, ceased to serve efficiently the city as a whole. He sought to determine what facilities and institutions were necessary for domestic life as such; how many people were needed to support an elementary school, a shopping center, a church, or other institutions; and by what rearrangement of the street pattern a coherent neighborhood could be created with every necessary local function within walking distance of the dwelling. With the aid of plans and elevations, Perry pushed beyond the work of the Chicago competition and attempted to describe an ideal unit, a fully equipped neighborhood. Some of the features of this ideal plan could not, perhaps, stand up under careful examination; but in the establishment of the proper distance from the remotest home to playground, park, or school, and in his suggestion that major traffic routes must be routed around, not through, a neighborhood unit, not least by dedicating ten per cent of the area to local parks and playgrounds, Perry made no small contribution to the reorganization of the modern city.

Even before Perry had published his work on the neighborhood unit, Messrs. Stein and Wright, in their plans for Sunnyside Gardens, Long Island, though confined by the existing gridiron street pattern, had created a neighborhood in which the playgrounds and open spaces and small meeting halls were treated as an integral part of the housing development; and in Radburn they carried this mode of planning, not without consultation with Perry and various school authorities, into their designs for the whole community.

Radburn, conceived in 1928 and largely built during the next three years, embodied in its planning the new concept of the neighborhood as a complete unit. The main traffic roads of

the town went around, not through, the units: the movement of pedestrians was mainly along a spinal green that
formed the inner core of the town, and, by its very constitution, furthered face-to-face acquaintance; at the center
of each neighborhood was an elementary school, with its
recreation field and its swimming pool; and the shops and
services were gathered in a shopping center, with a parking
place for cars, instead of being dispersed along a traffic
avenue. The population of the neighborhood unit was cal-
culated in terms of the number of families needed to support
an elementary school. Because New York authorities con-
sulted then favored big schools, elaborately equipped, from
seventy-five hundred to ten thousand was accepted as the
normal population of a neighborhood; and this has led to
a certain imitative rigidity as to the proper size of a neighborhood unit. Except where the density is unreasonably
high, five thousand would seem to me to be an upper limit,
beyond which one should seek to create a new neighborhood;
but there is no lower limit, except in terms of the facilities
a smaller group can afford. As with the city itself, the main
thing to recognize in neighborhood units is that there is
an upper limit of growth and extension; and that, to define
the unit and keep it in form, there must be both a civic
nucleus to draw people together and an outer boundary to
give them the sense of belonging together.

Perry's concept of the neighborhood unit carried a step
further the earlier notion, first introduced in Germany, of
dividing a city into specialized zones. Treating the domestic
quarters of the city as a functional zone, to be differentiated
in plan, because of its different needs, from the industrial or
commercial zones, he established likewise the need for a
nuclear treatment of the domestic zone, since the acceptable
dimensions of a neighborhood depended upon such relationships as a quarter-mile walk to a local playground or a half-
mile walk to the local school, to say nothing of such in-

determinate though limited distances as those a housewife will willingly walk to do her marketing or shopping. All this seems like such elementary common sense that one wonders that anyone should seriously challenge it. Where such spatial relations are flouted—as they so often are in the spotty, inconsecutive, irrational 'planning' of our time—the members of the community pay for it in extra time and expense and inconvenience, in putting further burdens on the transportation system, in paying extra assessments for otherwise extravagant streets and traffic avenues, or in simply doing without facilities that properly belong within a residential quarter. The neighborhood is based, essentially, on the needs of families; particularly on the needs of mothers and children from the latter's infancy up to adolescence; as well as upon the needs of all age groups for having access to certain common cultural facilities: the school, the library, the meeting hall, the cinema, the church. To have all these institutions within easy reach of the home is a guarantee of their being steadily used by all the members of the family, while to have them scattered and unrelated, especially in distant parts of the city, is to discourage their constant use and often, when children must be cared for, to prevent their use entirely—except at the price of family neglect.

In one of his attacks on the neighborhood unit principle Reginald Isaacs maps an area in Chicago covered by a typical family's activities: the map shows a theoretical self-contained neighborhood center devoid of any social facilities, apparently, except a school and a food shop, while most of the actual activities of the family (if the diagram has been drawn to scale) take place from two miles to twenty miles away from this area. On the basis of this diagram, he asks: Can any one neighborhood contain all the activities of a typical family? That is a specious question. As soon as one breaks down these activities one sees that they fall into two divisions. One consists of occasional activities, like a visit to a distant friend, or to a distant forest preserve on a holiday, or specialized shopping or daily work in an industrial plant necessarily outside the neighborhood—all activities which no one in his senses would propose to concentrate within a single neighborhood. But the other activities, the use of the health clinic, the library, the movies, a church, a park, a playground, a variety of shops, now found in every case outside the neighborhood, demonstrate how much of the time and energy of an urban denizen is wasted in unnecessary transportation, since there is not one of these activities that could not, with benefit, be relocated in a neighborhood unit. Even if no further advantages of face-to-face association and friendly intercourse and political cohesion followed from neighborhood planning, one could easily justify it on economic terms alone.

If the problem of urban transportation is ever to be solved, it will be on the basis of bringing a larger number of institutions and facilities within walking distance of the home; since the efficiency of even the private motorcar varies inversely with the density of population and the amount of wheeled traffic it generates.

All this does not mean that the neighborhood actually is or ideally should be a self-contained unit. The fact is that no social organization, from the family to the state, is wholly self-contained or self-enclosed. The biggest metropolis, in fact, is no more self-sufficient than the neighborhood; for not merely is it dependent upon distant sources of energy, food, raw materials, and products, but, in the case of certain surgical operations, for example, even the biggest of cities may not provide the skill that has been developed in some smaller center. The only functions with respect to which the neighborhood unit is relatively self-contained are the domestic functions or those activities that spring from them. For neighborhood units are built around the home and they should be so designed as to give the fullest advantages of housewifely and parental cooperation and result in the greatest measure of freedom, pleasure, and effectiveness in meeting the needs of family life at every stage of growth.

In short, the notion that the existence of a neighborhood unit presents an obstacle to the wider use of the city does not bear examination: rather it is only by the decentralization of as many activities as possible into local units that the centralized facilities can be kept from becoming congested and ultimately unusable. Sometimes this decentralization may be effected through a bit of mechanical apparatus, as when millions, with the aid of television, are present at a football match that could not possibly be watched by more than fifty thousand people; but at other times, the decentralization must take the form of creating and siting within the local area the appropriate organ of the common life.

From the nature of the case, neighborhood planning can be more easily achieved in new areas, where the whole site must be laid out, than in old quarters, where the very existence of established streets and property lines makes fresh planning difficult. Likewise, it is easier to achieve when the land is held by an urban authority or a development corporation than where it has already been broken into small individual parcels. But even in old neighborhoods, not yet sufficiently blighted or bombed to become 're-development areas,' it is possible to take the first step toward neighborhood integration through the redesign of the central nucleus, partly through pulling together on a more adequate site plan institutions that had been set down more or less at random, partly by abetting the deliberate recentralization of institutions now available to the residents of a neighborhood only by going to a distant part of the city.

The efficacy of many central institutions lapses, so far as the inhabitants of distant areas are concerned, because of the long journey their use demands: even when people are willing to make that journey—as they so long remained loyal to the big department stores—the very heaping up of facilities in the central organization often leads to inefficiency, if only because of the need for selling bulkier goods by sample and warehousing the product in a distant part of the city. In America, and first of all in the big cities, department stores have begun since the early nineteen-thirties to distribute their activities in branch shops in the suburbs, though when I suggested this necessity to the President of Macy's in 1929, he dismissed it as an absurd dream, since the very basis of success, he believed, lay in having 'everything under one roof.' But what has begun to take place with department stores applies almost to every other important metropolitan activity: the same principle, of decentralization into communal and neighborhood units, applies to museums, libraries, hospitals—above all, to hospitals and medical clinics.

Except for highly specialized needs, all of these institutions should seek to multiply facilities scaled to neighborhood use. In the case of childbirth, for example, the neighborhood maternity unit would be preferable to delivery within both the dwelling house, already too cramped for space and often too insistent in the demands made on the mother, and the distant hospital, which, except in cases that promise surgical difficulty, provides nothing that a local institution could not give, and, on the contrary, presents many disadvantages for both the patient and the family. In all of these departments Perry's thinking, excellent as it was in the twenties, has now to be carried beyond the bounds of current practice. Neighborhood unit organization seems the only practical answer to the giantism and inefficiency of the overcentralized metropolis. To preserve specialized institutions for their unique and specific services, which should be available to the whole region, they must be relieved of the heavy burden of performing, in addition, purely parochial functions. There would be no place for the scholar in the Central Library in New York if there were not local libraries, united into a metropolitan system, in every district in the city. This theorem has a wide application; and it justifies from the standpoint of the greater unit the principle of neighborhood decentralization.

The creation of a neighborhood involves something more than the planning on a different pattern than that which has hitherto characterized the undifferentiated big city; for it also demands the orderly provision and relationship in both space and time of a group of neighborhood institutions, such as schools, meeting halls, shops, pubs, restaurants, and local theaters. This calls for the continued activity of a public authority. It is the existence of a full complement of these latter facilities that transforms a spontaneous neighborhood into what one may properly call a neighborhood unit. Ideally, the neighborhood unit, then, would take an old form of association, never entirely suppressed even in the inorganic type of city, and reorganize it on a pattern that both amplifies and enriches daily activity. In doing this, so far from disrupting the functioning of the city as a whole, it rather makes more effective that larger association, since the bigger unit need no longer try to combine the functions of the local community and the larger community, in one muddled, undifferentiated pattern.

The fact—let me emphasize again—that many of the significant activities of the city are occasional ones, and lie outside the neighborhood, or that a large part of an adult's life may be spent far beyond his own domestic precincts, does not lessen the importance of neighborhood functions. Nor does the coming and going of the population of a big city lessen the formative result of good neighborhood design. Where in the city does the population come and go more rapidly than in the university, which turns over most of its population completely every four years? Yet who would deny that the orderly grouping of buildings and the concentration of student interests within the university precinct is itself a part of the educational process, and powerfully molds the lives that submit to it, even for a brief period? Universities whose separate departments were strewn over a great metropolitan area would lack both the economy and the *esprit de corps* a compact precinct gives.

Needless to say, the acceptance of the neighborhood principle does not by itself solve the problems of design: on the contrary, it raises many interesting new problems. Perhaps the first question of importance is what degree of isolation should be accorded the neighborhood, apart from the inevitable separation made by major traffic arteries. In cities like Pittsburgh, whose strong topographical features have broken it up into well-marked neighborhoods, so unrelated that even the high school student finds his high school within his own neighborhood, one notes the danger of a spirit of 'isolationism,' and the more satisfactory the neighborhood, the greater the danger of the self-complacency and the psychological self-enclosure. (In Philadelphia this has even stood in the way of multiple bridging of the Schuylkill, in order to join by direct highways the 'Main Line' suburbs and Germantown and Chestnut Hill; each, rather, prefers to 'keep itself to itself.') Messrs. Stein and Wright, in Radburn, designed their neighborhoods so as to overlap, with the shopping center serving as the point of fusion and intermixture, and by means of underpasses they bound together their neighborhoods by a continuous green core, which served as both park and pedestrian promenade. Both these devices seem preferable to the absolute isolation imposed by wide wedges of greenbelt in some of the British New Towns. When a greenbelt is employed to define a neighborhood, should it not be treated more economically and formally, so as to bring the neighborhoods, at the same time, into closer relationship?

The second problem is how far the tendency toward status and class affiliation should be permitted—abetted as they have been in recent years in the United States by zoning ordinances and deed restrictions—and how far should the neighborhood, as well as the city, be planned as a mixed community with housing for both upper- and lower-income groups? My own experience of living in a non-segregated community, at Sunnyside Gardens, with a wide range of income groups (from twelve hundred to twelve thousand dollars a year) living side by side, has led me to believe that this is the best kind of community. In terms of educating the young and of making the institutions of democracy work, the arguments are entirely in favor of a mixed community. Here another principle may be invoked, which applies, it seems to me, to other parts of the design: the principle that the neighborhood should, as far as possible, be an adequate and representative sample of the whole. I would apply this notion so far as to question the soundness of creating residential quarters on such a scale that local shops and markets and public restaurants and taverns were more than a quarter mile distant from the center. In other words, most of the activities that, in more specialized form, enter into the adult's world should be represented, in simpler modes, in the local community. This would give a variety to the neighborhood unit that is too often absent in new housing developments. The mixture of social and economic classes within a neighborhood should have its correlate in a mixture of housing types and densities of occupation. One of the best examples of the architectural advantages of such mixture is in the Lansbury Neighborhood in London, which has a charm and variety, despite its one hundred and thirty-six inhabitants per residential acre, that much more open schemes, at a flat forty-eight to the acre, often lack.

At the beginning, not every neighborhood can be fully equipped with all the social apparatus necessary for a full domestic and communal life. It would seem, accordingly, a matter of prudence to allow, in the areas set aside for local institutions, a certain amount of undetermined space, for later occupancy. Thus an occasional 'island,' in a local street plan, might allow space for a church, a cinema, or a group of shops, whose existence could not be provided for in the original layout. Until occupied, such free space might serve for allotment gardens. Still another matter that should be a subject of experiment in neighborhood planning is the degree in which the interests of children and adults can and should be combined. The modern community, particularly in England and America, has drifted into the acceptance of age segregation: the young and the old, in their hours of recreation, have little to do with each other. But in France and Italy, on the boulevards or in the open squares, young and old coexist together. In the Piazza Navona at Rome, for example, the adults meet and gossip and eat together, while within sight of them, the young play their games and go about their own affairs, occasionally coming back to 'home base' for comfort or reassurance or a bite to eat.

In the Peckham Health Centre the custom that the families should share the same recreation center and be within sight of each other was established, as a step forward toward family integration; and this would seem to lead to a much healthier relation, morally speaking, than one which either divorces the young from any kind of supervision or gives the function of the family to a paid supervisor. There is room for fresh urban invention here: a new kind of urban open space, more completely liberated from wheeled traffic than the Italian piazza or the market place of Harlow, more intimate than the Parisian boulevard or the market place at Hemel Hempstead; but surrounded with the kind of facilities and institutions that would bring parents and children within sight and call of each other during their leisure hours, so that the parents need not be too strictly confined to the home, nor the children permitted to be completely on the loose. The reintegration of the family, in this fashion, should be one of the serious concerns in planning for the new neighborhood unit.

All these matters in turn raise further problems of architectural treatment: the height and scale of buildings, the relation of open spaces to occupied spaces, of exposure and enclosure. Here there is much fresh thinking to be done, as a basis for design; for in reaction against the congestion of the great city, our architects and planners now tend to sacrifice sociability and concentration to mere openness. In the effort to achieve roominess they have forgotten how, in urban terms, to create rooms, that is, public enclosures adapted to particular urban functions. In the neighborhood, if anywhere, it is necessary to recover the sense of intimacy and innerness that has been disrupted by the increased scale of the city and the speed of transportation. Here the cul-de-sac, the court, even the cloister, have to be rethought by the modern architect in new terms, and recaptured in original designs, adapted to our present needs. No mere sighs of admiration, however voluminous, for the Piazza San Marco will produce the kind of public space the modern city and the modern neighborhood need.

Let me sum up. The neighborhood is a social fact; it exists in an inchoate form even when it is not articulated on a plan or provided with the institutions needed by a domestic community. By conscious design and provision the neighborhood may become an essential organ of an integrated city; and the discussion of the problems raised by neighborhood design will lead to solutions that will carry further the movement begun theoretically in Perry's studies, carried out concretely at Radburn, and applied on a large scale in the British New Towns. Has not the time come for a much more comprehensive canvass of the social functions of the neighborhood, for a more subtle and sympathetic interpretation of the needs of urban families at every stage in the cycle of human growth, and a more adventurous exploration of alternative solutions?

*Town Planning Review* (Liverpool), January 1954.

# 5

# Landscape and Townscape

During the last generation a change has taken place in our conception of open spaces in relation to the urban and regional environment. People in the nineteenth century were conscious, primarily, of the hygienic and sanitary function of open spaces. Even Camillo Sitte, a leader in the esthetic appreciation of cities, called the inner parks of the city 'sanitary greens.' In order to offset the increasing congestion and disorder of the city, great landscape parks were laid out, more or less in the fashion that the aristocracy had promoted for their private country estates. The recreational value of these landscape parks was indisputable; and, in addition, they served as barriers against the spread of the city as an unbroken urbanoid mass. But except for a leisured minority, people visited these parks only on Sundays and holidays; and no equivalent effort was made to provide more intimate open spaces in each neighborhood, where the young might dig and romp, where adults might relax, from time to time, all through the week, without making a special journey.

Given the high densities for dwellings that have prevailed in big cities, it was natural, no doubt, that there should be an emphasis on the biological necessity for open spaces: this recognized the value of sunlight, fresh air, free movement in promoting health, and the psychological need for the sight and smell of grass, bushes, flowers, trees, and open sky. The park was treated, not as an integral part of the urban environment, but as a place of refuge, whose main values derived from the contrast with the noisy, crowded, dusty, urban hive. So impoverished were most cities, except where they inherited aristocratic parks, open residential squares, and playing fields from previous centuries, that open spaces came to be treated as if their value was directly proportional to their area—without too much regard for their accessibility, their frequency of use, or their effect in altering the texture of urban life. Those who felt increasingly deprived of the gardens and parks essential to urban living moved, if they had the means, to a spacious leafy suburb; and in the very act of seeking this all-too-simple solution, they permitted the city itself to become further congested and pushed the open country ever farther away from its center.

Today our appreciation of the biological function of open spaces should be even deeper, now that their function in sustaining life is threatened by radioactive pollution and the air itself around every urban center is filled with scores of cancer-producing substances. But in addition, we have learned that open spaces have also a social function to perform that the mere demand for a verdant refuge too often overlooks.

To understand how important the social role of open spaces is, we must take into account three great changes that have taken place during the last century. First, the change in the mode of human settlement brought about by fast transportation and instantaneous means of communication. As a result, physical congestion is no longer the sole possible way of bringing a large population into intimate contact and cooperation. From this has come another change: a change, wherever sufficient land is available at reasonable prices, in the whole layout of the city: for in the suburbs that have been growing so rapidly around the great centers the buildings exist, ideally, as free-standing structures in a parklike landscape. Too often the trees and gardens vanish under further pressure of population, yet the sprawling, open, individualistic structure, almost anti-social in its dispersal and its random pattern, remains. The third great change is the general reduction of working hours, along with an increasing shift of work itself from industrial occupations to services and professional vocations.

Instead of being faced with a small leisured class, we have now to provide recreational facilities for a whole leisured population. And if this emancipation from incessant toil is not to become a curse, we must create a whole series of alternatives to the sedatives and anesthetics now being offered —especially the anesthesia of locomotion at an ever-higher rate of speed and an even lower return in esthetic pleasure and meaningful purpose. In meeting this challenge, we may well re-examine the experience of the historic aristocracies who, when not engaged in aimless violence and destruction, devoted so much of their energies to the audacious transformation of the whole landscape. Once we accept the challenge of creating an environment so rich in human resources that no one would willingly leave it even temporarily on an astronautic vacation, we shall alter the whole pattern of human settlement. Ebenezer Howard's dream of Garden Cities will widen into the prospect of a garden civilization.

Now very little of the planning that has been projected or achieved during the last generation has taken this new situation into account. Indeed, the chief work that has been done in urban extension and in highway building has been under a curious compulsion to serve the machine rather than to respond to human needs. Unless fresh ideas are introduced, the continued growth of loose suburban areas will undermine our historic cities and deface the natural landscape, creating a large mass of undifferentiated, low-grade urban tissue, which, in order to perform even the minimal functions of the city, will impose a maximum amount of private locomotion, and, incidentally, push the countryside even farther away from the sprawling suburban areas.

This kind of openness and low density is another name for social and civic disintegration, such as we find in cities like Los Angeles. Meanwhile, the great landscape parks in the heart of our old cities too often become neglected, though a long motor ride often leads to a far less attractive destination. While this is happening, the more distant recreation areas by woods, lake, or sea are left to stagger under a weekend congestion that robs that facility of its recreative value, for the motorcar brings to such distant areas the combined population, not just of a single city, but of a whole region.

As a result of these changes, in particular our overattention to movement and our underattention to settlement, the very words 'park' and 'field' have taken on new meanings. 'Park' now usually means a desert of asphalt, designed as a temporary storage space for motorcars; while 'field' means another kind of artificial desert, a barren area planted in great concrete strips, vibrating with noise, dedicated to the arrival and departure of planes. From park and field unroll wide ribbons of concrete that seek to increase the speed of travel between distant points at whatever sacrifice of esthetic pleasures or social opportunities. And if our present system of development goes on, without a profound change in our present planning concepts and values, the final result will be a universal wasteland, unfit for human habitation, no better than the surface of the moon. No wonder people play with projects for exploring outer space: we have been turning the landscape around our great cities into mere launching platforms, and our long daily journeys in the cramped interiors of motorcars are preparatory trips for the even more cramped and comatose journeys by rocket.

Perhaps the first step toward regaining possession of our souls will be to repossess and replan the whole landscape.

To turn away from the processes of life, growth, reproduction, to prefer the disintegrated, the accidental, the random to organic form and order is to commit collective suicide; and by the same token, to create a counter-movement to the irrationalities and threatened exterminations of our day, we must draw close once more to the healing order of nature, modified by human design.

The time has come, then, to conceive alternatives for the classic and romantic clichés of the past, and for the even more sterile clichés of the mechanical 'space-eaters,' who would destroy all the esthetic resources of the landscape in their effort to enable tens of thousands of people to concentrate at a distant point at the same time; and who, when their weekend tourists finally reach such a point, can only reproduce the congested facilities and the banal amusements of the community they have made such a desperate effort to escape. It is not by a mere quantitative increase in the present park facilities, but by a comprehensive change in the whole pattern of life, that we shall realize to the full the social function of open spaces.

And first, one must think of open recreation spaces, outside the existing urban areas, as no longer adequately represented by a few landscape parks or wild reservations, however large: nothing less than a whole region, the larger part of which is in a state of natural growth and useful cultivation, will suffice to meet the needs of our new-style recreation, open to the larger part of the population. The most important public task, around every growing urban center, and far beyond, is to reserve permanent open areas, capable of being maintained for agriculture, horticulture, and related rural industries. These areas must be established in such a fashion as to prevent the coalescence of one urban unit with another. Within its metropolitan area, this has been the notable accomplishment of Stockholm, and in no small degree of the Netherlands as an ecological regional entity. Witness the call of the multi-colored bulb fields at flowering time in spring.

Though the provision of urban greenbelts in part meets our new requirements, we must now think not of greenbelts alone but of a permanent green matrix, dedicated to rural uses whether it comes under public control or remains in private hands. For weekend recreation, the whole regional landscape has become, in fact, the landscape park. That area is far too large to be acquired for park purposes alone; for its upkeep, if solely under state or municipal control, would overburden the largest budget. But by firm legal regulations, the land may be zoned permanently for rural uses in a fashion that will maintain its recreational value, provided both highway system and recreational facilities are planned so as to disperse the transient population of visitors.

The new task for the landscape architect is to articulate the whole landscape so that every part of it may serve for recreation. Besides persuading public authorities to stabilize agricultural land uses by zoning and urban tax abatement so that it will not, without public authorization, be used for residential or industrial building, the task of the landscape architect will be to design footpaths, picnicking grounds, pedestrian pleasances along river fronts, beaches, and woodland groves in such a fashion as to give public access to every part of the rural scene, without undue disturbance to the daily economic round. One must think of continuous strips of public land weaving through the whole landscape and making it usually accessible both to nearby residents and to holiday visitors. There is the beginning of this new process of using the whole landscape as a recreational facility in the layout of bicycle paths in the Netherlands; and there remains in certain parts of England, as a residue from an older era, a system of public footpaths over hill and dale, through field and wood, that needs only to be broadened into somewhat wider strips, no more than twenty or sometimes fifty feet, to provide amply for public needs without encroaching too heavily on agricultural uses.

The same kind of planning would even apply to the motor road, once the object was to achieve, not the maximum amount of speed, but the maximum amount of relaxation and beauty in slow drives designed to open up views, and persuade the motorist, not to seek a more distant point at high speed, but to linger where shade and rich foliage and spicy air are his without further effort. Even in the design of faster highways, those recreational values that have nothing to do with speed can be brought into play by the resourceful landscape architect. Thus the design of the Taconic Parkway in New York State, following the ridgeway in great curves, heavily planted with flowering bushes, opening wide views from time to time over the valley below, offers special rewards to the sensitive motorist.*

While our facilities for mass transportation are responsible for opening up the whole region as a recreational area and public park, the landscape architect must boldly challenge the transportation authorities and highway engineers who have made a fetish of speed and who, in order to justify the extravagant costs of their enterprise, seek to attract the heaviest load of traffic. Speed is the vulgar objective of a life devoid of any more significant kind of esthetic interest. But if our rational object is to disperse traffic and avoid congestion, we must round out our highway system, not by building more speedways, but by laying out or rehabilitating minor roads designed for just the opposite purpose; namely, to tempt the motorist to slow down, to stretch his legs and relax, to spend more time in enjoying the natural beauties near at hand, and

* This praise refers to the original design. Since then the New York State highway engineers have, in their one-eyed fixation on speed, flattened out these curves wherever possible, even substituting ugly steel balks for green division strips.

less time in trying to reach some more distant point where
thousands of other motorcars will converge.

Our ability to turn the whole regional landscape into a
collective park, with its recreation facilities dispersed and
easy to reach, will be determined by the success of public
authorities in making misused or untidy parts of the landscape more attractive, and by setting aside as public recreation grounds a sufficient number of small areas to prevent any
congestion or overuse in any particular spot. The government
might well offer subsidies to individual farmers and land-
owners for participating in larger public landscaping schemes,
as well as by paying outright for widened rights of way and
providing the gates and stiles and fences needed to keep the
urban visitor within bounds. Something of the same system
that the Italians have worked out to police their roads, with
individual stations at intervals, occupied by a permanent road-
worker and his family, might well be applied to ensure the
proper care of the landscape.

In this task of applying landscape design to the whole
region, in order to make it available to every kind of recreation, we must find a place for both the extrovert and the
introvert; for those whose enjoyments are often enhanced
by a public setting and the presence of other people, and
those whose deepest impulses lead to withdrawal and solitary
exploration and quiet contemplation. Today, in most countries, we tend to overplay the role of mass movements and
mass satisfactions and mass attendance at spectatorial sports.
We forget the need to offset the pervasive compulsions of
the crowd by providing plenty of space for solitary withdrawal. But man, as Emerson observed, needs both society
and solitude; and no small part of the social function of
open spaces is *to remain open,* not crowded with people
seeking mass recreation.

In this regional provision for open spaces I can detect no
difference whatever between the needs of the most con-

gested metropolis and those of the country town or the open suburb. For mass transportation, by rail, by public bus, and by motorcar, has extended the field of recreation far beyond the local community and has, at least potentially, widened the area of choice. The surest mark of bad planning is that, in the very effort to meet one kind of mass demand, the planner is tempted to set up a single standard of success, that of quantitative use, and to overlook the need for variety and choice. If this goes on, our mass recreation areas will become as standardized, as monotonous, as lacking in psychological stimulus of any kind, as the urban quarters people want relief from. Good planning, on the other hand, as it widens the field of recreation, in order to meet the demands of a bigger population commanding greater leisure, must be more concerned to achieve a fuller differentiation of both human activities and landscape forms, bringing out the unique resources of each spot—here a winding river, there a striking view, or, in another place, an historic village with a good inn, whose character must be preserved by swinging motor roads and carparks widely around the village, instead of letting them pile up in its center. The autumn visits to the vineyards that used to go on in the Napa Valley of California, like the visits to the blossoming apricot orchards once possible in the Santa Clara Valley, may have more recreational value than a visit to an idle landscape sacred to park custodians. In allowing such land to be swallowed up by speculative builders our 'great metropolises' are depleting their most precious recreational resources.

So much for the larger conception of open spaces, as conceived on a new regional pattern, with a permanent green matrix of open areas, preserved for both local residents and visitors. If we take the necessary political measures to establish this green matrix, a large part of the pressure to escape from the congested city to a seemingly more rural suburb will be relieved, for the rural values that the suburb sought to achieve by strictly private means—and actually could achieve only for a prosperous fraction of the population—will become an integral feature of every urban community.

Two complementary movements are now necessary and possible: one is that of tightening the loose and scattered pattern of the suburb, turning it from a purely residential dormitory into a balanced community, approaching a true garden city in its variety and partial self-sufficiency, with a more varied population and with sufficient local industry and business to support it; and the other is that of loosening the congestion of the metropolis, emptying out part of its population, introducing parks, playgrounds, green promenades, private gardens, into quarters that we have permitted to become indecently congested, void of beauty, and often positively inimical to life. Here, too, we must think of a new form of the city, which will have the biological advantages of the suburb, the social advantages of the city, and new esthetic delights that will do justice to both modes.

Now the great function of the city is to give a collective form to what Martin Buber has well called the I-and-Thou relation: to permit—indeed, to encourage—the greatest possible number of meetings, encounters, challenges, between varied persons and groups, providing as it were a stage upon which the drama of social life may be enacted, with the actors taking their turn, too, as spectators. The social function of open spaces in the city is to bring people together; and as Raymond Unwin demonstrated at Hampstead Garden Suburb—and Henry Wright and Clarence Stein even more decisively at Radburn—when both private and public spaces *are* designed together, this mingling and meeting may take place, under the pleasantest possible conditions, in the neighborhood. Unfortunately, the very congestion of the city produced a reaction on the part of sensitive people that made them overemphasize a purely quantitative ideal of open spaces; and under the influence of suburban practices, which made privacy and spatial aloofness a mark of upper-class status, many of our new communities in both America and Europe are far too loose and sprawling to serve their social purposes. Socially speaking, too much open space may prove a burden rather than a blessing. It is the quality of the open space—its charm and its accessibility—that counts for more than gross quantity.

The problem of the archetypal suburb today is to trade some of its excessive biological space (gardens) for social space (meeting places): that of the congested city is just the opposite, it must introduce into its overbuilt quarters sunlight, fresh air, private gardens, public squares, and pedestrian malls, which will both fulfill the social functions of the city and make it as favorable a place as was the older suburb for establishing a permanent home and bringing up children. The first step in making our older cities habitable is to reduce their residential densities, replacing decayed areas now occupied at a density of two hundred to five hundred persons per acre with housing that will permit parks and gardens as an integral part of the design, at densities not higher than a hundred, or at most, in quarters with a large proportion of childless people, of one hundred and twenty-five to one hundred and fifty persons per acre.

Let us not be deceived by the appearance of the spatial openness that can be achieved by crowding many families into fifteen-story apartment houses. Abstract visual open space is not the equivalent of functional open space that may be used as playgrounds and private gardens. Here again a variety of uses—and therefore a variety of esthetic forms —is the mark of skillful planning and expressive design. Row after row of great slabs or towers, even though set apart far enough to avoid casting a shadow on each other, create a poor environment for any kind of recreation, for they rob the area of sunlight and destroy the intimate and familiar human scale, so vital to the young child, and so pleasant, for that matter, to the adult.

In the restoration or fresh creation of urban open spaces there is room for much fresh experiment and bold design, which will depart from both traditional models and those that have become the fashionable clichés of contemporary form. And in this field each city should suggest a different answer: what is appropriate for Amsterdam with its great water resources would not be equally possible in Madrid. We do not merely need grand plans, conceived freshly, for entirely new neighborhoods where we have cleared away acres of slum. We also need piecemeal solutions that can be applied on a small scale, seizing each small opportunity that will go toward the fulfillment over the years of a much larger design.

When I ask myself what immediate improvement would make my own city, New York, more attractive to live in again, I find two answers: rows of shade trees on every street, and a little park, a quarter or even an eighth of an acre, in each block, preferably near the middle. When I think of another familiar city, Philadelphia, I would turn the back alleys into green pedestrian malls, threading through the city, now widening into pools of open space surrounded by restaurants, cafés, or shops, all insulated from motor traffic. And what applies to individual blocks applies to neighborhoods. To have any value for recreation they, too, must be insulated from the traffic avenues and motorways: the parts of the neighborhood should be joined together by green ribbons, pedestrian malls, and pleasances, such as that admirable park Olmsted designed for the Back Bay Fens of Boston, taking advantage of a little river and a swamp to create a continuous band of green, uniting more than one neighborhood.

The one great requirement for open spaces in urban centers is to insulate them from the fumes, the noise, and the distracting movement of motor traffic. The neighborhood, not the individual building block, is now the unit of urban design, and all fresh schemes both for open spaces and for traffic, to be worthy of approval, must separate the pedestrian completely from the motorcar. When this can be done from the beginning as was first decisively achieved at Radburn, New Jersey, the motor roads that give access to buildings may be reduced in area and partly eliminated; while the space that is so saved within the superblock and the neighborhood may be dedicated to a public park. When these measures are taken, a much more economic and socially valuable use of the land can be made, without the wastage in excessive roads and setbacks and verges one finds in the British New Towns—admirable though they often are in their adequate, indeed sometimes overgenerous, provision for greenbelts and private gardens.

What I have been saying about the social function of open spaces can now be briefly summed up. For weekend recreation we must treat the whole region as a potential park area and make it attractive at so many points that the hideous congestion of the slowly unwinding procession of weekend traffic will be minimized, or disappear entirely in a more lacy network of regional distribution. As for daily use, the same requirements for open space now apply to both the most congested cities and the most sprawling suburbs: for the first must be loosened up for the sake of health and pleasure, while the second must become more concentrated and many-sided for the sake of a balanced social life. In the cities of the future, ribbons of green must run through every quarter, forming a continuous web of garden and mall, widening at the edge of the city into protective greenbelts, so that landscape and garden will become an integral part of urban no less than rural life, for both weekday and holiday uses.

*Landscape,* Winter 1960–1961.

# 6

# The Highway and
# the City

When the American people, through their Congress, voted last year for a twenty-six-billion-dollar highway program, the most charitable thing to assume about this action is that they hadn't the faintest notion of what they were doing. Within the next fifteen years they will doubtless find out; but by that time it will be too late to correct all the damage to our cities and our countryside, to say nothing of the efficient organization of industry and transportation, that this ill-conceived and absurdly unbalanced program will have wrought.

Yet if someone had foretold these consequences before this vast sum of money was pushed through Congress, under the specious guise of a national defense measure, it is doubtful whether our countrymen would have listened long enough to understand; or would even have been able to change their minds if they did understand. For the current American way of life is founded not just on motor transportation but on the religion of the motorcar, and the sacrifices that people are prepared to make for this religion stand outside the realm of rational criticism. Perhaps the only thing that could bring Americans to their senses would be a clear demonstration of the fact that their highway program will, eventually, wipe out the very area of freedom that the private motorcar promised to retain for them.

As long as motorcars were few in number, he who had one was a king: he could go where he pleased and halt where he pleased; and this machine itself appeared as a compensatory device for enlarging an ego which had been shrunken by our very success in mechanization. That sense of freedom and power remains a fact today only in low-density areas, in the open country; the popularity of this method of escape has ruined the promise it once held forth. In using the car to flee from the metropolis the motorist finds that he has merely transferred congestion to the highway; and when he reaches his destination, in a distant suburb, he finds that the countryside he sought has disappeared: beyond him, thanks to the motorway, lies only another suburb, just as dull as his own. To have a minimum amount of communication and sociability in this spread-out life, his wife becomes a taxi driver by daily occupation, and the amount of money it costs to keep this whole system running leaves him with shamefully overcrowded, under-staffed schools, inadequate police, poorly serviced hospitals, underspaced recreation areas, ill-supported libraries.

In short, the American has sacrificed his life as a whole to the motorcar, like someone who, demented with passion, wrecks his home in order to lavish his income on a capricious mistress who promises delights he can only occasionally enjoy.

For most Americans, progress means accepting what is new because it is new, and discarding what is old because it is old. This may be good for a rapid turnover in business, but it is bad for continuity and stability in life. Progress, in an organic sense, should be cumulative, and though a certain amount of rubbish-clearing is always necessary, we lose part of the gain offered by a new invention if we automatically discard all the still valuable inventions that preceded it. In transportation, unfortunately, the old-fashioned linear notion of progress prevails. Now that motorcars are becoming universal, many people take for granted that pedestrian movement will disappear and that the railroad system will in time be abandoned; in fact, many of the proponents of highway building talk as if that day were already here, or if not, they have every intention of making it dawn quickly. The result is that we have actually crippled the motorcar, by placing on this single means of transportation the burden for every kind of travel. Neither our cars nor our highways can take such a load. This overconcentration, moreover, is rapidly destroying our cities, without leaving anything half as good in their place.

What's transportation for? This is a question that highway engineers apparently never ask themselves: probably because they take for granted the belief that transportation exists for the purpose of providing suitable outlets for the motorcar industry. To increase the number of cars, to enable motorists to go longer distances, to more places, at higher speeds has become an end in itself. Does this overemployment of the motorcar not consume ever larger quantities of gas, oil, concrete, rubber, and steel, and so provide the very groundwork for an expanding economy? Certainly, but none of these make up the essential purpose of transportation, which is to bring people or goods to places where they are needed, and to concentrate the greatest variety of goods and people within a limited area, in order to widen the possibility of choice without making it necessary to travel. A good transportation system minimizes unnecessary transportation; and in any event, it offers a change of speed and mode to fit a diversity of human purposes.

Diffusion and concentration are the two poles of transportation: the first demands a closely articulated network of roads—ranging from a footpath to a six-lane expressway and a transcontinental railroad system. The second demands a city. Our major highway systems are conceived, in the interests of speed, as linear organizations, that is to say, as arteries. That conception would be a sound one, provided the major arteries were not overdeveloped to the exclusion of all the minor elements of transportation. Highway planners have yet to realize that these arteries must not be thrust into the delicate tissue of our cities; the blood they circulate must, rather, enter through an elaborate network of minor blood vessels and capillaries.

In many ways, our highways are not merely masterpieces of engineering, but consummate works of art: a few of them, like the Taconic State Parkway in New York, stand on a par with our highest creations in other fields. Not every highway, it is true, runs through country that offers such superb opportunities to an imaginative highway builder as this does; but then not every engineer rises to his opportunities as the planners of this highway did, routing the well-separated roads along the ridgeways, following the contours, and thus, by this single stratagem, both avoiding towns and villages and opening up great views across country, enhanced by a lavish planting of flowering bushes along the borders. If this standard of comeliness and beauty were kept generally in view, highway engineers would not so often lapse into the brutal assaults against the landscape and against urban order that they actually give way to when they aim solely at speed and volume of traffic, and bulldoze and blast their way across country to shorten their route by a few miles without making the total journey any less depressing.

Perhaps our age will be known to the future historian as the age of the bulldozer and the exterminator; and in many parts of the country the building of a highway has about the same result upon vegetation and human structures as the passage of a tornado or the blast of an atom bomb. Nowhere is this bulldozing habit of mind so disastrous as in the approach to the city. Since the engineer regards his own work as more important than the other human functions it serves, he does not hesitate to lay waste to woods, streams, parks, and human neighborhoods in order to carry his roads straight to their supposed destination. As a consequence the 'clover-leaf' has become our national flower and 'wall-to-wall con-crete' the ridiculous symbol of national affluence and techno-logical status.

The fatal mistake we have been making is to sacrifice every other form of transportation to the private motorcar—and to offer as the only long-distance alternative the airplane. But the fact is that each type of transportation has its special use; and a good transportation policy must seek to improve each type and make the most of it. This cannot be achieved by aim-ing at high speed or continuous flow alone. If you wish casual opportunities for meeting your neighbors, and for profiting by chance contacts with acquaintances and colleagues, a stroll at two miles an hour in a relatively concentrated area, free from vehicles, will alone meet your need. But if you wish to rush a surgeon to a patient a thousand miles away, the fastest motorway is too slow. And again, if you wish to be sure to keep a lecture engagement in winter, railroad trans-portation offers surer speed and better insurance against being held up than the airplane. There is no one ideal mode or speed: human purpose should govern the choice of the means of transportation. That is why we need a better transportation *system*, not just more highways. The projectors of our national highway program plainly had little interest in transportation. In their fanatical zeal to expand our high-ways, the very allocation of funds indicates that they are ready to liquidate all other forms of land and water trans-portation.

In order to overcome the fatal stagnation of traffic in and around our cities, our highway engineers have come up with a remedy that actually expands the evil it is meant to overcome. They create new expressways to serve cities that are already overcrowded within, thus tempting people who had been using public transportation to reach the urban centers to use these new private facilities. Almost before the first day's tolls on these expressways have been counted, the new roads themselves are overcrowded. So a clamor arises to create other similar arteries and to provide more parking garages in the center of our metropolises; and the generous provision of these facilities expands the cycle of congestion, without any promise of relief until that terminal point when all the business and industry that originally gave rise to the congestion move out of the city, to escape strangulation, leaving a waste of expressways and garages behind them. This is pyramid building with a vengeance: a tomb of concrete roads and ramps covering the dead corpse of a city.

But before our cities reach this terminal point, they will suffer, as they now do, from a continued erosion of their social facilities: an erosion that might have been avoided if engineers had understood MacKaye's point that a motorway, properly planned, is another form of railroad for private use. Unfortunately, highway engineers, if one is to judge by their usual performance, lack both historic insight and social memory: accordingly, they have been repeating, with the audacity of confident ignorance, all the mistakes in urban planning committed by their predecessors who designed our railroads. The wide swathes of land devoted to cloverleaves and expressways, to parking lots and parking garages, in the very heart of the city, butcher up precious urban space in exactly the same way that freight yards and marshalling yards did when the railroads dumped their passengers and freight inside the city. These new arteries choke off the natural routes of circulation and limit the use of abutting properties, while at the points where they disgorge their traffic they create inevitable clots of congestion, which effectively cancel out such speed as they achieve in approaching these bottlenecks.

Today the highway engineers have no excuse for invading the city with their regional and transcontinental trunk systems: the change from the major artery to the local artery can now be achieved without breaking the bulk of goods or replacing the vehicle: that is precisely the advantage of the motorcar. Arterial roads, ideally speaking, should engirdle the metropolitan area and define where its greenbelt begins; and since American cities are still too impoverished and too improvident to acquire greenbelts, they should be planned to go through the zone where relatively high-density building gives way to low-density building. On this perimeter, through traffic will bypass the city, while cars that are headed for the center will drop off at the point closest to their destination.

Since I don't know a city whose highways have been planned on this basis, let me give as an exact parallel the new semicircular railroad line, with its suburban stations, that bypasses Amsterdam. That is good railroad planning, and it would be good highway planning, too, as the Dutch architect H. Th. Wijdeveld long ago pointed out. It is on relatively cheap land, on the edge of the city, that we should be building parking areas and garages: with free parking privileges, to tempt the commuter to leave his car and finish his daily journey on the public transportation system. The public officials who have been planning our highway system on just the opposite principle are likewise planning to make the central areas of our cities unworkable and uninhabitable.

Now, as noted before, the theory of the insulated, high-speed motorway, detached from local street and road systems, immune to the clutter of roadside 'developments,' was first worked out, not by highway engineers, but by Benton MacKaye, the regional planner who conceived the Appalachian Trail. He not merely put together its essential features, but identified its principal characteristic: the fact that to achieve speed it must bypass towns. He called it, in fact, the Townless Highway. (See 'The New Republic,' March 30, 1930.) Long before the highway engineers came through with Route 128, MacKaye pointed out the necessity for a motor bypass around the ring of suburbs that encircle Boston, in order to make every part of the metropolitan area accessible, and yet to provide a swift alternative route for through traffic.

MacKaye, not being a one-eyed specialist, visualized this circuit in all its potential dimensions and developments: he conceived, accordingly, a metropolitan recreation belt with a northbound motor road forming an arc on the inner flank and a southbound road on the outer flank—the two roads separated by a wide band of usable parkland, with footpaths and bicycle paths for recreation. In reducing MacKaye's conception to Route 128, without the greenbelt and without public control of the areas adjacent to the highway, the 'experts' shrank the multi-purpose Bay Circuit into the typical 'successful' expressway: so successful in attracting industry and business from the center of the city that it already ceases to perform even its own limited functions of fast transportation, except during hours of the day when ordinary highways would serve almost as well. This, in contrast to MacKaye's scheme, is a classic example of how not to do it.

Just as highway engineers know too little about city planning to correct the mistakes made in introducing the early railroad systems into our cities, so, too, they have curiously forgotten our experience with the elevated railroad—and, unfortunately, most municipal authorities have been equally forgetful. In the middle of the nineteenth century the elevated seemed the most facile and up-to-date method of introducing a new kind of rapid transportation system into the city; and in America, New York led the way in creating four such lines on Manhattan Island alone. The noise of the trains and the overshadowing of the structure lowered the value of the abutting properties even for commercial purposes; and the supporting columns constituted a dangerous obstacle to surface transportation. So unsatisfactory was elevated transportation even in cities like Berlin, where the structures were, in contrast to New York, Philadelphia, and Chicago, rather handsome works of engineering, that by popular consent subway building replaced elevated railroad building in all big cities, even though no one could pretend that riding in a tunnel was nearly as pleasant to the rider as was travel in the open air. The destruction of the old elevated railroads in New York was, ironically, hailed as a triumph of progress precisely at the moment that a new series of elevated highways were being built, to repeat on a more colossal scale the same errors.

Like the railroad, again, the motorway has repeatedly taken possession of the most valuable recreation space the city possesses, not merely by thieving land once dedicated to park uses, but by cutting off easy access to the waterfront parks, and lowering their value for refreshment and repose by introducing the roar of traffic and the bad odor of exhausts, though both noise and gasoline exhaust are inimical to health. Witness the shocking spoilage of the Charles River Basin parks in Boston, the arterial blocking off of the Lake Front in Chicago (after the removal of the original usurpers, the railroads), the barbarous sacrifice of large areas of Fairmount Park in Philadelphia, the insistent official efforts, despite public disapproval, to deface the San Francisco waterfront.*

One may match all these social crimes with a hundred other examples of barefaced highway robbery in every other metropolitan area. Even when the people who submit to these annexations and spoliations are dimly aware of what they are losing, they submit without more than a murmur of protest.

* The fact that the aroused citizens of San Francisco not only halted the engirdlement of the Bay but now also demand that the present structure be torn down may prove a turning point in the local community's relations with an entrenched and high-handed bureaucracy. An encouraging example to all other cities similarly threatened. In November 1967 the New York 'Times' headlined the happy news: "U.S. Road Plans Periled by Rising Urban Hostility."

What they do not understand is that they are trading a permanent good for a very temporary advantage, since until we subordinate highway expansion to the more permanent requirements of regional planning, the flood of motor traffic will clog new channels. What they further fail to realize is that the vast sums of money that go into such enterprises drain necessary public monies from other functions of the city, and make it socially if not financially bankrupt.

Neither the highway engineer nor the urban planner can, beyond a certain point, plan his facilities to accommodate an expanding population. On the over-all problem of population pressure, regional and national policies must be developed for throwing open, within our country, new regions of settlement, if this pressure, which appeared so suddenly, does not in fact abate just as unexpectedly and just as suddenly. But there can be no sound planning anywhere until we understand the necessity for erecting norms, or ideal limits, for density of population. Most of our congested metropolises need a lower density of population, with more parks and open spaces, if they are to be attractive enough physically to retain even a portion of their population for day-and-night living; but most of our suburban and exurban communities must replan large areas at perhaps double their present densities in order to have the social, educational, recreational, and industrial facilities they need closer at hand. Both suburb and metropolis need a regional form of government, working in private organizations as well as public forms, to decentralize their strangled resources and facilities, so as to benefit the whole area.

To say this is to say that both metropolitan congestion and suburban scattering are obsolete. This means that good planning must work to produce a radically new pattern for urban growth. On this matter, public policy in the United States is both contradictory and self-defeating. Instead of lowering central area densities, most urban renewal schemes, not least those aimed at housing the groups that must be subsidized, either maintain old levels of congestion, or create higher levels than existed in the slums they replaced. But the Home Loan agencies, on the other hand, have been subsidizing the wasteful, ill-planned, single-family house, on cheap land, ever remoter from the center of our cities; a policy that has done as much to promote the suburban drift as the ubiquitous motorcar.

In order to cement these errors in the most solid way possible, our highway policy maximizes congestion at the center and expands the area of suburban dispersion—what one might call the metropolitan 'fall-out.' The three public agencies concerned have no official connections with each other: but the total result of their efforts proves, once again, that chaos does not have to be planned.

Motorcar manufacturers look forward confidently to the time when every family will have two, if not three, cars. I would not deny them that hope, though I remember that it was first voiced in 1929, just before the fatal crash of our economic system, too enamored of high profits even to save itself by temporarily lowering prices. But if they don't want the motorcar to paralyze urban life, they must abandon their fantastic commitment to the indecently tumescent chariots they have been putting on the market. For long-distance travel, the big car, of course, has many advantages; but for town use, let us insist upon a car that fits the city's needs: it is absurd to make over the city to fit the swollen imaginations of Detroit. The Isetta and the Gogomobil have already pointed the way; but what we need is a less cramped but still compact vehicle, powered by electricity, delivered by a powerful storage cell, yet to be invented: the exact opposite of our insolent chariots.* Maneuverability and parkability

* Both the cell and the car are now, a decade later, on the way.

are the prime urban virtues in cars; and the simplest way to achieve this is by designing smaller cars. These virtues are lacking in all but one of our current American models. But why should our cities be destroyed just so that Detroit's infantile fantasies should remain unchallenged and unchanged?

If we want to make the most of our national highway program, we must keep most of the proposed expressways in abeyance until we have done two other things. We must replan the inner city for pedestrian circulation, and we must rebuild and extend our public forms of mass transportation. In our entrancement with the motorcar, we have forgotten how much more efficient and how much more flexible the footgoer is. Before there was any public transportation in London, something like fifty thousand people an hour used to pass over London Bridge on their way to work: a single artery. Mass public transportation can bring from forty to sixty thousand people per hour, along a single route, whereas our best expressways, using far more space, cannot move more than four to six thousand cars, and even if the average occupancy were more than one and a half passengers, as at present, this is obviously the most costly and inefficient means of handling the peak hours of traffic.

As for the pedestrian, one could move a hundred thousand people, by using all the existing streets, from, say, downtown Boston to the Common, in something like half an hour, and find plenty of room for them to stand. But how many weary hours would it take to move them in cars over these same streets? And what would one do with the cars after they had reached the Common? Or where, for that matter, could one assemble these cars in the first place? For open spaces, long distances, and low densities, the car is now essential; for urban space, short distances, and high densities, the pedestrian.

Every urban transportation plan should, accordingly, put the pedestrian at the center of all its proposals, if only to facilitate wheeled traffic. But to bring the pedestrian back into the picture, one must treat him with the respect and honor we now accord only to the automobile: we should provide him with pleasant walks, insulated from traffic, to take him to his destination, once he enters a business precinct or residential quarter. Every city should heed the example of Rotterdam in creating the Lijnbaan, or of Coventry in creating its new shopping area. It is nonsense to say that this cannot be done in America, because no one wants to walk.

Where walking is exciting and visually stimulating, whether it is in a Detroit shopping center or along Fifth Avenue, Americans are perfectly ready to walk. The legs will come into their own again, as the ideal means of neighborhood transportation, once some provision is made for their exercise, as Philadelphia is now doing, both in its Independence Hall area and in Penn Center. But if we are to make walking attractive, we must not only provide trees and wide pavements and benches, beds of flowers and outdoor cafés, as they do in Zurich: we must also scrap the monotonous uniformities of American zoning practice, which turns vast areas, too spread out for pedestrian movement, into single-district zones, for commerce, industry, or residential purposes. (As a result, only the mixed zones are architecturally interesting today despite their often frowzy disorder.)

Why should anyone have to take a car or a taxi and drive miles to get domestic conveniences needed every day, as one must often do in a suburb? Why, on the other hand, should a growing minority of people not be able again to walk to work, by living in the interior of the city, or, for that matter, be able to walk home from the theater or the concert hall? Where urban facilities are compact, walking still delights the American: does he not travel many thousands of miles just to enjoy this privilege in the historic urban cores of Europe? And do not people now travel for miles, of an evening, from the outskirts of Pittsburgh, just for the pleasure of a stroll in Mellon Square? Nothing would do more to give

life back to our blighted urban cores than to reinstate the
pedestrian, in malls and pleasances designed to make circulation a delight. And what an opportunity for architecture!

While federal funds and subsidies pour without stint into
highway improvements, the two most important modes of
transportation for cities—the railroad for long distances and
mass transportation, and the subway for shorter journeys—are
permitted to languish and even to disappear. This is very
much like what has happened to our postal system. While
the time needed to deliver a letter across the continent has
been reduced, the time needed for local delivery has been
multiplied. What used to take two hours now sometimes takes
two days. As a whole, our postal system has been degraded
to a level that would have been regarded as intolerable even
thirty years ago. In both cases, an efficient system has been
sacrificed to a new industry, motorcars, telephones, airplanes;
whereas, if the integrity of the system itself had been respected, each of these new inventions could have added
enormously to the efficiency of the existing network.

If we could overcome the irrational drives that are now
at work, promoting shortsighted decisions, the rational case
for rebuilding the mass transportation system in our cities
would be overwhelming. The current objection to mass
transportation comes chiefly from the fact that it has been
allowed to decay: this lapse itself reflects the general blight
of the central areas. In order to maintain profits, or in many
cases to reduce deficits, rates have been raised, services have
decreased, and equipment has become obsolete, without
being replaced and improved. Yet mass transportation, with
far less acreage in roadbeds and rights of way, can deliver at
least ten times more people per hour than the private motorcar. This means that if such means were allowed to lapse in
our metropolitan centers—as the interurban electric trolley
system, that beautiful and efficient network, was allowed to

disappear in the nineteen-twenties—we should require probably five to ten times the existing number of arterial highways to bring the present number of commuters into the city,
and at least ten times the existing parking space to accommodate them. In that tangled mass of highways, interchanges,
and parking lots, the city would be nowhere: a mechanized
nonentity ground under an endless procession of wheels.
Witness Los Angeles, Detroit, Boston—indeed, every city
whose municipal officials still stubbornly equate expressways,
high-rise buildings, and parking facilities with urban progress.

That plain fact reduces a one-dimensional transportation
system, by motorcar alone, to a calamitous absurdity, as far
as urban development goes, even if the number of vehicles
and the population count were not increasing year by year.
Now it happens that the population of the core of our big
cities has remained stable in recent years: in many cases, the
decline which set in as early as 1910 in New York seems to
have ceased. This means that it is now possible to set an
upper limit for the daily inflow of workers, and to work out
a permanent mass transportation system that will get them in
and out again as pleasantly and efficiently as possible.

In time, if urban renewal projects become sufficient in number to permit the design of a system of minor urban through-
ways, at ground level, that will bypass the neighborhood, even
circulation by motorcar may play a valuable part in the total
scheme—provided, of course, that minuscule-size town cars
take the place of the long-tailed dinosaurs that now lumber
about our metropolitan swamps. But the notion that the
private motorcar can be substituted for mass transportation
should be put forward only by those who desire to see the
city itself disappear, and with it the complex, many-sided
civilization that the city makes possible.

There is no purely engineering solution to the problems
of transportation in our age: nothing like a stable solution is
possible without giving due weight to all the necessary ele-

ments in transportation—private motorcars, railroads, air-planes and helicopters, mass transportation services by trolley and bus, even ferryboats, and finally, not least, the pedestrian. To achieve the necessary over-all pattern, not merely must there be effective city and regional planning, before new routes or services are planned; we also need eventually—and the sooner the better—an adequate system of federated metropolitan government. Until these necessary tools of control have been created, most of our planning will be empirical and blundering; and the more we do, on our present premises, the more disastrous will be the results. What is needed is more thinking on the lines that Robert Mitchell, Edmund Bacon, and Colin Buchanan have been following, and less action, until this thinking has been embodied in a new conception of the needs and possibilities of contemporary urban life. We cannot have an efficient form for our transportation system until we can envisage a better permanent structure for our cities. And the first lesson we have to learn is that the city exists, not for the facile passage of motorcars, but for the care and culture of men.

*Architectural Record*, April 1958.

# 7

# The Disappearing City*

Nobody can be satisfied with the form of the city today. Neither as a working mechanism, as a social medium, nor as a work of art does the city fulfill the high hopes that modern civilization has called forth—or even meet our reasonable demands. Yet the mechanical processes of fabricating urban structures have never before been carried to a higher point: the energies even a small city now commands would have roused the envy of an Egyptian Pharaoh in the Pyramid Age. And there are moments in approaching New York, Philadelphia, or San Francisco by car when, if the light is right and the distant masses of the buildings are sufficiently far away, a new form of urban splendor, more dazzling than that of Venice or Florence, seems to have been achieved.

Too soon one realizes that the city as a whole, when one approaches it closer, does not have more than a residue of this promised form in an occasional patch of good building. For the rest, the play of light and shade, of haze and color, has provided for the mobile eye a pleasure that will not bear closer architectural investigation. The illusion fades in the presence of the car-choked streets, the blank glassy build-

* This and the following four articles came out as a series in the 'Architectural Record' and form a unit.

ings, the glare of competitive architectural advertisements, the studied monotony of high-rise slabs in urban renewal projects: in short, new buildings and new quarters that lack any esthetic identity and any human appeal except that of superficial sanitary decency and bare mechanical order.

In all the big cities of America, the process of urban rebuilding is now proceeding at a rapid rate, as a result of putting both the financial and legal powers of the state at the service of the private investor and builder. But both architecturally and socially the resulting forms have been so devoid of character and individuality that the most sordid quarters, if they have been enriched over the years by human intercourse and human choice, suddenly seem precious even in their ugliness, even in their disorder.

Whatever people made of their cities in the past, they expressed a visible unity that bound together, in ever more complex form, the cumulative life of the community; the face and form of the city still recorded that which was desirable, memorable, admirable. Today a rigid mechanical order takes the place of social diversity, and endless assembly-line urban units automatically expand the physical structure of the city while destroying the contents and meaning of city life. The paradox of this period of rapid 'urbanization' is that the city itself is being effaced. Minds still operating under an obsolete nineteenth-century ideology of unremitting physical expansion oddly hail this outcome as 'progress.'

The time has come to reconsider the whole process of urban design. We must ask ourselves what changes are necessary if the city is again to become architecturally expressive, and economically workable, without our having to sacrifice its proper life to the mechanical means for keeping that life going. The architect's problem is again to make the city visually 'imageable'—to use Kevin Lynch's term. Admittedly, neither the architect nor the planner can produce, solely out of his professional skill, the conditions necessary for building and rebuilding adequate urban communities; but their own conscious reorientation on these matters is a necessary part of a wider transformation in which many other groups, professions and institutions must in the end participate.

The multiplication and expansion of cities which took place in the nineteenth century in all industrial countries occurred at a moment when the great city builders of the past —the kings and princes, the bishops and the guilds—were all stepping out of the picture; and the traditions that had guided them, instead of being modified and improved, were recklessly discarded by both municipal authorities and business enterprisers.

Genuine improvements took place, indeed, in the internal organization of cities during the nineteenth century: the first substantial improvements since the introduction of drains, piped drinking water, and water closets into the cities and palaces of Sumer, Crete, and Rome. But the new organs of sanitation, hygiene and communication had little effect on the visible city, while the improvements of transportation by railroad, elevated railroad, and trolley car brought in visual disorder and noise and, in the case of railroad cuts and marshalling yards, disrupted urban space as recklessly as expressways and parking lots do today. In both the underground and the aboveground city, these new gains in mechanical efficiency were mainly formless, apart from occasional by-products like a handsome railroad station or a bridge.

In consequence, the great mass of metropolitan buildings since the nineteenth century has been disorganized and formless, even when it has professed to be mechanically efficient. Almost until today, dreams of improvement were either cast into archaic, medieval, classic, or renascence molds, unchanged except in scale, or into purely industrial terms of mechanical innovations, collective 'Crystal Palaces,' such as H. G. Wells pictured in his scientific romances, and even Ebenezer Howard first proposed for a garden city shopping mall. In America, despite the City Beautiful movement of the nineties, urban progress is still identified with high buildings, wide avenues, long vistas: the higher, the wider, the longer, the better.

Current suggestions for further urban improvement still tend to fall automatically into a purely mechanical mold: gouging new expressways into the city, multiplying skyscrapers, providing moving sidewalks, building garages and underground shelters, projecting linear Roadtowns, or covering the entire area with a metal and plastic dome to make possible total control of urban weather—on the glib theory that uniform conditions are 'ideal' ones. So long as the main human functions and purposes of the city are ignored, these subsidiary processes tend to dominate the architect's imagination. All the more because the resulting fragments of urbanoid tissue can be produced anywhere, at a profit, in limitless quantities. We are now witnessing the climax of this process.

The great exception to the routine designs for nineteenth-century urban expansion was the replanning of the center of Paris. Paris became in fact *the* model nineteenth-century city. Here, in a consistent organic development that began under Colbert and was carried to a temporary climax under Baron Haussmann during the Second Empire, a new central structure was created—first in the handsome monumental masonry of the Seine embankment, and then in the great boulevards and new parks. By creating a new outlet for sociability and conversation in the tree-lined promenade and the sidewalk café, accessible even to older quarters that were still dismally congested and hygienically deplorable, the planners of Paris democratized and humanized the otherwise sterile Baroque plan. The beauty and order of this new frame, which at once preserved the complexities of the older neighborhoods and opened up new quarters threaded with broad public greens, attracted millions of visitors to Paris and—what was more im-

portant—helped increase the daily satisfaction of its inhabitants.

But while Paris improved its rich historic core, it lost out
in form, as badly as London or Berlin, Philadelphia or
Chicago, on its spreading periphery. The vitality and individuality that had been heightened by the boulevards, parks,
and parkways of Paris were dependent upon historic institutions and many-sided activities that the new quarters lacked.
Left to themselves, these residential quarters were deserts of
pretentious monotony. Today central Paris, too, is being an-
nihilated by the same forces that produce the vast areas of
urban nonentity that surround the living core of our own
big cities. These forces are choking Paris today as they
have choked cities in the United States, as new as Fort Worth
and as old as Boston.

Not the weakest of these destructive forces are those that
operate under the guise of 'up-to-date planning,' in extravagant engineering projects, like the new motorways along
both banks of the Seine—a self-negating improvement just as
futile as the motorways that have deprived Boston and Cambridge of access to their most convenient and potentially most
delightful recreation area along the Charles. This new order
of planning makes the city more attractive temporarily to
motorcars, and infinitely less attractive permanently to human
beings. On the suburban outskirts of our cities everywhere in
both Europe and America, high-rise apartments impudently
counterfeit the urbanity they have actually left behind.
Present-day building replaces the complex structure of the
city with gray masses of gritty 'urbanoid' tissue.

This formless urbanization, which is both dynamic and
destructive, has become almost universal. Though it utilizes
one kind of structure in metropolitan renewal projects and a
slightly different kind in suburbia, the two types have bas-
ically the same defect. They have been built by people who
lack historical or sociological insight into the nature of the

city, considered as anything but the largest number of consumers that can be brought together in the most accessible manufacturing and marketing area.

If this theory were an adequate one, it would be hard to account for the general exodus that has been taking place from the center of big cities for the last generation or more; and even harder to account for the fact that suburbs continue to spread relentlessly around every big metropolis, forming ever-widening belts of population at low residential density per acre, ever further removed from the jobs and cultural opportunities that big cities are by their bigness supposed to make more accessible. In both cases, cities, villages, and countryside, once distinct entities with individuality and identity, have become homogenized masses. Therewith one of the main functions of architecture, to symbolize and express the social idea, has disappeared.

During the last generation an immense amount of literature on cities has belatedly appeared, mostly economic and social analysis of a limited kind, dealing with the subsidiary and peripheral aspects of urban life. Most of these studies have been entirely lacking in concrete architectural understanding and historical perspective. Though they emphasize dynamic processes and technological change, they naïvely assume that the very processes of change now under observation are themselves unchanging; that is, that they may be neither retarded, halted, nor redirected nor brought within a more complex pattern that would reflect more central human needs and would alter their seeming importance.

For the exponents of aimless dynamism, the only method of controlling the urban processes now visible is to hasten them and widen their province. Those who favor this automatic dynamism treat the resultant confusions and frustrations as the very essence of city life, and cheerfully write off the accompanying increase in nervous tensions, violence, crime, and health-depleting sedatives, tranquillizers, and atmospheric poisons.

The effect of this literature has been, no doubt, to clarify the economic and technical processes that are actually at work in Western urban society. But that clarification, though it may help the municipal administrator in performing his daily routines and making such plans as can be derived from five-year projections, has so far only served to reinforce and speed up the disruptive processes that are now in operation. From the standpoint of the architect and the city planner, such analysis would be useful only if it were attached to a formative idea of the city; and such an idea of the city is precisely what is lacking.

'Idea' comes from the original Greek term for 'image.' Current proposals for city improvement are so imageless that city-planning schools in America, for the last half-generation, have been turning out mainly administrators, statisticians, economists, traffic experts. For lack of an image of the modern city, contemporary 'experts' covertly fall back on already obsolete clichés, such as Le Corbusier's Voisin plan for Paris. Following the humanly functionless plans and the purposeless processes that are now producing total urban disintegration, they emerge, like the sociologist Jean Gottmann, with the abstract concept of 'Megalopolis'—the last word in imageless urban amorphousness. And unfortunately, people who have no insight into the purposes of urban life have already begun to talk of this abstraction as the new 'form' of the city.

The emptiness and sterility of so much that now goes under the rubric of modern city design is now being widely felt. Hence the interest that has been awakened by books like Jane Jacobs' 'The Death and Life of Great American Cities,' with its keen appreciation of some of the more intimate aspects of urban life, and with its contrasting criticism, largely deserved, of radical human deficiencies in the standardized, high-rise, 'urban renewal' projects.

The fact is that twentieth-century planning still lacks a fresh multi-dimensional image of the city, partly because we have not discussed and sorted out the true values, functions and purposes of modern culture from many pseudo-values and apparently automatic processes that promise power or profit to those who promote them.

What has passed for a fresh image of the city turns out to be two forms of anti-city. One of these is a multiplication of standard, de-individualized high-rise structures, almost identical in form, whether they enclose offices, factories, administrative headquarters, or family apartments, set in the midst of a spaghetti tangle of traffic arteries, expressways, parking lots, and garages. The other is the complementary but opposite image of urban scatter and romantic seclusion often called suburban, though it has in fact broken away from such order as the nineteenth-century suburb had actually achieved, and even lacks such formal geometric coherence as Frank Lloyd Wright proposed to give it in his plans for Broadacre City. As an agent of human interaction and co-operation, as a stage for the social drama, the city is rapidly sinking out of sight.

If either the architect or the planner is to do better in the future, he must understand the historical forces that produced the original miscarriage of the city, and the contemporary pressures that have brought about this retreat and revolt.

*Architectural Record,* October 1962.

# 8

# Yesterday's City of
# Tomorrow

In the preceding chapter I dealt with the continued dissolution of the city into an amorphous, overmechanized urbanoid mass, lacking both esthetic identity and social character.
Even the biggest metropolises seem fatally doomed by this
process, if we allow it to continue. Private transportation by
motorways, during the last two decades, instead of assisting
the reorganization and reintegration of urban life on a
regional scale, has only lengthened distances, slowed down
transportation within the city, and dispersed useful facilities
that were once close at hand and constantly available.
Therewith the city and all its organs have been dissolving
into the amoeboid nonentity miscalled Megalopolis.

Meanwhile, the major reaction against the misdemeanors
of the city has been the escape to Suburbia. For more than
a century, families that were content to do without the
social advantages of the city profited by the cheap land and
the natural landscape to create a biologically more adequate
environment, with full access to all the things now missing
from the city: sunlight, untainted air, freedom from mechanical noises, ample lawns and gardens, accessible open country
for walks and picnics; finally, individual houses, specially
designed for family comfort, expressive of personal taste.

This impulse to have closer contact with the rural scene was fed by the literature of the Romantic movement, from Rousseau on to Thoreau; but it did not originate there. For the rich families of Florence, Rome, and Venice, in the fifteenth and sixteenth centuries, did not wait for either Romanticism or the railroad age to build their country villas in Fiesole, in Frascati, or on the Brenta. What marks the modern age is that both the impulse and the means of achieving it have become universal.

Though the ultimate outcome of this suburban retreat on a large scale has proved to be a non-city, if not an anti-city, just because of the very isolation and separation it proudly boasted, one must not underestimate its architectural results or its great human attraction; in fact, no adequate image of the emerging city will arise until these are both fully reckoned with. From William Morris' Red House to the shingle-houses of H. H. Richardson, W. R. Emerson, and their colleagues, from Frank Lloyd Wright's prairie houses on to the work of Voysey, Parker, and Baillie-Scott, from Olmsted's Riverside and Roland Park to Unwin's Hampstead Garden Suburb, most of the fresh forms of domestic architecture and planning grew out of the suburb. This still holds true today: not merely in houses, but in shopping centers, school complexes, industrial parks. Apart from purely industrial architecture, like the cotton mills of Manchester or the early skyscrapers of Chicago, no other environment has proved so encouraging to positive architectural expression as the suburb.

Though the original values of the suburb have been fast disappearing in the welter of the ever-spreading conurbation, the image that was left behind has had an influence upon urban planning. This is the image of a new kind of city, the 'City in a Park'; more open in texture than the more crowded cities of the past, with permanent access to gardens and parks for all the inhabitants of the city, not just for the dominant minority. That influence has expressed itself in three different conceptions of the contemporary city, advanced by three distinguished architects and planners, Raymond Unwin, Frank Lloyd Wright, and Le Corbusier. Though radically different in their human background and purpose, all three conceptions have a common denominator: an unqualified demand for more space. In this article I shall confine myself to the work of Le Corbusier. If space and speed, mass production and bureaucratic regimentation were all that were necessary to form a new image of the modern metropolis, Le Corbusier would already have provided an adequate solution.

Most architects, during the last thirty years, and certainly most architectural and planning schools, have been dominated by the powerful propaganda and experimental achievement of this singular man of genius, Le Corbusier. If anyone put forward what seemed a fresh and original conception of the City of Tomorrow, it was this redoubtable leader. Though that conception has gone through a series of changes, corresponding to changes that have taken place likewise in his architecture, certain main features stand out, and will probably for a while continue to have influence, even if the master should abandon them. And though no one city, except Chandigarh, shows the full range of his influence, his thought has run so closely along the grain of our age that fragments of it are scattered everywhere.

The chief reason for Le Corbusier's immediate impact lies in the fact that he brought together the two architectural conceptions that separately have dominated the modern movement in architecture and city planning: the machine-made environment, standardized, bureaucratized, 'processed,' technically perfected to the last degree; and to offset this, the natural environment, treated as so much visual open space, providing sunlight, pure air, green foliage, and views.

Not the least attraction of Le Corbusier's thought to his

contemporaries was that in bringing these two together, he paid no more attention to the nature of the city and to the orderly arrangements of its constantly proliferating groups, societies, clubs, organizations, institutions, than did the real-estate broker or the municipal engineer. In short, he embraced every feature of the contemporary city except its essential social and civic character. This failure to understand the function of the city as a focal meeting place extended to the C.I.A.M., which commissioned a book on the city in which the functions of the city that concerned the planner were reduced to housing, work, recreation, and industry; and it was not until this group belatedly produced its symposium on the 'Heart of the City' that the city's special social attributes, as a meeting place, were at last recognized.*

In his first presentation of the City of the Future, Le Corbusier overemphasized its new mechanical facilities, and equated urban progress with geometrical order, rectilinear planning, and mechanized bureaucratic organization. Enchanted by the possibilities of modern steel and concrete construction, Le Corbusier first presented a picture of a modern city like Paris, transformed into his new image: an image of free-standing, sixty-story office buildings, set in open spaces, as the central feature, with multiple high-speed transportation routes at many levels, feeding into this center, and long series of apartment houses, uniform in height, forming an undifferentiated residential district outside the bureaucratic core. This new unit would hold three million inhabitants, the equivalent of Paris. Le Corbusier's Voisin plan (1922–1925) was superimposed on the center of Paris: he proposed to tear down the historic core of Paris, as confused, unsanitary, pestilent, preserving only a few ancient monuments, and packing all its multifarious activities into uniform structures.

* See J. L. Sert, 'Can Our Cities Survive?' Cambridge, Mass.: Harvard University Press, 1942.

In his readiness to demolish the historic quarter of Paris and replace it with these towering isolated buildings, Le Corbusier's imagination worked like a bulldozer on an urban renewal project. In the name of efficiency, he paid no attention to the actual functions and purposes of the structures he proposed to rehouse, or to historic buildings that by their individual character give form and continuity to the life that goes on within them. In short, he ignored the main office of the city, which is to enrich the future by maintaining in the midst of change visible structural links with the past in all its cultural richness and variety. In proposing prudently to preserve a handful of historic buildings as isolated monuments, Le Corbusier overlooked the fact that no small part of their value and meaning would disappear, once they were cut off from the multitudinous activities and associations that surrounded them; that, in fact, it was people, not space, that they needed if they were even properly to be seen.

In placing his emphasis on the vertical, rather than the horizontal, elements of city design, Le Corbusier was fascinated, not only by the general possibilities of technology, but also by the desire to give a more rigorous Cartesian expression to the American skyscraper. He had returned, most probably without any consciousness of it, to the form of the early Chicago skyscrapers, and had removed, not merely the romantic pinnacles and setback towers that had followed, but also the visual jumble and congestion. His novel proposal was to combine the new order of height with something that had never been seriously suggested before, a palatial increase of open space, in the form of a park, between the buildings.

In that simple act, Le Corbusier wiped out the complex tissue of a thousand little and not so little urban activities that cannot be economically placed in tall structures or function efficiently except at points where they are encountered at street level and utilized by a multitude of people going about their business at all times of the day.

The extravagant heights of Le Corbusier's skyscrapers had no reason for existence apart from the fact that they had become technological possibilities; the open spaces in his central areas had no reason for existence either, since on the scale he imagined there was no motive during the business day for pedestrian circulation in the office quarter. By mating the utilitarian and financial image of the skyscraper city to the romantic image of the organic environment, Le Corbusier had, in fact, produced a sterile hybrid.

But perhaps the very sterility of Le Corbusier's conception was what has made it so attractive to our age. In American cities tall buildings came into existence not simply as a convenience for business enterprise, but as a mode of increasing land values and the opportunities for highly profitable large-scale building and speculation; and even when the business towers provided too little floor space in proportion to elevator space to be profitable, they served by their very extravagance as a form of commercially valuable advertisement. The tall building was accepted in America as a standardized substitute, with convertible units of space, for more functional plans and elevations that might require a more generous—that is, expensive—allotment of land along with a more exacting design.

By stressing the visual openness between tall buildings, offsetting the low coverage with ever-higher structures, Le Corbusier seemed to have satisfied two hitherto irreconcilable conditions: higher densities with higher rents on one hand, and greater exposure to light and air, along with a greater sense of open space, however unusable except to the eye. This pattern could be reduced to a mechanical formula and repeated anywhere precisely because it paid so little attention to the variety of human needs and the complexities of human association. That failing largely accounts for the present success of Le Corbusier's formula. But applied to urban renewal projects it has proved a disastrous success, on which Jane Jacobs has said almost the last word, though her own counter-proposals, to increase densities and encourage haphazardness, are equally unsound, and quite as willfully negligent of urban realities.

Le Corbusier's early images of the city were supplemented by later designs that could be carried out on a more modest scale: his plan in the nineteen-thirties for the little town of Nemours in North Africa, with its geometric grouping of domino structures, set the fashion for high-rise slabs. Both images in turn have had a massive impact upon the minds of today's architect–city planners. The postwar housing estates of the London County Council record that influence at its best, sometimes in more ingratiating forms than he had pictured—as in the Alton estate at Roehampton, on land already richly landscaped by the original suburban owners— but also at its worst, as in their overemphatic repetitions of his Unity House slab in another area.

In the United States the standard urban renewal projects fostered by the federal government have been designed in a similar socially heedless fashion. Le Corbusier meanwhile has kept on modifying his original proposals, which were exclusively metropolitan and bureaucratic. In more recent statements since 1945 he has envisaged small, better balanced, more self-contained communities, as complementary members of the metropolis; and in Chandigarh he even took over from Albert Mayer and Matthew Nowicki, the first planners, the outlines of the Radburn plan, with its series of neighborhood superblocks and its inner green walkways.

But the gigantic scale of that city demands a completely motorized population: that is the mischief of excessive openness. Though Le Corbusier's buildings are low, his walks are long, and the central public buildings swim in space under a torrid summer sun whose heat further penalizes pedestrian circulation. The misplaced openness of Le Corbusier's new capital turns the great buildings and monuments into isolated works of sculpture, exhibited as in a high outdoor museum. They are meant to be visited piously or admired occasionally at a distance: not to serve as intimate architectural companions in the daily traffic of the city, visible at all times, with sufficient detail to hold the eye and refresh the spirit even under intimate inspection. In its excessive, official openness this plan vies with Walter Burley Griffin's purely suburban conception of the Australian capital of Canberra: but already it is plain that Griffin's plan is the better one.

Le Corbusier was, of course, right in thinking that the functions of business and transportation could be more efficiently handled in structures especially designed to fit modern needs; he was right, too, in thinking that a basic pattern of order is essential to the full enjoyment of the city, particularly in our own age, in which a multitude of sensual and symbolic stimuli—print, sound, images—at every hour of the day, would produce overwhelming confusion if the general background were equally confused. So, too, he was correct in thinking that the skyscrapers of New York or Chicago should be thinned out, if they were to be visible from street level, or if the traffic avenues were to remain usable; and further, that sunlight, pure air, vegetation, along with order and measure, were essential components of any sound environment, whether urban or rural.

But in his contempt for historic and traditional forms, Le Corbusier not merely lost continuity with the past but likewise any sense of how much of the present he was also losing. His new conception of the City in a Park misconceived the nature and functions of both city and park.

The monotony of Le Corbusier's favored forms has expressed the dominant forces of our ages, the facts of bureaucratic control and mechanical organization, equally visible in business, in industry, in government, in education. That fact itself constituted one of its meretricious attractions. But until Le Corbusier theoretically destroyed the historic tissue of the city, with its great complexity of form and its innumerable variations even within the fixed geometry of the gridiron plan, the prevailing bureaucratic pattern had been modified by many human, sometimes all-too-human, departures. The old skyscrapers of Wall Street or the Loop may have been anarchic in their efforts to pre-empt space or claim attention, but they did not present the faceless conformist image of present-day Park Avenue. As for urban compositions that have been more directly influenced by Le Corbusier's idea of the City in a Park—the collection of office buildings in the Pittsburgh Triangle, for example—they might as well be in a suburb as in the city itself. Even the open space around these buildings has become meaningless in terms of light and air, for all-day fluorescent lighting and air conditioning flout the one benefit that would justify this type of plan.

Unmodified by any realistic conception of urban functions and urban purposes, apart from the bureaucratic process itself, Le Corbusier's City in a Park turns out in fact to be a suburban conception. By its very isolation of functions that should be closely connected to every other aspect of city life, and by its magnification of the forces that govern metropolitan life today, it can be detached from the organic structure of the city and planted anywhere. Even the space around Le Corbusier's skyscrapers has an ambivalent function, for the City in a Park has now taken a more acceptable, commercially attractive form, and has become a City in a Parking Lot.

When we follow this whole process through, we discover that the freedom of movement, the change of pace, the choice of alternative destinations, the spontaneous encounters, the range of social choices and the proliferation of marketing opportunities, in fact, the multifarious life of a city, have been traded away for expressways, parking space, and vertical circulation. It is not for nothing that so many of the new urban housing projects, filled with twenty-story skyscrapers, are called villages: the conformities they demand, the social opportunities they offer, are as limited as those of a village. These islands of habitation in the midst of a sea of parking lots might have densities of five hundred inhabitants a residential acre, and be part of a megalopolitan complex holding tens of millions of inhabitants, but the total mass still would lack the complex character of a city.

In short, the City in a Park does nothing to foster the constant give and take, the interchange of goods and ideas, the expression of life as a constant dialogue with other men in the midst of a collective setting that itself contributes to the animation and intensity of that dialogue. The architectural blankness of such a city mirrors the only kind of life possible under it: over-all control at the top, docile conformity at the bottom.

While Le Corbusier's image of the city is still often regarded as the last word in modern design, it combines, in fact, the three chief mistakes of the nineteenth century. These misconceptions destroyed the classic form of the city, as it had existed almost from the beginning, and replaced it with a succession of urban and suburban wastelands: anticities.

The first mistake was the overvaluation of mechanization and standardization as ends in themselves, without respect to the human purpose to be served. The second was the theoretic destruction of every vestige of the past, without preserving any links in form or visible structure between past and future, thereby overmagnifying the importance of the present and at the same time threatening with destruction whatever permanent values the present might in turn create, and nullifying any lessons that might be learned from its

errors. This is the error of the 'disposable urban container.'
Finally, Le Corbusier's concept carried to its extreme the
necessary reaction against urban overcrowding: the mistake
of separating and extravagantly overspacing facilities whose
topographic concentration is essential for their daily use.

Now that a sufficient number of adaptations of Le Corbusier's leading concepts are in existence, we begin to have
an insight into both their social and their esthetic limitations;
for the two are, in fact, closely connected. The visual open
space that this planning produces has no relation to the
functional open space, space as used for non-visual purposes,
for meeting and conversation, for the play of children, for
gardening, for games, for promenades, for the courting of
lovers, for outdoor relaxation. At the high density of two
hundred and fifty to five hundred people per acre, what
seems by the trick of low coverage an ample provision of
open space turns out to be miserly.

The esthetic monotony of these high-rise dominoes is, in
fact, a reflection of their social regimentation: they do not
represent, in architectural form, the variety that actually
exists in a mixed human community; uniformity and conformity are written all over them. Such freedom, such family
intimacy, such spontaneous utilization of the natural environment, and such architectural identity as even the old-fashioned
railroad-suburb offered have been forfeited without any
equivalent return.

The City in a Park, as so far conceived by Le Corbusier
and his followers, is a blind alley. Yet its basic ingredients,
the more adroit use of present-day mechanical facilities and
the constant respect for the natural conditions for health and
child nurture, must play a part in any better image of the
future city. Neither high-rise structures, vertical transportation, spatial separation, multiple expressways and subways,
nor wholesale parking space will serve to produce a community that can take advantage of all the facilities modern

civilization offers and work them into an integrated urban form. Even when assembled together in orderly fashion they still do not constitute a city. Before the architect can make his contribution to this new form, his private services to his client must be combined with a better understanding of the nature and functions of the city as a device for achieving the maximum amount of human cooperation and crystallizing in more durable and visible form the whole creative process.

*Architectural Record,* November 1962.

# 9

# Megalopolis as
# Anti-City

The bureaucratic ideals of standardization, regimentation, and centralized control have left their mark on all our urban planning for the last half century: the city, to paraphrase Aristotle, has become Organization Man writ large.

In reducing the realities of living organisms and human societies to calculable financial abstractions—square feet of rentable space, acres of traffic interchanges, miles of superhighways, millions of taxable real estate—the constructors and administrators of our modern, machine-conditioned metropolises have overlooked the essential task of the city. That task is to provide the maximum number of favorable opportunities for large populations to intermingle and interact, to interchange their human facilities and aptitudes as well as their economic goods and services, to stimulate and intensify by frequent contact and collaboration many common interests that would otherwise languish.

This neglect of the corporate activities and personal participations of the city derives from a new situation. Except for the extractive industries, production and consumption can now be carried on almost anywhere. The more mechanized and automatic the economic operations, the less need they have of the city's human abundance and cultural variety.

More than half a century ago the prophetic eye of H. G. Wells pointed out in 'Anticipations' that, with the railroad and the motorcar—and soon, he foresaw, the airplane—the population would become 'delocalized' and mobile. He pictured detached villas and factories spread all over the countryside, entirely released from the gravitational field of the big city.

This pressure toward total dispersion has been embodied in two different concepts of urban design that still keep on cropping up. The earliest was that of the Spanish engineer Soria y Mata: he proposed in the eighties to create a continuous 'linear city' by extending the existing centers systematically along their major routes of transportation, to form continuous urban belts. This idea was revived in 1910 by an American engineer, Edgar Chambless, in a book called 'Roadtown,' and the notion in turn was reformulated once more by Le Corbusier, before it was given a grim practical expression in some of the Soviet Russian industrial settlements of the thirties.*

In an entirely undirected but diagrammatic fashion, Roadtown has automatically grown up along the major highways of America; an incoherent and purposeless urbanoid nonentity, which dribbles over the devastated landscape and destroys the coherent smaller centers of urban or village life that stand in its path. Witness among a thousand other examples the Bay Highway between San Francisco and Palo Alto. Roadtown is the line of least resistance; the form that every modern city approaches when it forgets the functions and purposes of the city itself and uses modern technology only to sink to a primitive social level.

The other model for urban dispersion was that put forward by Frank Lloyd Wright in his design for Broadacre

* For the latest sophisticated version of Megalopolis—and, incidentally, the final *reductio ad absurdum*—see C. A. Doxiadis, 'Ecumenopolis: Toward the Universal City.' Athens: Doxiadis Associates, 1961.

City, with the square western section and quarter-section doing duty for the purely linear traffic road. This plan took a self-sufficient family dwelling as the unit of urban development, and placed it on a plot of from one to three acres, repeating this unit, as one might easily do on the flat prairie, with similar rectangular plots spatially regimented to serve such minimal social institutions as might survive. On the scale of Broadacre City, fewer than eight hundred families—at most some three thousand people—would occupy a site as large as New York's Central Park.

This fantasy of Wright's was based on both his wholesome appreciation of the hygienic and domestic values of rural life, and his feudal contempt for the many-sided corporate and institutional life of the city. In the name of the first, he was ready to shrink the acreage of productive soils and break down the special human values of the rural landscape, with the functional divisions of meadow, pasture, and woodland, of cultivated land and wild land, in order to give every house and family a subsistence garden; and he was no less ready to break down the natural coagulations of life in villages and country towns, in a new fashion that made every social activity call for long-distance transportation and therefore the incessant use of the motorcar.

Wright's handsome imaginative design for Broadacre City was never carried out except in piecemeal form. But the idea itself has indirectly had a devastating success, since it merely represented in a coherent, disciplined pattern the random forces, mechanical and financial, that have been disintegrating the city.

In short, what Wright proposed as the City of the Future proved to be what his countrymen, during the next thirty years, would turn into our dismal sub-suburban present, abetted as they have been by exuberant highway building and expansive motorcar production. The upper-income group image of urban dispersion is the green ghetto of the exurban community, just far enough beyond the metropolitan center and its spreading suburban belt to be able to zone its territory for housing at a minimum density of one family to the acre. The high price of such remote lots automatically turns the farmer into a real-estate speculator, and results, as in California, in the slaughter of the orchards, vineyards, and market gardens that once gave both health and delight—to say nothing of fresh food—to the nearby urban communities. Every year, according to Dr. Marion Clawson, a million acres of agricultural land are taken over for housing, largely scattered in green acres, and another million acres are withheld from farming through speculation and social erosion.

The result is not a new kind of city on a supermetropolitan scale, but an anti-city; not merely destitute of urban attributes, but also inimical to the most important of them—the unification of specialized vocations and interests in order to produce a more stimulating and creative common life. And instead of producing the maximum amount of freedom and spontaneity, this scattering of the metropolitan population over the remoter parts of the countryside confines its working members for ever-longer periods to a mobile cell, travelling ever-longer distances to the place of work or to achieve even a few of the social and interpersonal relations that the city once provided at one's elbow.

On the surface Frank Lloyd Wright's ideal of the self-sufficient rural household in a thinned-out pattern of settlement might seem to be a large-scale domesticated fulfillment of Thoreau's Walden; but actually he had projected in elegant geometric form a regime as antithetic to Walden as Skinner's 'Walden Two' or his own later 'skyscraper a mile high.' Walden was at least attached to Concord, and Concord in turn to Cambridge and Boston: so even in isolation Thoreau partook of the multi-dimensional social life of the city.

❖

The anti-city that is now being produced by the reckless extension of standardized expressways, standardized roadside services, and standardized residential subdivisions—all greedily devouring land—dilutes to the point of complete insolvency all the valuable urban functions that require a certain density of population, a certain mixture of activities, a certain interweaving of economic necessities and social occasions. Despite all that, this negative image has proved, especially during the last two decades, to be a highly attractive one; so powerful that many people already identify it, despite its brief history and meager promise, with the 'American way of life.'

The reason is not far to seek, for the anti-city combines two contradictory and almost irreconcilable aspects of modern civilization: an expanding economy that calls for the constant employment of the machine (motorcar, radio, television, telephone, automated factory, and assembly line) to secure both full production and a minimal counterfeit of normal social life; and as a necessary offset to these demands, an effort to escape from the overregulated routines, the impoverished personal choices, the monotonous prospects of this regime by daily withdrawal to a private rural asylum, where bureaucratic compulsions give way to exurban relaxation and permissiveness, in a purely family environment as much unlike the metropolis as possible. Thus the anti-city produces an illusory image of freedom at the very moment all the screws of organization are being tightened.

Though the anti-city, almost by definition, is hardly imageable, its scattered parts are often esthetically attractive and humanly rewarding. Moreover, as a practical expedient, the anti-city has at its disposal the combined forces of highway engineers, motorcar manufacturers, real-estate developers, and lending institutions: all the more favored because its very randomness avoids the need for disciplined cooperation and municipal coordination. Because the anti-city is by nature fragmentary, any part can be built by anybody any-where at any time. This is the ideal formula for promoting total urban disintegration.

Not the least factor in this development, certainly in America, is the persistent residue of the curious pioneer be-lief in space and mobility as a panacea for the ills of social life. In a recent discussion of the siting of a new university in California, which has been endowed with thousands of acres at the outskirts of a small, well-situated coastal town, Santa Cruz, I found I was almost alone in favoring a compact de-velopment in close proximity to the existing facilities of the town. Most of the administrators, under the current doctrine of space for space's sake, favored a much looser grouping of buildings, miles away from the center of the town, with a faculty housing subdivision even more remote and more segre-gated. Characteristically, this scattering would necessitate the building of a special motor road and the sacrifice of valuable university land to parking.

When the sense of the city's reason for existence is lacking, there is nothing to keep the parts from spreading ever farther away, not merely from the metropolitan centers but also from each other. This has become the 'space age' with a vengeance: in architecture space has become a substitute for urban design. In opting for the anti-city, the architect and the businessman play into each other's hands. Great business enterprises tend more and more to operate like self-sufficient feudal enclaves, watchfully regulating the activities of their employees in the interest of their health, working efficiency, and future promotion. By moving into the open country, a corporation can plan self-contained facilities, on land hith-erto unbuilt on, and occupy acres at a lower price than the city demands for square feet. In this new anti-urban pattern, each agency has its own self-contained plant, surrounded by broad acres of parking lot, often with its own bowling alley, its own medical clinic, its own hospital; while its employees draw upon the marketing facilities of a shopping center equally insulated in space.

These conditions have proved highly attractive to the architect, too. Even if he does not share Frank Lloyd Wright's delight in the rural background as such, he too easily falls for the attraction of empty acres upon which his individual creation will stand gloriously alone: no longer cramped by inadequate frontages, by insufficient land, or by too exacting urban building codes and zoning regulations; no longer in danger, either, of being defaced or obliterated by the building next door. The archetypal model for this overspaced existence is the airport.

This lonely eminence is a powerful lure; all the more so because the new rural office buildings, the new industrial parks, sometimes even the new shopping centers, and, above all, the new schools and college campuses can, in fact, often show a much higher level of design than their constricted metropolitan equivalents. Apart from the architect's freedom, one of the reasons for his readiness to desert the city is that with land so cheap, a proportionately greater part of the budget can be spent on the building and the landscaping. Unfortunately, this distinction too often is nullified by the immense paved void of parking lot, and the esthetic result is sullied by regiments of motorcars in the foreground.

Actually, the conditions provided by the anti-city are not so favorable in the long run for any purpose as either the architect or the businessman imagines. This spatial openness, on close examination, proves to be social enclosure and constriction; and too often the architect himself, in obedience to the dominant bureaucratic principle, nullifies the advantages of his ample acres by designing a sealed-in, air-conditioned building, whose blank, Venetian-blinded façade turns its back on the landscape and mocks its very openness with a tightly closed inner court. Alternately, the plethora of space may go to the architect's head and cause him to produce loose, rambling plans and vacuous incoherent structures, as over-spaced as his parking lots. What the modern architect needs for a better model is an image of variety and multiformity and social complexity and concentration that neither the bulldozed landscape of Roadtown nor the systematic dispersal of Broadacre City provides. Only the historic city can bring him back this image or the life that it stands for.

Both Roadtown and Broadacre City have provided such persistent images for the City of the Future that one must pause for a moment to show how, despite their professions of spatial and social liberation, and their effort to bring urban settlements closer to the agricultural and recreational areas of the countryside, they actually have only introduced the typical vices of the overgrown and overregimented metropolis in a new form. For first of all, both concepts attempt to break down the most fundamental of all organic limitations: the functional limits of growth. Every organic form has, as Aristotle pointed out, an upper and a lower limit of growth; and this applies, as he also pointed out, even to purely physical utilities, like ships, because if a ship is too big it is not maneuverable or seaworthy, and if it is too small it cannot carry a sufficient cargo. In the case of cities, this natural limitation had, until the seventeenth century, rarely been overpassed: except for a few Romes and Babylons, the city by its very size and form expressed the need for social concentration.

Not merely do these anti-urban concepts destroy the social forms of the city, they likewise destroy the natural variety in the size and architectural structure of communities, a variety determined by a multitude of conditions: local population, agriculture, topography, productive industry, transportation, and cultural affiliations. There is a wide choice in the style of life as between a solitary villa, an agricultural hamlet, a country village, and a country town on one side, though they all have the common attribute of ample areas for gardens and for play, and these in turn are different from the more urban styles of the small industrial town, the suburb, the seaport, the small provincial city with a base of its own, the satellite town, dependent upon the metropolis, and the metropolis itself, with its historic concentrations of culture. As long as this wide range of settlement is maintained, with its corresponding assortment of sizes, all limited by function and need, every type of human character, every kind of industrial and cultural interest, can be satisfied somewhere. To concentrate on a single urban type, even though it be as big and far-reaching as a New York, a London, or a Tokyo, is to wipe out a valuable store of human potentialities.

Since form is conditioned by these other factors, the greatest wealth of architectural and town planning forms is possible. The anti-city image has only one form: a negation of complexity, ecological variety, and intimate social cooperation. Each fragment duplicates, with massive monotony, the limited premises upon which the negative image was based.

Finally, these images of total urban dispersal destroy by their very premises another significant organic characteristic, which in the city takes a special institutional form: the power of the attractive nucleus to serve as a magnet for concentrating a diversity of functions and purposes. Without such a nucleus, aided by many sub-nuclei, urban life lacks organs for mixing, meeting, mobilization. The essence of the city is its ability by its very form to focus human activities, and to make visible by symbolic magnification the true nature of the human condition and the human prospect. Historic cities, above all, great metropolises, thanks to the accumulations of time and sentiment, have powerful nuclei, which magnetize not merely their own inhabitants but also people from distant regions. For many special occasions their magnetic field has now become planetary. The absence of such social foci in the anti-city actually puts an end to necessary urban functions and imposes a uniform pattern of life, derived at second or third hand from some distant metropolitan center that still retains the surviving vestiges of the city's social properties.

The total result of these defects is to do away with natural variety, with urban individuality, with human choice. But from the standpoint of the other essential function of the city, as a container of human culture, the diluted and homogenized environment of the anti-city proves an even greater sociological absurdity. For the capacity of the urban container should vary with the total amount of experience and culture that must be transmitted from generation to generation. Part of this heritage is carried forward in institutional and symbolic form, represented by buildings, archives, records, libraries, for which the city serves as permanent storehouse; and an even larger part of it is transmitted directly through human agents, by daily face-to-face transactions and conversations, by direct observations and imitations, and by chance encounters as well as deliberate meetings. The size and design of the urban container must vary directly with the size and complexity of this total heritage.

If our civilization is worth while maintaining, with all its vocational differentiation and cultural variety—historic, scientific, religious, humanistic—two urban conditions must be laid down: one, a many-dimensioned container capable of maintaining this richness and complexity and of distributing, over wider areas in space and time and over larger populations, the cultural wealth that urbanization both stores and helps to increase. The other condition is the creation of highly attractive focal points—cities in the historic sense, striking in form and character—where a diversity of organizations, institutions, associations, along with primary family and neighborhood groups, necessary to maintain this complex social order, can come together and profit by the constant give-and-take.

No secondary modes of intercourse, neither the printed

page, nor the tape recorder, nor the telephone, nor television, can take the place of that direct face-to-face intercourse whose occasions the city, when it remains close to the human scale, multiplies. Without an urban container deliberately planned for such intercourse, the dominant economic and technical pressures of our time tend to form a multitude of overspecialized, non-cooperating, and non-communicating enclaves, whose spatial remoteness and social segregation favor the totalitarian automatism of our time.

As an instrument for disrupting the processes of culture and ultimately arresting human development, the anti-city seems little less than a slow-acting equivalent for a nuclear catastrophe. The reduction of organic social complexity in the anti-city makes its scattered population incapable of carrying on its tasks with greater mental stimulus than that of a village: the mechanical conformity that this life exacts, by its utter dependence upon remote centrally controlled and secondary modes of intercourse, is quite as deadening as the social conformity of the tradition-bound village—and much harder to escape. This disurbanized random scattering of population is current technology's ultimate gift to totalitarian absolutism and its centralized remote control.

Even if the anti-city embraced a population as numerous as Gottmann's Megalopolis—that is, the whole population of the Atlantic seaboard—the total cultural capacity of this atomized container would still be less than that of any single metropolis in a healthy state. Though the isolated institutional parts might be as hyper-productive as those computers whose output is already too abundant to be efficiently assembled and intelligently interpreted, the cultural creativity that fosters further human development is bound to drop, within a generation or two, toward zero.

The first institutions to feel the effect of this failure will be the great corporations that are now so often, single-handedly, escaping from the overgrown metropolis. Not least does this hold for the various research agencies whose members, from day to day, see only their own kind, hear only echoes of their own ideas, and more and more live in a mental isolation-ward inhabited only by other specialists, equally cut off from human realities. In sheer self-defense, the directors of these institutions will have to send their staffs periodically, as the Bell Telephone Company has been sending its too sedulously trained junior executives, back to the university, to have a therapeutic injection of dynamic ideas that the city once spontaneously generated.

In view of all this, the nature of the modern city needs to be re-examined: a new pattern of urban integration more capable of utilizing the immense energies that modern man now commands must be invented. We can no longer think, in old-fashioned terms, of a 'metropolis of three million people,' for that no longer corresponds to the range of urban cooperation; nor shall we improve the situation by thinking of a pseudo-metropolis of three billion, for such an agglomeration would effectually wipe out one of the most important components of the city: its own visible structure, its identifiable groups and persons, and its natural landscape with all its appropriate cultural and recreational uses. We must rather seek a new over-all pattern for both the small-scale and the large-scale unit. The expression and linking together of these units is the task of modern urban design.

The large unit must be on a regional scale: sufficiently big to stabilize the essential rural occupations and provide a permanent green matrix, within which further urban colonization may take place. This concept, not of a *metropolitan* region dominated by a single center and continuous in structure with it, but of a regional framework capable of embracing cities of many sizes, including the central metropolitan center and giving each urban unit the advantages of the whole, has still to be worked out. But I have sketched in its main outlines under the title 'The Invisible City,' in 'The City in History.' This larger structure, unlike the present clumsy magnification of the old Stone Age container, is rather an open network, comparable to the electric power grid, which utilizes both small and big units to form a greater interdependent system.

With a regional grid, the smallest urban unit will be able to make demands and draw on all the resources of the largest unit in a two-way system of intercourse and cooperation. But to create such a larger system, one must begin with a reorganization of small units, by introducing balance, self-government, organic growth, and a dynamic, self-renewing form into the neighborhood, the precinct, the city, and into all the institutional components of the city, which have become clumsy and disorganized through unregulated overexpansion. The first effective steps toward creating such local units have already been made; and I shall consider them next.

*Architectural Record*, December 1962.

*Postscript.* If these strictures apply to the popular conception of Megalopolis as "the future form of the city," they apply even more severely to Dr. C. A. Doxiadis' proposal to accept a single ultimate world city, Ecumenopolis, as he calls it, as the only kind of urban reservoir capable of holding the rising population flood. The present rate of population growth, with its threat of a general overpopulation of the whole planet, not just India and China, is notoriously alarming. But it is likewise somewhat alarming to find that an experienced city planner like Dr. Doxiadis regards the formation of such an urbanoid nonentity as the only possible way of meeting this threat. There is no scientific ground for such fatalism, and no reason whatever to embrace this proposal.

Population changes, as this generation has reason to know, are unpredictable; and as far as present extrapolations of population-increase go, their information, since it is based solely on the past, gives no guidance for the future, except in the stern warning to take suitable counter-measures. As Albert Mayer has put it in his 'The Urgent Future,' "Trend is not Destiny." The intelligent response to present population pressures is not to plan for urbanizing every possible acre of the planet but to apply the resources of science, politics, morals, and religion to forestall this prospective catastrophic increase and bring about a population equilibrium, without invoking a succession of world plagues or nuclear catastrophes—both of which are far more probable events than the construction of Ecumenopolis.

In conceiving this urbanoid planetary unit, in defiance of ecological principles, though doubtless in conformity with his personal conception of Ekistics, Dr. Doxiadis has in fact only combined in a single gigantic fantasy the two antipodal nightmares of our age: total congestion and total dispersion—which is another way of saying 'total extermination.' His statistical premises are patently unsound, his deductions unwarranted, and his solution absurd. But conceivably this ultimate nightmare may perform the one useful function of all nightmares: before it becomes too painful it may wake us up.

# 10
# Beginnings
# of Urban Integration

The two favored images of the city today are the products of a complementary process of regimentation and disintegration. One of them is the City in a Parking Lot, a collection of high-rise slabs and towers linked by multi-laned expressways; the other is the Anti-City, alias Megalopolis, a by-product of urban decomposition, which in the pursuit of nature denatures the countryside and mechanically scatters fragments of the city over the whole landscape.

Whether the urban container explodes upward, in profitably congested 'urban renewal' projects, or outward, in suburban and exurban subdivisions, the result is an increasingly homogenized urbanoid mass that lacks the complex social and cultural attributes of the city, at the same time that it levels down the geological and ecological character of the natural landscape and lowers its agricultural potential.

The problem of finding an adequate form for the modern city is increased by the very powers the highway engineer and the architect command when they willingly serve the economic forces making for disintegration. Today the chief mode of urban destruction comes from misdirected construction. This paradox cannot be resolved by holding that formlessness is the determining feature of contemporary urban form. Yet some of our younger architects and planners have been making sketches for an anti-city on the assumption that randomness, accident, deformation, fragmentation —like crime, violence, extermination—have the same order of value as function, purpose, integration, health, moral character, or esthetic design.

This tendency finds ample support, unfortunately, not merely in the fashionable *avant-garde* literature and drama of our time, but in the practice of some of the most sensitive contemporary painters and sculptors who keep on telling us that the only order possible is willful disorder, that the only valid image of man himself is a horror-skeleton derived from the Nazi extermination camps, and that the only imageable urban form, apart from a collective underground shelter, would be the deliberate equivalent of the debris left by a nuclear bomb. Elizabeth Close's satiric commentary on 'Design by Chance,' published in the May 1962 number of the 'Journal of the American Institute of Architects,' is too close to reality to be funny. If a chimpanzee, a psychotic, and a museum-qualified painter are equally capable of achieving a 'modern' painting, the forces that are now vomiting the wreckage of the city over the landscape are doubtless sufficient to produce the 'modern' form of the city—formless by intention.

If we are not to follow these irrational forces to their methodical conclusion—the effacement of human culture and the annihilation of man himself—the explosive elements that are now at work must be harnessed to a different and more human set of purposes. As with the mixture that composes gunpowder, the individual components in this urban explosion are in themselves innocuous: motor transportation, mass production, instantaneous communication, automation, are all potentially effective agents for human development, provided that it is the welfare of man, not the untrammeled expansion of his mechanical instruments, that one has in view. Even their explosive mixture, again like gunpowder, may prove serviceable for better human purposes provided we have adequate social instruments to control the explosion, and a rational target to aim at.

The paramount urban problem today is to invent an adequate urban container which will do for our complex and many-sided culture what the original Stone Age container did for the far simpler cooperations and communications of earlier societies. This problem cannot be answered, then, merely by pointing to the existing metropolis, or the conurbation, or the 'megalopolis,' and calling one of these the new container, though these big units do, in fact, point to the scale in which an effective multi-centered container must be conceived and the vast range of specialized functions and human purposes that must be brought together.

More than a generation before all the dimensions of this problem had become visible, the first tentative step toward an answer was made by Ebenezer Howard. In his concept of the garden city, he restored many of the essential elements that the city, in its mechanical expansion and dispersion, in its human regimentation and biological depression, had lost; for he returned to the human scale, and he conceived of a means of increasing size and complexity of social relations without destroying this scale.

The projector of this urban form was not an architect, a planner, or a painter, but an inventor of machines. His dry little prospectus—it is little more than that—'Garden Cities of Tomorrow,' first published in 1898, started many fresh ideas sprouting in other minds; and some of the original seeds that remained dormant are now ready at last to germinate. But the idea itself made headway swiftly. By 1904 the first New Town, Letchworth Garden City, was founded.

If I feel obliged once more to outline Howard's leading

ideas, it is only because the popular view of them, even in planning circles, is often based, not on his proposals, but upon the strange aberrations of his critics, whose resistance takes the form of attributing to him preconceptions, methods and goals precisely the contrary to those he held. Even Howard's followers have sometimes given to his tentative proposals a rigidity of form and a finality of purpose he did not himself value; for his was an experimental mind, and the worst homage one could do to his way of thinking would be to assume that his experiment is already fixed and finished.

What Howard proposed was both a new image of the modern city and an organic method of handling its continued growth. The new image was that of a city limited in size, not by natural obstacles or poor economic resources or military necessity, but by a deliberate social intention and by the very nature of the contents and purpose of the plan. He sought to handle the problem of continued population growth by continued colonization in a series of self-contained towns with a sufficient variety of industrial, agricultural, and professional occupations to give work to the larger part of their own populations.

These new cities, in contrast to the current mode of urban expansion, were to be limited in area, in density and in population. Howard estimated that the desirable size for such a town would be about thirty thousand, with two thousand more inhabitants engaged in market gardening and other rural occupations in the permanent greenbelt that surrounded it and gave the community its visible definition. The number of acres and of people he deemed adequate was a first approximation. It is not any single population figure, but the desirability of establishing limits for the concrete, visible urban form that is important.

The main feature of Howard's idea, apart from the limitation of population and area, was a notion that he himself introduced with the very concept of the new city: the city was not only to be small enough to be manageable and accessible, but big enough to have variety and diversity. At this point he made a decisive departure both from the plans of the 'industrial villages' that were being built by a few British manufacturers, bent solely on improving housing conditions of their workers, and from those of the ordinary residential suburb, wholly dependent for diversity upon a distant urban center.

Howard's prospectus was so fully given over to the practical details of launching such a city that he himself barely sketched in its more fundamental ideas. But if the words 'balance' and 'organic unity' and 'social mixture' are lacking in Howard's book, they underlie the whole conception, and I do him no injustice in emphasizing them, though he himself rather stressed the municipal ownership and control of the land, as a means of maintaining the new pattern.

In outlining a more organic form of the city, Howard sought at the same time to unite town and country: he rightly understood their interdependence and complementarity. In proposing more spacious surroundings both for the buildings and the town as a whole, Howard was only democratizing a process that the aristocracy had long observed in establishing their own quarters in the city. The luxury of space, particularly the luxury of great parks and gardens, was historically the great aristocratic contribution to the city; and Howard felt, again rightly, that for the sake of health and delight the garden and the park were an integral part of every quarter of the city.

In the nineteenth century this spacious mode of planning had been achieved only in the health spa and the suburb; but by now it has become a basic requirement of all urban design. Howard felt, indeed, that one of the great benefits of building new towns on a large scale would be to reduce the pressure of metropolitan population sufficiently to make it possible to replan every part of London, and make it as attractive and habitable again as it still is around its green core of parks and tree-filled squares.

In aiming to deal with the dual problems of congestion and overgrowth Howard had, almost by accident, rediscovered the essential nature of the city itself. The main ingredient of this conception was a population large enough to be diversified; diversified enough to be economically and socially balanced, and balanced sufficiently to permit most of the daily needs of the community to be satisfied within the city's limits, and yet have secure immediate access to the open country and to other cities.

But Howard was no small-town isolationist. Not for a moment did he suppose that a single community of thirty-two thousand people could satisfy all modern man's social and cultural needs, or provide a sufficient variety of economic opportunities. Nor did he underestimate the special advantages of large numbers and plentiful capital resources, though he suspected that the great metropolis exacted too high a price for supplying them. On the contrary, in his chapter on 'Social Cities' Howard pointed to a higher order of organization: a new kind of openwork metropolis, with ten such communities grouped around a larger city at the center, bound closely by public rapid transit, commanding a population within the range of three hundred and fifty thousand.

Here Howard suggested that such a constellation of cities or 'town clusters' would have social and cultural advantages that no small town could offer. But he saw—as many advocates of continued metropolitan expansion and dispersion still do not see—that as the size of the total regional population increases, its component parts must be gathered together in more concentrated and coherent containers, built to a human scale, with sufficient autonomy to assume responsibilities and make demands, as no scattered, disorganized population can.

To make order again out of the present metropolitan

explosion we must begin with its antithesis: a small-scale urban implosion or assemblage of urban elements. Only by first unifying the parts can a larger whole, the 'urban grid,' a highly organized regional network of cities and urban institutions, come into existence.

If I have correctly interpreted the significance of the Garden City, why is it that Howard's leading ideas have often been violently caricatured or disdainfully ignored? Apart from sheer human perversity, there are two reasons for this. The first is that Howard, as a public character, was a far bigger man than his book; and it was his genius for action as well as a certain meagerness of sociological and historic background that kept him from expressing in more effective literary form the full implications of his ideas. That task was left largely to his followers, particularly Unwin, Purdom, Osborn, Stein, and myself.

The second reason was that Ebenezer Howard had no pretensions to being a planner and he offered no plans: all his illustrations are plainly labelled as diagrams. In so far as he himself suggested any concrete forms for the new city, they were closer in spirit to Joseph Paxton than to William Morris, and were more or less adaptations of the common forms of his own time: a central park as in London; an elongated glass shopping arcade, like that built in Milan or many other European cities; a greenbelt, collectively owned, such as had always existed, though usually without public protection, around country towns and railroad-suburbs. As to the residential area, if Howard had an image of the city, it was nearer to that of an early Victorian development in London, Ladbroke Grove, than to the cities that came actually to be built as demonstrations of his idea.

The first translation of Howard's idea into an actual urban form was the work of Raymond Unwin and Barry Parker, two young planners who did not fully share Howard's old-fashioned delight in Victorian invention and mechanical progress: for they were under the corrective humanizing influence of William Morris, and were more interested in recapturing the genial older traditions of domestic architecture than in finding a fresh, striking image for a new kind of city as a whole.

As an historian of city design and a planning theorist, Raymond Unwin was the outstanding figure of his generation, for he carried further the pioneer innovations of Frederick Law Olmsted, and since he had both the literary facility and the cultural background that Howard lacked, his vision of the new town carried greater authority. Unwin's analysis of the human insufficiency and economic waste of the 'standard by-law street' imposed by English legislation to achieve a minimum of sanitation and order is a classic little pamphlet: for he showed in residential neighborhoods that capital was being wastefully sunk into an excessive number of streets, paved for heavy traffic that did not exist, and mechanical utilities that were not needed, which could have been turned to better account by eliminating a large number of through streets and converting the space so saved into playgrounds and gardens.

To Unwin's demonstration, carried further by Clarence Stein and Henry Wright in Sunnyside and Radburn, we owe in large part the adoption of the superblock, which has liberated the architect from the rigid constraints of the building lot, the narrow block and the uniform building line.

Unfortunately, the plan for Letchworth Garden City was uninspired. In leaning backward to avoid the stark simplicity of Howard's diagrams, the planners managed to avoid any positive visual expression of the idea itself. And though much of the domestic architecture was more fresh and vigorous than anything of comparable cost being built at the time, and an occasional factory, set in the midst of these houses, like the Spirella corset plant, was admirable in design, the total architectural effect was mediocre, and as far as the idea went, esthetically unconvincing. Neither the plan nor the structures articulated the differentiated but balanced structure of the new city. Visually, the garden displaced the city.

As a result of this architectural indecisiveness, the handsomely cultivated gardens and open spaces far outshone the architecture and served as the identifying mark of the new idea, though the garden was only one of many ingredients in Howard's new urban formula. In form Letchworth Garden City now seems a cross between a modernized country town and a spread-out contemporary suburb. Unwin's later Hampstead Garden, a suburb which had no pretensions to being a city, turned out to be far more coherent and handsomely urbane, perhaps partly under the influence of Sir Edward Lutyens. In a word, the still-fermenting New Town wine was poured, at the beginning, into a too familiar suburban milk bottle. That archaic image has retarded the acceptance of the idea itself.

This overemphasis upon the gardens and open spaces was doubtless a natural reaction against the dreary deserts of pavement, with trolley poles and lamp standards taking the place of trees, that stood as drab symbols of mechanical progress. But by its very overemphasis it shifted attention from Howard's main idea, which was that of social manifoldness, balance of urban and rural opportunities, functional completeness. As a result the Garden City came to be tied up in many people's minds, even in those of its most powerful proponents, with a general housing standard of twelve to fourteen houses per residential acre. This notion was further stereotyped by Unwin himself, for as chief architect to the English Ministry of Health, Unwin introduced this standard on a national scale for public housing estates. He advocated this density for the sensible but limited purpose of providing a subsistence garden for every working-class family. And it is this standard layout, not the garden city, that spread everywhere in England from the nineteen-twenties on.

Though Howard himself experimentally promoted group housing design for communal living, the single-family house-and-garden of fixed dimensions became a standard, or rather an overstandardized, requirement. When Welwyn Garden City was built some fifteen years later, the Georgian revival was in full swing, and the planner, Louis de Soissons, achieved greater charm and coherence here than Letchworth possessed. Yet, except for the admirable industrial zone, the emphasis was again on private functions and traditional forms and ample greenery, rather than on association and intercourse, on public functions, on focal meeting places and social intermixture, all of which call for the pedestrian scale and a more close-textured design.

This failure to convey a more coherent image probably slowed down the acceptance of the idea, but in recent years it has been partly corrected. Indeed, at the very moment that Letchworth was being built, Tony Garnier, in his ideal plans for a new industrial city on the Rhone, was often closer in his architectural forms to the fresh image of the New Town than were Unwin and Parker. A generation later Ernst May, once an assistant of Unwin's, came still closer to a valid form in the satellite settlement of Römerstadt, near Frankfurt am Main. Today the planners of the New Town of Cumbernauld, near Glasgow, though they have overreacted against both the excessive spacing and neighborhood segregation of the first batch of British New Towns, are approaching in architectural form—without resorting to high-rise structures—the compactness that is needed to make daily encounters and mixtures between people and groups not merely possible but inevitable. In time, both lack of historic structures and lack of modern examples will be overcome: the new image itself will come clear.

*Architectural Record,* January 1963.

# 11

# Social Complexity and Urban Design

The key to a fresh architectural image of the city as a whole lies in working toward an organic unit of urban order which will hold together its component parts through successive changes in function and purpose from generation to generation. While such an archetypal image can never be fully realized, this concept of the city as a whole, restated in contemporary terms, will help to define the character of each institutional structure.

In general outline, though not in dramatic architectural form, such a unit was first achieved in the British New Towns, for these were the first towns since the Middle Ages to attempt to incorporate in a unified whole all the necessary features of the social and natural environment. Contrary to prevalent opinion, England's two pioneer New Towns, originally called Garden Cities, built by private corporations under the restriction of limited dividends, have been an economic success. Though their growth was at first slow, it was sound. And in far more rapid fashion, the fifteen British New Towns built since 1947 in accordance with Ebenezer Howard's principles, now with government aid, have been even more strikingly successful. In many of their factory precincts, and in some of their new town centers, they vie with Coventry, Rotterdam, and Vällingby in delineating the beginning of a fresh urban form. Already nearly five hundred thousand people live in these salubrious towns, planned to contain from fifteen thousand to ninety thousand people each; and ultimately they will hold a million. In the past year, three more New Towns have been started in Britain.*

Plainly Howard's method of nucleating and integrating urban functions, in units scaled to human needs and purposes to which bureaucratic and mechanical functions are subordinated, has proved viable even under a regime more or less committed to expanding these separate functions and profiting by their continued growth. The new quarters in existing cities that have achieved anything like a comparable gain in health, social diversity, family-centered amenity, and varied economic opportunity are those which, like the rebuilt Borough of Stepney in London, have followed most closely the New Town formula of mixture, balance, and limitation of density.

Today the municipal corporation of Glasgow, which for long obstinately resisted the new idea of urban growth by colonization instead of the usual method of congestion and conglomeration, has reversed itself. Glasgow is now controlling its further population growth by building New Towns; and its first full-size town, Cumbernauld, is now approaching completion. If there has been any flaw in this development, it is only that it has proceeded so rapidly that the planners and architects—too often bound by obsolete standards imposed by the Ministry of Transport and local government authorities—have not been able to incorporate the results of past experiments and recent urban experience in their designs.

Now this organic principle of urban growth and organization does not apply only to that part of the population

---

* By 1968 twenty-two New Towns were built or in process, not counting extensive additions to the two original New Towns, Letchworth and Welwyn.

which can no longer be packed into the existing metropolitan centers. One of the great causes for the wholesale exodus now taking place into the suburbs is that those who can make a choice are no longer content to put up with depleted physical environment and the often degraded social conditions of our 'great American cities.' If the big cities hope to hold their population and continue to perform those special functions that depend upon large numbers of people, they themselves must have some of the spaciousness, the order, and the variety in their intimate, small-scale units that the New Town concept has brought into existence. Fortunately, the method Howard initiated can be applied equally to the redevelopment of the existing metropolitan centers.

Limitation of numbers and density, mixture of social and economic activities, internal balance, the interplay of usable open spaces with occupied spaces, the restoration of parks, gardens, and green walkways as integral parts of the urban environment—these are the keys to overcoming the congestion and disorganization of the big city and restoring its general habitability. So essential are these processes in creating new urban forms that many critics who parade as Howard's sworn enemies have nevertheless adopted his guiding principles under another name.

Thus in 'Communitas,' Paul and Percival Goodman, after shelving Howard respectfully as a bourgeois back number, restate a major part of his thesis as their own original contribution. Thus Le Corbusier, after contemptuously dismissing the British Garden City, comes forth with his own 'Vertical Garden City' as an alternative and uses the advanced mechanical facilities of a skyscraper to achieve the all-too-limited associations of a mere village. Thus again Dr. E. A. Gutkind, whose recent book on 'The Twilight of Cities' spurns the Garden City and the New Town as an obsolete Victorian concept, projects as alternative a multitude of garden townlets, or infra-garden cities, as his way of handling regional dispersal. All these proposals represent a lower order of urban organization and association than Howard's.

Even Jane Jacobs, after idiotically characterizing Howard as a would-be destroyer of the city, proposes to restore the essential urban qualities that have been lost through over-congestion and overexpansion by dividing the metropolis into self-governing 'districts,' with their own local economic enter-prises and social opportunities. Mrs. Jacobs' districts are de-signed not merely to welcome the diverse activities that Howard insisted on for the Garden City, but they turn out even to have the same suggested population, some thirty thousand. That number, incidentally, is the very size that Leonardo da Vinci hit upon when he proposed to the Duke of Milan to relieve the congestion and foul disorder of six-teenth-century Milan by designing ten cities of thirty thou-sand population each.

In short, Mrs. Jacobs atones for her sedulous ignorance of Howard's work by unconsciously becoming his disciple, at least for half his urban program. And for similar valid reasons the recent Royal Commission report on the govern-ment of London proposed to reorganize that unwieldy mass into semiautonomous boroughs of approximately equal size, around two hundred thousand, all cooperating within a larger regional framework. This gives support to Mrs. Jacobs' sug-gestion that one hundred thousand is perhaps the right size for a 'district' in a big metropolis like New York; but here again she touches on the upper limits of the actual New Towns! What she chooses to call a district is in fact an in-tegrated city.

No adequate image of the emerging city can be formed without reference both to the most enduring and valuable features of historic cities as well as to the fresh departures and fresh opportunities that our modern age, with its im-mense stores of knowledge, wealth, and power, has opened up. Not least, we must carefully evaluate the many experiments in urban design made during the last century, from Ladbroke Grove (London) to the latest suburban shopping center.

Yet as a result of the ferment in planning thought that Howard started, we can now draw the following conclusions. First, the useful, manageable, visible, reproducible, and—not least important—humanly lovable city must range somewhere between thirty thousand and three hundred thousand people. Beyond that size, if we are not to enter the realm of de-personalized mechanisms, the unit of organization becomes not the city but the region. Second, its own area and population must be limited in order to be able to set a limit to its component parts. The maintenance of diversity and balance between all essential urban functions, biological, economic, and cultural, is the only effective means of controlling the insensate dynamism of separate institutions that, concerned solely with their own expansion, tend to separate themselves from the whole and to grow inordinately at the expense of the whole. To ensure these results Howard introduced a third essential feature that his superficial imitators leave out: the public ownership of the land and the permanent retention of increased land values by the community.

Like personalities and organisms, cities are devices for reducing the now otherwise limitless energies at our command to just those quantities that will promote a self-governing and self-developing mode of life. Localized oversize in any single institution, whether it is a business corporation, a hospital, or a university, is a sign that the city has ceased to perform one of its most essential modern functions: the control of one-sided growth.

Thus the new conception of the city, as a balanced organization and an integrated structure, maintaining unity in diversity and continuity in change, is essential for controlling excessive quantities, whether of population or physical power.

For having achieved the first glimpse of this organic principle of urban order, Ebenezer Howard will perhaps be remembered even longer than the 'first' Greek town planner, Hippodamus. Though many historic cities embodied this idea, this is the first age in which it has come clearly into consciousness.

Those of us who are pursuing further the train of constructive thought that Howard so largely started and Raymond Unwin and Barry Parker first carried out cannot be content with any present embodiments of their ideas, though we no doubt have a duty to defend them from libelous caricature and ignorant abuse. Still less do we wish to make the existing New Towns a standard pattern for all urban integration, duly codified by law. Such a stereotyping of the idea would eliminate the very richness and variety of concrete detail that is inherent in the notion of a city. For the city is nothing less than a collective personality whose character reflects its unique combination of geographic, economic, cultural, and historic factors. As William Blake put it, "One law for the lion and the ox is oppression."

Admirable though the New Towns of Britain have proved, in contrast with the raucous disorder and standardized blight of so many metropolitan areas, no existing examples can be considered as final. Many rectifications and improvements remain to be made both in detail and in their general pattern. And meanwhile, some seemingly decisive innovations made elsewhere, like the American suburban shopping center and the specialized industrial park, have already disclosed their own grave liabilities, which stem mainly from their boasted detachment from the city.

Apart from this, thanks to a century of historic investigation whose results have at last come to a head in the works of Pierre Lavedan, Ernst Egli, and myself, the essential value of old forms can now be properly appreciated, and some of these forms, hitherto rejected as obstacles to 'progress,' can be preserved either to maintain continuity or to serve as a departure for further renovations. For much has recently been learned about the social nature of the city and the meaning of its diversity that suggests further revisions, adaptations, and innovations. Some of Jane Jacobs' fresh observations on these matters deserve to be heeded, even by those who are not drawn to her concrete planning proposals.

But first we must remove a current superstition: namely, the notion that the form and content of the city must primarily serve its technology and support its 'expanding economy.' This assumption turns the true order upside down. Perhaps the primary function of the city today is that of bringing technology itself into line with human purpose, reducing speed, energy, quantification to amounts that are humanly assimilable and humanly valuable.

Along these lines there has been a considerable amount of fresh architectural and social invention, which awaits embodiment in the larger framework of the city. Thus the separation of fast-moving vehicles from the pedestrian—the Radburn principle, or, more anciently, the Venice principle —not merely facilitates these two complementary modes of circulation, both still necessary, but also releases building from the old uniform lot-and-block pattern. This makes it possible to plan superblocks and precincts and neighborhoods so as to serve a variety of functions related in space and form to the needs of the users, rather than to an arbitrary street pattern. That gives the architect in the city proper some of the freedom in composition that he has had only in the suburbs. So, too, the new pedestrian shopping mall, as in Coventry, Rotterdam, and Stevenage, has already demonstrated advantages that neither the old shopping avenue nor the isolated suburban shopping center, wallowing in a sea of parking space, can provide.

Still other innovations call for critical assessment and

doubtless for further modification or for alternative solutions. Some of them, like the urban greenbelt, the Radburn plan of a continuous internal park, or the Perry conception of the balanced neighborhood unit, have now been sufficiently tested to provide useful data for judgment. Not least the notion of a single ideal residential density calls for further reconsideration; for, even before the polemic of the 'Architectural Review' against 'prairie planning,' it had become clear, as I pointed out in 1953, that the British New Towns had been overspaced, and that the hygienic and recreational advantages of abundant open spaces must be integrated with the social and domestic needs for cohesion, intimacy, and spontaneous association, which demand somewhat higher densities and the preservation of the pedestrian scale.

For all their notable improvements, the over-all designs of the British New Towns are at last ready for detailed and discriminating criticism on the basis of their actual performance. One of the principal factors to be reconsidered is their density. As a result of a uniformly low residential coverage, under mandate of legislation, along with an over-plenitude of wide roads and verges, to say nothing of the acres of playing fields demanded by education authorities, plus neighborhood greenbelts, which are actually more often wide wedges, the planners of New Towns have even forfeited the domestic convenience of the neighborhood unit itself. This space wastage must be challenged even more severely in many current American projects, from new university campuses to the new project of El Dorado Hills near Sacramento, California, which has been conceived as a collection of semi-urban villages that more or less correspond, in fact, to Dr. Gutkind's ideal pattern. All this calls for more judicious criticism than it has yet received from any quarter, in the light of a more social conception of the city.

Meanwhile, many older inventions in planning call for fresh expression. The nineteenth-century boulevard or parkway, in which pedestrians and vehicles shared the same space, has long been obsolete, but its latest specialized form, the expressway, must be routed out of the city, if the city is to have a life of its own. Once the expressway enters the city, it undertakes an impossible task of canalizing into a few arteries what must be circulated through a far more complex system of arteries, veins, and capillaries: only the fullest use of the whole system, restored for general circulation, with public vehicles undertaking the major burden, will rectify the mistakes of monotransportation in urban areas. As for the discarded element in the boulevard—the green walkway— it must be restored as a separate system, detached from wheeled vehicles, as is now being done in the Society Hill district of Philadelphia. For the same reason, that other by-product of the boulevard, the sidewalk café—now ruined by the noise and fumes of motor traffic—must take refuge in tiny neighborhood parks, such as those in Central Athens, though they might easily survive as a socially enlivening feature in the interior of a superblock.

These many innovations and rectifications call for increasing integration in formal designs, which will set a new pattern for each part of the city. But to demand a clean-minted urban image from the work of a single architect, or even a single generation, is to misunderstand the essentially cumulative nature of the city. An organic image of the city requires for its actual fulfillment a dimension that no single generation can ever supply: it requires time, not merely an individual lifetime, but many collective lifetimes. Neither as a seemingly unchangeable spatial object outside of time, nor as a disposable container, good only for the brief period necessary for financial amortization, can the city perform its essential function. The now popular concept of the city as a disposable container, to be replaced at a profit every decade or every generation, in order to feed an expanding economy, denies the most valuable function of the city as an organ of social memory; namely, its linking up the generations, its bringing into the present both the usable past and the desirable future.

No organic urban design for any larger urban area accordingly can be completed once and for all, like a Baroque city established by royal fiat, by wiping out all existing structures and replacing them by the fashionable current model. This futurist method would put the city at the mercy of five-year-old knowledge and five-year-old minds, and the resulting loss of memory is no less a serious impairment to the life of the city than the loss of memory in people whose brains have been injured by shock or senility. In a sense, then, there can be no single modern architectural form of the city. Part of what was modern fifty years ago is by now vitally historic and as worthy of sedulous preservation as any ancient building in so far as it still serves new uses, while other examples of what was once modern have long been obsolete and should be removed; indeed, what looks brightly modern only for the year in which it was built is usually out of date before it is finished.

In contrast to the position taken by Paul Ylvisacker and others, a more organic view of the city holds that the greater the inherent dynamism of science, technics, and finance, today, the greater need there is for a durable urban container. For as I pointed out in 'The City in History,' when the container changes as rapidly as the contents, neither can perform their necessary but complementary functions. Here at last we have, I believe, an essential key to sound urban and architectural design today: it must not merely welcome variety and complexity in all their forms, environmental, social, and personal, but it must also deliberately leave a place for continued rectification, improvement, innovation, and renewal. When soundly designed, such an urban form will be fulfilled, not spoiled, by the increment of each succeeding generation, as the medieval city was in fact improved by interpolating squares and buildings that mirrored the new spatial order of the Renaissance.

Now the cities of the past often overemphasized continuity. Their builders entombed life in all-too-massive permanent structures and in even more rigid routines that resisted growth and prevented the necessary modifications each generation must make. But the cities of today have just the opposite vice: while their neglected quarters fester, their favored 'dynamic' areas are too ephemeral to foster human growth and cultural continuity. Once time and organic complexity are taken seriously as components of design, it is plain that the replacement of outworn areas is a delicate process; and while it must go on constantly in small measures, it must not be fatally limited to superficial reformations that do not interfere with any fresh larger designs. Among the many postwar plans for rebuilding half-ruined cities, those made for Manchester by its town surveyor, Rowland Nicholas, have stood out by reason of the fact that their proposals for the redesign of partly wrecked areas, filled with obsolete buildings and wasteful streets, were conceived as a complex process in time: demolition and rebuilding were provided for in a series of stages, covering a period of forty years. Such planning, which does justice to the future without forgetting the past, happily exemplifies an organic approach that can handle, and profit by, any degree of complexity and diversity.

This analysis perhaps clarifies the failure of Howard's concept of the Garden City or New Town to find at once an appropriate architectural expression. Our age tends to think of complexity in purely mechanical terms, and to reduce social and human relations to simplified abstract units that lend themselves easily to centralized direction and mechanical control. Hence the brilliantly sterile images that Le Corbusier and Miës van der Rohe projected, images that magnify power, suppress diversity, nullify choice, have swept across the planet as the 'new form of the city.' This identification of modern form with uniform high-rise buildings, which one finds too often even in recent surveys of modern architecture, should be as outmoded as the bureaucratic animus to which it pays homage. Such oversimplification of form is now eating the heart out of our projects of urban renewal, and has had even more disastrous results in such new cities as Brasilia.

By contrast, a new image of the city which does justice to all its dimensions can be no simple overnight job: for it must include the form-shaping contributions of nature, of river, bay, hill, forest, vegetation, climate, as well as those of human history and culture, with the complex interplay of groups, corporations, organizations, institutions, personalities. Let us not then unduly regret our slowness in arriving at an expressive and unified form for the modern city.

The minds that are fully at home in all these dimensions of modern life are few, and in any quantity they have still to be formed. Certainly they are not yet being equipped and disciplined by our leading architectural and planning schools; nor are there enough leaders in business and government to provide them the opportunities they need. Yet once a more organic understanding is achieved of the complex interrelation of the city and its region, the urban and the rural aspects of environment, the small-scale unit and the large-scale unit, a new sense of form will spread through both architecture and city design. In both spheres, instead of creating closed and complete forms, there will be a deliberate attempt to provide space for further constructive effort and development.

This series began with the obvious proposition that even our biggest and richest cities today fall short of the ideal possibilities that our age has opened up. We have not had the imagination or the forethought to use the immense energies modern man now commands: our architects have frittered them away on constructive trivialities and super-fluities that have often defaced the environment without improving the human condition or the architectural form.

To counteract this miscarriage of effort, we looked about for a fresh image of the city, as conceived by the influential planners and architects of the last half century, Le Corbusier, Frank Lloyd Wright, and Raymond Unwin, and we found that the only model that did justice to the complexity of the city was that offered in purely diagrammatic form by Ebenezer Howard, the founder of two Garden Cities. Be-cause the New Town principle was not invented during the last five years, the more fashionable academic minds regard it as obsolete and flirt with a formless 'Megalopolis' or a mechanically conceived 'Ecumenopolis' as an ultimate form. Yet even the new towns that have been built on Howard's abstract principles have hardly as yet provided a fresh image, in terms of present-day potentialities and the future needs of the emerging city.*

Part of the reason for all these shortcomings became evi-dent when we considered that organic complexity requires the dimension of time; and that even in the design of the British New Towns not sufficient time has yet elapsed to incorporate and integrate all that we know now about the nature of cities, and the value of the various urban inventions that have been produced during the last century. Thus we see that a truly modern design for a city must be one that allows for both its historic and social complexity, and for its continued renewal and reintegration in time. No single instantaneous image, which reflects the needs of a particular moment, can encompass the feelings and senti-ments that bring the generations together in working part-nership, binding the past that has never died to the future that is already in process of gestation.

* But see J. R. James and Andrew Derbyshire, 'Planning for the 1970's,' in the R.I.B.A. 'Journal,' October 1967.

This interpretation of urban form indicates that the same cultural factors underlie both the possibility of renewal in existing cities, however big, and the building of new towns, however small. As energy and productivity increase, a larger proportion will be available for the humanization of man; and this task, despite many ominous contrary indications today, is still the essential task of the city. Only those who seek to respond to this challenge will be able to give the city an adequate form: a form that will bring within the range and grasp of every citizen the wider world on which his life and well-being depend.

*Architectural Record,* February 1963.

# 12

# Megalopolitan Dissolution vs. Regional Integration

Under the vague, somewhat evasive title 'Change: Challenge: Response,' New York State has come out with a basic plan and policy for the future development of its cities, agricultural areas, and recreation and forest reserves, over a period of the next sixty years. The publication of this report should clear the air of the largely meaningless noises that have grown in volume during the last decade on the subject of metropolitan planning and urban renewal: noises that reach a pitch of confused emptiness in the term 'Megalopolis,' treated as if it were a new kind of city, instead of the urbanoid mishmash that it actually is.

Nothing of similar consequence to the arts of improving the environment has been published since the announcement of the Tennessee Valley Authority. While the computers are busily turning out more sophisticated traffic counts, population predictions, and mobility estimates, proving that nothing can be done except to 'go with' and accelerate the forces that are already in motion, the Office of Regional Development has introduced a hitherto unused factor not embraced by computers or by computer-directed intelligences: human imagination and purpose.

The special quality of this report appears in the very

first section, which shows the present situation of New York State in the perspective of the whole world community and of the great changes in population growth, technology, and urbanization which underlie all plans for improvement. The very existence of New York and its great port depended, as the planners of the Erie Canal first saw, upon forces and movements that have never been entirely under local control.

Planners who lack this perspective remain as bewildered as Robert Moses over the fact that his traffic remedies have worsened the conditions they sought to alleviate. They are baffled by the insight of Benton MacKaye, who in 'The New Exploration' observed that in order to overcome the traffic congestion of Times Square it might be necessary to reroute the shipment of wheat through the Atlantic ports. So, too, the Federal Housing Administration's mistaken loan policy, which favored suburban builders, has done almost as much as Detroit to turn our cities into gaping parking lots.

The quality of imaginative insight lifts much of this planning report—but alas! not all—from the level of the dismally probable to that of the hopefully possible. Instead of accepting wholly the current tendency to allow short-sighted highway engineers, motorcar manufacturers, and realty developers to create conditions that no public authority is able to remedy except by beginning all over again, they show, rather, the necessity for a policy of land planning and urban development on a regional scale, carried out under the authority of the state executive. They seek to control disorderly metropolitan growth in already congested areas by spreading urban and industrial development over the entire state.

In getting down to regional bedrock, this report re-establishes the vital contribution made by the first 'Report on a Plan for the State of New York,' issued by the New York State Housing and Regional Planning Commission in 1926. The new proposals do not merely build upon the work that was so well done almost forty years ago, but go further in the direction of regional integration. In certain basic assumptions, it is true, the new report has accepted without challenge the belief that intensified mechanization and ever-accelerating locomotion will remain the one constant in an otherwise changing world. In overlooking the human reactions to this process, already visible, they unnecessarily weaken both their historic analyses and their constructive proposals.

But even in its present form, this portfolio is an important public document. Let no one be put off by its deplorable Madison Avenue 'presentation' in seven colors of type and four of paper: a format that might make one unfairly suspect that a piddling idea has been inflated into a staggering sales prospectus to lure an unwary investor or flatter the ego of some corporation executive. If, however, the essential ideas that are embodied in this report are understood and carried into action, they should have a widespread effect upon the whole pattern of urbanization. And if some of its serious weaknesses are corrected, it might serve as a model program for urban and regional development everywhere.

What gives this new development policy special authority is the fact that it reunites two aspects of planning that should never have been separated, even in the mind: cities and their regional matrix. As the geographer Mark Jefferson observed long ago, city and country are one thing, not two things; and if one is more fundamental than the other, it is the natural environment, not the man-made overlayer.

The biggest metropolis cannot expand beyond the limits of its water supply; and even when it wipes out the valuable reserves of countryside close at hand, instead of zealously preserving them, its inhabitants are still dependent for recreation and change of scene on some more distant area. Unfortunately, the more distant the area, the less open to daily common use, the more tedious to reach by motorcar, the more costly to get to by plane, and the more empty it will ultimately be of recreation value, since crowds of people from other areas will likewise be drawn to it—thus turning the most striking natural landscape into a kind of recreation slum, like Yellowstone in mid-summer.

By recognizing that the conservation of the countryside is an essential part of any sound policy of urbanization, this report challenges the false premises of Jean Gottmann's statistical nonentity, 'Megalopolis,' with his picture of cities dissolving into an interminable mass of undifferentiated urban tissue, stretching from Maine to Georgia, and from Buffalo to Chicago. No city, however big, can hold its own against this mode of dissolution and disintegration, and no policy of highway building or urban renewal will prove otherwise than destructive until a regional framework can be established which will give form to all our diversified economic and cultural activities.

The outlining of this new framework is the first step toward a balanced urban development. The authors of the New York State report have taken this decisive step. What the clotted metropolis did in the past, the region will have to do in the future.

But in still another respect, the report breaks fresh ground; or, rather, it comes back to the classic report of 1926, which in turn was based on an earlier analysis of the present planning situation, published in May 1925 as the Regional Planning number of the 'Survey Graphic.' For the present planners emphasize that any large coordinated effort at planning lies beyond the scope of municipal action in any one city, however large: it rests on bringing together in a working partnership a multitude of municipal, county, state, and even federal agencies, and in persuading individual property owners and private corporations to work within the general pattern. Unfortunately, the regrouping of urban units within the regional setting cannot take place automatically through the unregulated operation of private interests—for it must halt or reverse many present economic tendencies that work against a sound urban development.

Not a little of the large-scale planning and construction being done today, by highway departments, municipalities, and housing agencies, comes to nothing, or worse than nothing, for lack of any agreed social purposes: many radical changes are made, such as that which is now turning Long Island, New York City's last nearby seashore recreation area, into a mere expressway bypass, merely to provide fat jobs and profits to construction companies and speculative builders, while many essentials of conservation are neglected just because they contribute nothing to the insensate dynamism of our affluent society.

Too often our most active planning agencies, for lack of any clearly defined social ends, cancel each other out. Thus, in New York City one municipal department has been commissioned to reduce the amount of air pollution. Meanwhile, the Traffic Commissioner and the Port of New York Authority, abetted by the State Highway Department, have been zealously working to bring an ever greater number of motor vehicles into the city. But not merely are the poisonous exhausts from motorcars a major cause of air pollution, but the amounts of nitric oxide and lethal carbon monoxide in New York's air have doubled during the last year. This in turn defeats the municipal drive to abate cancer and heart disease, since the medical evidence that directly connects cigarette smoking with these diseases applies likewise to the concentration of dangerous motor exhausts.

Up to now planners, with only a few exceptions, have assumed that cities, or at least big metropolises, could be treated as if they were self-contained units. If they lacked the space needed to improve conditions in the existing mu-

nicipal area, then the remedy was to widen the periphery
and take in such independent towns, suburbs, or swathes of
open land as were accessible. Metropolitan government has
been put forward as if it were a cure-all for our present
confusion: but the city of Philadelphia has had metropolitan
government for more than a century without showing the
least benefit from it.

The process of metropolitan extension and aggrandize-
ment has gone on steadily in New York, London, Paris, Rome,
and Tokyo without producing anything except congestion,
blight and urban decay; and the fact that the same processes
are now at work in some forty-one other metropolitan
areas in the United States does not improve the prospects
for urban living or human development: quite the contrary.
This situation was analyzed clearly for the first time in the
1926 'Report on a Plan for the State of New York' already
referred to; and to understand what the new development
policy has added to that report, one may profitably take a
look at that classic original document, and the background
thinking that made it possible.


The extraordinarily rapid growth of both New York
State and New York City during the nineteenth century
increased the magnitude of their problems and the enormity
of their mistakes. But likewise, it brought about an early
series of efforts to correct them. Thus New York City
introduced the first pure water supply from distant sources
in the Croton system, 1842; mass transportation, first by elevated railway, 1869; improved tenement house designs (Alfred T. White), 1877; housing by neighborhood communities, Forest Hills, 1909; and public housing for the lower-
income groups, 1927.

Some of these remedies, like mass transportation and
public housing, turned sour, because their effect was to add
to the already formidable congestion; other efforts, like

Forest Hills, did not catch on, for what was meant originally to be an experiment in workers' housing proved so expensive that the new housing estate was turned into a superior suburb for the well-to-do. But in the early nineteen-twenties a fresh start was made, in two radically different directions, by two different groups, both using the term 'regional' in an entirely different context.

The first group was that created to produce a 'Regional Plan for New York.' This organization was under the directorship of an experienced planner, Thomas Adams, backed by the financial resources of the Russell Sage Foundation. With a freedom no single municipal agency possessed, this group focussed attention upon the metropolitan area of New York, an area then covered by a circle with a forty-mile radius. With little difficulty, their economists showed that, since this was a highly concentrated market, the intensive urbanization of the entire area was inevitable: indeed, the more people here, the bigger the market and the greater the commercial prosperity. On those terms, there was no reason to look beyond the metropolitan area for a solution of New York's problems.

The other group, the Regional Planning Association of America, challenged both the premises and the conclusions of the Russell Sage group. This association was founded in 1923; it consisted of a handful of architects, planners, economists, 'geotects,' and writers who believed that the new forces that were already visible—giant power, the telephone, the radio, the motorcar—had made metropolitan congestion obsolete, and necessitated a large-scale regional coordination of the institutions that were almost automatically producing the wrong type of urban development in the wrong place for the wrong purpose.

One of the members of this little group, Clarence Stein, persuaded Governor Alfred E. Smith to create the New York State Housing and Regional Planning Commission;

and another member, Henry Wright (senior), became its planning consultant. In 1926 this commission brought out its final report on the regional development of New York State, past, present, and possible.

This report shifted the focus of interest and political authority from a single metropolis to the whole state, with its highly diversified regional components. Viewing the state as a whole, it traced the early development of the state through two periods, the first that of water power, canals, and highroads, with a fine balance of industry and population, the second that of the railroad and the steam engine, with an overconcentration of population in the principal port terminuses, Buffalo and New York.

Instead of carrying metropolitan concentration further, Wright showed that if new technical facilities were utilized, and old human values were respected, a better development of the whole state would be possible, with a diffusion of power and the building of many new urban centers that would form part of a larger regional complex. This would not merely restore the balance between town and country, but also make it possible for the whole population everywhere to have the advantages of genuine city life, without the dreary drill of long subway rides, crowded tenement quarters, insufficient play space, and a constant expenditure of municipal funds upon repairing conditions that would, in a better-ordered environment, never have come into existence.

This was the first time any public body had taken a broad historic and geographic view of urban development. In its method of approach, it broke with all one-sided specialist attempts to deal only with piecemeal problems and patchwork solutions. Instead of wiping out urban variety by taking for granted that a single model, Megalopolis, would take its place, Henry Wright's contribution was to demonstrate that a multi-centered approach would not only give fresh life to every part of the state but also would re-lieve the population pressures upon the Empire City itself and so, for the first time, give it opportunity to catch up with its human arrears.

Despite its apparent failure and its long neglect, this report remains the basic American document in regional planning; and nothing that covers a smaller area of life deserves to be called regional planning. Though the many planning and housing agencies created under President Frank-lin D. Roosevelt failed to understand the new approach made by Wright, Stein, and their colleagues, the ideas be-hind it were too sound to be indefinitely buried. If Wright's report now comes back, through the Office of Regional Development, with renewed authority, it is perhaps because the purely metropolitan or anti-regional approach of all the specialized planning agencies has done nothing to coun-teract the cataclysmic economic forces that are now pro-ducing something close to total urban chaos, in which pur-poseless violence and bare-faced criminality and meaning-less 'happenings' contradict all the professed boasts of an advancing civilization. Art and architecture have both be-gun to tell the same story, embracing accident and chance, belittling purposeful order and humane design. Behind the smooth bureaucratic and technological façade, chaos con-tinues to widen, for only machines can prosper in the en-vironment we are now mechanically and electronically cre-ating.

The analysis on which the new development policy is based begins, in effect, at the point where the report of 1926 left off. Henry Wright had shown that the valleys of the Hudson and the Mohawk were necessarily the backbone of any surface transportation system; but the zone of settle-ment was not confined to the strip immediately served by the railroad, since now the motorcar, the telephone, the radio, and the electric grid gave equal advantages to a much wider zone, where a network of new communities, and revivified older towns, would have, if properly organized, all the advantages of a metropolitan community without the disadvantages of congestion. The building of new towns to attract industries and population was the first means of coping with metropolitan overgrowth.

The new report points out that three patterns of growth can now be detected. First: the expansion of the hitherto minor metropolitan areas of Rochester, Syracuse, Utica, Rome, and the tri-city complex of Schenectady, Albany and Troy. The second process, largely a result of highway development, is the inter-linking not only of the cities but also of the major valley areas, which opens up an even larger area of settlement. This in turn leads to a possible further expansion of both smaller communities and remoter areas of the state, in order to take care of the current increase of population.

To handle these three kinds of change, the report has made a major advance by dividing the state into ten great regions, each with its own metropolitan center. In de-limiting these areas, the planners have given weight to both geographic and historic realities, adroitly retaining the existing counties and combining them in such a fashion as to balance environmental resources and make fuller use both of natural opportunities and the existing pattern of urban settlements. There was a beginning of such regional differentiation back in the nineteen-twenties, when the Niagara Frontier Council, the Capital District Regional Planning Association, and the Central Hudson Association were formed; but now the planners propose to make these regional divisions part of the political structure of the state.

By this one stroke the Office of Regional Development has clarified and given concrete expression to the term 'regional city'; it shows that it is actually a congeries of cities, big and small, including hamlets, villages, and townships, and that in this new pattern the maintenance of open spaces and rural resources is as important as the presence of economic and cultural opportunity. Unfortunately, though the writers have grasped the main factors in regional development, they are still under the spell of metropolitan expansion, with its tendency to establish centralized control. As a result, among the fifteen proposals they make for carrying out a regional policy, they fail to emphasize the three that are essential to any sufficient transformation: Regional Councils, Land Control, and New Towns. On these three matters, the nearly forty years that separate the first and the second reports seem to have taught the policymakers all too little.

Let me speak more specifically about these weaknesses, for unless they are remedied this report will be so much elegantly printed waste paper.

In the last half century, we have had enough experience with advisory commissions in city planning to learn how little influence they exercise. If regional development is to fare better, the state will have to set up competent regional authorities, with powers of planning, capital investment, and corporate action similar to those exercised by, say, the Port of New York Authority: in addition, regional legislatures will be necessary to see that such authorities do not get out of hand. Advisory regional councils are certainly not enough.

All the report's proposals for rehabilitating the existing metropolitan areas and planning new cities rest upon control of the land. To propose only a "codification and classification" of existing laws on land use control, as the report does, is to evade the issue: for if the existing laws were sufficient, land planning and land utilization would be done by the state and regional governments for the benefit of the whole community. New Jersey's admirable 'Green Acre' program to acquire three hundred thousand acres for conservation and outdoor recreation is already handicapped not only by speculative land-grabbing and price-raising but by local authorities seeking to retain taxable properties.

There is no use talking about the preservation of recreation areas and other open spaces when the mere announcement of such a purpose is sufficient to push up speculative land values beyond the reach of the state's budget. What we need are regional authorities with the power to put an embargo on uses of land that do not conform to public policy. Even in heavily settled areas like the Ruhr district of West Germany, such an embargo has proved effective. Since 1920, the authorities there have been able to keep that highly congested area from clotting into a single industrial mass: they have not merely kept forty per cent of the area in forests and farms, but have even added to the open area.

Finally, the changeover from metropolitan congestion to regional distribution cannot be achieved without building new towns—balanced communities, not residential suburbs —on a large scale. This was the policy put forward by Clarence Stein and his associates in the early nineteen-twenties and embodied in Wright's sketches for the further development of the state. But at that time, only two new towns of limited size had yet been built on Ebenezer Howard's principles in England. Forty years ago, the present report's suggestion of "a major study of the 'new cities' concept" would have been in order; but now that twenty towns are already being built in England under government auspices, and private developers have undertaken others recently in California, Virginia and Maryland, the sort of study advocated should have been an integral part of the present report. The next "basic step to action" is not to study the concept but to begin, experimentally, to build the towns.

Strangely, the graphic emphasis of this report falls on

what should *not* be done, treated as if it were something that could not possibly be avoided. The report accordingly wastes four huge pages to show the kind of urban development that its writers weakly believe is going to continue: the monotonous mass housing of the suburbs and the equally monotonous and even more inhumane mass housing in high-rise apartments, done under the comic name of 'Urban Renewal.' Instead of saying at this point, "This is what we must prevent," the report says confidently that five hundred thousand more people will be housed in the same dismal way. This is a betrayal of the basic regional concept. In the whole elaborate presentation, indeed, there is not a single picture of a well-planned town, or even of part of such a town. What the pictures unfortunately show could be summed up in Patrick Geddes' savage phrase: "More and more of worse and worse."

In a report whose main outlines are so sound, such weaknesses and contradictions as I have touched on cannot be treated lightly; for this report is nothing if it is not an educational document, and half the value of it is destroyed because the writers did not realize that the dominant tendencies in present-day urban development do not need encouragement, and that the main use of such a fresh conspectus is to point out the many desirable alternatives that actually exist. One of the best uses of statistical predictions is to call attention to undesirable consequences that may, with further thinking and planning, be avoided. Instead, the writers treat these predictions as instructions to continue repeating the same errors.

Behind the specific failures of this report stands a more central one which is all too common in most predictive statistical analyses: it treats statistical predictions as if they were commands. The report takes for granted, on the basis of the recent curve of population growth, that the number of people in New York State will rise from sixteen million in 1960 to some thirty million in 2020. This, then, becomes automatically a directive to prepare for such an expansion. To regard such statistics as final is only an excuse for succumbing to the inevitable, instead of taking necessary countermeasures to produce what is humanely desirable.

Actually, there are many unpredictable factors, from nuclear extermination to birth control, that may nullify this prediction: not the least important factor would be an intelligent reaction, by any large part of the population, to the prediction itself, if once its consequences were spelled out. The report, instead of cheerfully preparing for the expected thirty million, might at least have pointed out that such a population could not be accommodated without a drastic shortage of recreation space and general elbow room. Thus a more realistic canvass of the possibilities of life under such conditions might lead once more to the practice of family limitation that prevailed before 1940. Even while the report was being prepared, in fact, the number of births per thousand in New York State dipped from 25.3 in 1957 to 21.7 in 1963. Given another ten years, the population graph might be as different from the present one as those made in 1940 turned out to be.

Because it pays too much attention to statistical trends and probabilities, and not enough to fresh ideas and possibilities, except in the way of new mechanical inventions, this report lacks some of the essential virtues of the 1926 report. But the mistake that the framers of this report make is one that is common to a whole generation: it is the tendency to treat the technological forces and institutional practices now in operation as if they were immortal. When they plan on this assumption, they tend to make their most unwelcome predictions come true. But where they depart from this practice, as in the proposal for setting urban and rural growth within ten newly constituted regions, the Office of Regional Development opens up a new prospect for controlling the forces that are defeating and strangling sound urban development. For this reason, the report should have the widest possible circulation and promote the most extensive critical discussion. I know no other proposed innovation in public policy since the T.V.A. that more deserves earnest attention, not merely 'in New York, but in every other state of the Union: indeed, all over the world.

*Architectural Record,* March 1965.

# 13

# Home Remedies for
# Urban Cancer

Ever since 1948, when the national Urban Renewal Act was passed, the cities of this country have been assaulted by a series of vast federally aided building operations. These large-scale operations have brought only small-scale benefits to the city. The people who gain by the government's hand-outs are not the displaced slum dwellers but the new investors and occupants. In the name of slum clearance, many quarters of Greater New York that would still have been decently habitable with a modest expenditure of capital have been razed, and their inhabitants, along with the shopkeepers and tavern keepers who served them, have been booted out, to resettle in even slummier quarters.

Even in municipal projects designed to rehouse the displaced slum dwellers or people of equivalent low income, the physical improvements have been only partial and the social conditions of the inhabitants have been worsened through further social stratification—segregation, actually—of people by their income levels. The standard form of housing favored by the federal government and big-city administrators is high-rise slabs—bleak structures of ten to twenty stories. Superficially, these new buildings are an immense improvement over both the foul Old Law Tenements of New York and the New Law (1901) Tenements that covered the newer sections of the Bronx and the Upper West Side up to 1930. The latest model buildings are only two rooms deep; all the flats have outside exposure; the structures are widely spaced around small play areas and patches of fenced grass spotted with benches. Not merely are the buildings open to the sun and air on all sides but they are also as bugproof and verminproof as concrete floors and brick walls can make them; they have steam heat, hot and cold water, standard bathroom equipment, and practically everything a well-to-do family could demand except large rooms and doors for their closets; the absence of the latter is an idiotic economy achieved at the expense of the tenants, who must provide curtains.

These buildings, with all their palpable hygienic virtues, are the response to a whole century of investigation of the conditions of housing among the lower-income groups in big cities, particularly New York. Shortly after 1835, when the city's first deliberately congested slum tenement was built, on Cherry Street, the Health Commissioner of New York noted the appallingly high incidence of infant mortality and infectious diseases among the poor, and he correlated this with overcrowding of rooms, overcrowding of building plots, poor ventilation, and lack of running water and indoor toilet facilities. For a large part of the nineteenth century, in all big cities, housing conditions worsened, even for the upper classes, despite the common boast that this was 'the Century of Progress.' It was only because of the most massive effort by physicians, sanitarians, housing reformers, and architects that legislation established minimum standards for light, air, constructional soundness, and human decency.

Unfortunately, it turned out that better housing was more expensive housing, and at the rents the lower-income groups could afford no landlord could be tempted to invest. The most profitable rentals came from congested slum housing.

So pressing were the economic and sanitary problems in urban housing that when finally government aid on a large scale was secured, the dominant conception of good lower-income housing was naturally centered on physical improvements. Our current high-rise housing projects find their sanction in the need to wipe out more than a century of vile housing and provide space for people who have been living in slums holding three hundred to seven hundred people an acre. On sound hygienic terms, this demand can be met within the limited areas provided only by tall buildings whose grim walls are overshadowing ever-larger sections of Manhattan.

There is nothing wrong with these buildings except that, humanly speaking, they stink. What is worse, after a few years of occupancy, some of them stink in an olfactory sense, for children, out of mischief or embarrassment, often use the elevators as toilets. And the young have found the automatic elevators marvellous instruments for annoying adults; putting them out of order or stalling them has become a universal form of play. London County Council administrators have told me the same story about the conflict between high-rise urban esthetics and the spirit of youth in city elevator shafts. By the very nature of the high-rise slab, its inhabitants are cut off from the surveillance and protection of neighbors and passers-by, particularly when in elevators. In some housing projects, the possibility of casual violence, rape, even murder, a rising menace in all our big cities, is conspicuously present. The daily life of the inhabitants, besides being subject to the insistent bureaucratic regulation of the management, labors under a further handicap. Because of a long-standing rule, only lately removed, urban renewal projects could not provide marketing facilities to replace those they had wiped out; often the housewife had to trundle her heavy shopping bags many blocks and was denied the convenience of sending a small member of the family to the corner store.

In short, though the hygiene of these new structures was incomparably superior to anything the market had offered in the past—and in sunlight, air, and open view definitely superior to the congested superslums of the rich on Park Avenue—most of the other desirable facilities and opportunities had descended to a lower level.

From time to time in 'The New Yorker' I have pointed out these deficiencies in public housing in New York; as far back as 1942, when one of the first high-rise projects opened in the Navy Yard area of Brooklyn, I foretold that it would become the slum that it now notoriously is. But the person who has lately followed through on all the dismal results of current public housing and has stirringly presented them is Jane Jacobs, whose book 'The Death and Life of Great American Cities' has been an exciting theme for dinner-table conversation all over the country this past year. Though her examples of desirable urban quarters are drawn chiefly from New York—indeed, largely from a few tiny pockets of New York—the bad fashionable patterns she points to are universal.

A few years ago, Mrs. Jacobs stepped into prominence at a planners' conference at Harvard. Into the foggy atmosphere of professional jargon that usually envelops such meetings, she blew like a fresh, offshore breeze to present a picture, dramatic but not distorted, of the results of displacing large neighborhood populations to facilitate large-scale rebuilding. She pointed out a fact to which many planners and administrators had been indifferent—that a neighborhood is not just a collection of buildings but a tissue of social relations and a cluster of warm personal sentiments, associated with the familiar faces of the doctor and the priest, the butcher and the baker and the candle-

stick maker, not least with the idea of 'home.' Sanitary,
steam-heated apartments, she observed, are no substitute for
warmhearted neighbors, even if they live in verminous cold-
water flats. The chat across the air shaft, the little changes
of scene as a woman walks her baby or tells her troubles
with her husband to the druggist, the little flirtations that
often attend the purchase of a few oranges or potatoes, all
season the housewife's day and mean more than mere physical shelter. It is no real gain to supplant the sustaining
intimacies of long neighborhood association with the professional advice of a social worker or a psychiatrist, attempting by a wholly inadequate therapy to combat the trauma of
social dislocation.

Mrs. Jacobs gave firm shape to a misgiving that many
people had begun to express. But she saw more deeply
into the plight of both those who were evicted and those
who came back to living in homogenized and sterilized
barracks. These barracks had been conceived in terms of
bureaucratic regimentation, financial finagling, and administrative convenience, without sufficient thought for the diverse needs of personal and family life, thus producing a
human void that matched the new architectural void. In
this process, even valuable buildings, though cherished land-
marks in the life of the community, are often destroyed,
so that the operation may 'start clean,' without any en-
cumbrances.

Mrs. Jacobs' criticism established her as a person to be
reckoned with. Here was a new kind of 'expert,' very refreshing in current planning circles, where minds unduly
fascinated by computers carefully confine themselves to asking only the kinds of questions that computers can answer and
are completely negligent of the human contents or the
human results. This able woman had used her eyes and, even
more admirably, her heart to assay the human result of
large-scale housing, and she was saying, in effect, that these

toplofty barracks that now crowd the city's skyline and overshadow its streets were not fit for human habitation. For her, the new pattern of high-rise urban housing was all one—whether undertaken by municipal authorities to rehouse low-income groups displaced from their destroyed slum quarters, or by insurance companies to house, somewhat more spaciously and elegantly, carefully selected members of the middle classes and provide a safe, reasonably high return—or finally, by speculative investors and builders taking advantage of state aid and state subsidies to feather their private nests.

From a mind so big with fresh insights and pertinent ideas, one naturally expected a book of equally large dimensions. But whereas 'Sense and Sensibility' could have been the title of her Harvard discourse, what she sets forth in 'The Death and Life of Great American Cities' comes close to deserving the secondary title of 'Pride and Prejudice.' The shrewd critic of dehumanized housing and faulty design is still evident, and has applied some of her sharp observations and her political experience to the analysis of urban activities as a whole. But this excellent clinical analyst has been joined by a more dubious character who has patched together out of the bits and pieces of her personal observation nothing less than a universal theory about the life and death of our great—by 'great,' Mrs. Jacobs seems always to mean 'big'—American cities. This new costume of theory, though not quite as airy as the Emperor's clothes, exposes such large areas of naked unawareness that it undermines many of Mrs. Jacobs' sound statements. Some of her boldest planning proposals, indeed, rest on faulty data, inadequate evidence, and startling miscomprehensions of views contrary to hers. This does not make her book easy to appraise.

Before seeking to do justice to Mrs. Jacobs' work as a whole, I must say a word about her first chapter, in which she does not do justice to herself. Ironically, this doughty opponent of urban renewal projects turns out to have a huge private urban renewal project of her own. Like a construction gang bulldozing a site clean of all habitations, good or bad, she bulldozes out of existence every desirable innovation in urban planning during the last century, and every competing idea, without even a pretense of critical evaluation. She is sensibly opposed to sterile high-rise projects, but she is even more opposed to the best present examples of urban residential planning, such as Chatham Village, in Pittsburgh, and she seems wholly to misunderstand their nature, their purpose, and their achievement. Her misapprehension of any plans she regards as subversive of her own private concepts of urban planning leads her to astounding statements, and she even attempts to liquidate possible opponents by treating anyone who has attempted to improve the design of cities by another method as if such people were determined enemies of the city. To wipe out her most dangerous rival, she concentrates her attack on Sir Ebenezer Howard, the founder of the New Towns (Garden City) movement in England. Her handling of him is, for those who know anything of his biography, comic. Howard, it happens, devoted the last quarter century of his life to the improvement of cities, seeking to find by actual experiment the right form and size, and the right balance between urban needs and purposes and those of the rural environment. Under the rubric of the 'garden city,' he reintroduced into city building two important ideas: the notion that there was a functional limit to the area and population of a city; and the notion of providing for continued population growth by founding more towns, which would form 'town clusters,' to perform the more complex functions of a metropolis without wiping out the open recreational spaces and the rural activities of the intervening countryside. Fifteen such communities exist in England today as embodiments of his principle, mostly with populations ranging from sixty to ninety thousand people—a group of towns that will eventually hold a vast number of people working not as commuters to London but in their local factories and business enterprises. During the last year three more such towns have been founded in Britain alone.

Ebenezer Howard, Mrs. Jacobs insists, "set spinning powerful and city-destroying ideas. He conceived that the way to deal with the city's functions was to sort and sift out of the whole certain simple uses, and to arrange each of these in relative self-containment. He focussed on the provision of wholesome housing as the central problem to which everything else was subsidiary." No statement could be further from the truth. Mrs. Jacobs' wild characterization contradicts Howard's clearly formulated idea of the garden city as a balanced, many-sided, urban community. In the same vein, Mrs. Jacobs' acute dislike of nearly every improvement in town planning is concentrated in one omnibus epithet expressive of her utmost contempt: "Radiant Garden City Beautiful." Obviously, neither radiance (sunlight), nor gardens, nor spaciousness, nor beauty can have any place in Mrs. Jacobs' picture of a great city.

I shall say no more of Mrs. Jacobs' lack of historical knowledge and scholarly scruple except that her disregard of easily ascertainable facts is all too frequent. An English reviewer has charitably called her an *enfant terrible;* terrible or not, she has become a rampant public figure in the cities movement, and she has a sufficiently large uncritical following even among supposedly knowledgeable professors of planning to require a rigorous appraisal of her work lest all of it be accepted as holy writ.

"This book is an attack on current city planning and rebuilding." With these words Mrs. Jacobs introduces herself. An exhaustive critical analysis and appraisal of the torrent of urban renewal that has been reducing areas of

New York and other cities to gargantuan nonentities of high-rise buildings has been long overdue. To have someone look over the situation with her rude fresh eye seemed almost a gift from heaven. Unfortunately, her assault on current planning rests on an odd view of the nature and function and structure of big cities. Underneath her thesis— that the sidewalk, the street, and the neighborhood, in all their higgledy-piggledy unplanned casualness, are the very core of a dynamic urban life—lies a preoccupation that is almost an obsession, the prevention of criminal violence in big cities.

Despite the grandiloquent title of her book, Mrs. Jacobs' obsession prevents her from presenting a total view of the great metropolis, in life or in death: she beholds it just in fragments, especially the rundown fragment of Greenwich Village she has lived in and sentimentally overvalues. While she exults in the mere size of New York and the immense diversity of its activities, she overlooks even the most obvious price of that size in millions of dismal man-hours of daily bus and subway transportation and even longer commuter journeys by rail and car, just as she overlooks the endless rows and blocks and square miles of almost identical houses, spreading from Brooklyn to Queens, from Queens over Long Island, that have not the least touch of the diversity she finds so valuable in her own familiar Village quarters.

When the inhabitants of Greenwich Village go to work each day, they have the unique grace, in Mrs. Jacobs' rose-spectacled eyes, of performers in a ballet. But she has no epithet and no image for the daily walk to the subway station, or for the tense scrimmage and grim incarceration of the subway ride. She recognizes the existence of "gray areas," with their overpowering monotony. But she dogmatically attributes this to the low density of population, even though the post-1904 Bronx, one of the grayest of gray areas, is a high-density borough. And she ignores the appalling prison routine that most of the inhabitants of a great city have to follow, a state that in some measure accounts for some of the aggressive reactions that are now visible. Her great American city has as its sole background the humble life of a very special, almost unique historic quarter, Greenwich Village: for long a backwater whose lack of dynamism accounts for such pleasant features as it has successfully retained.

With Greenpoint and East New York, with the Erie Basin and Harlem, with Flatbush and Canarsie, Mrs. Jacobs' analysis has nothing to do. She does not even trace to its turbid source the violence overflowing into the area around Columbia University. Had Mrs. Jacobs been more aware of urban realities that long antedated high-rise housing, she would have admitted that the crime rate on Morningside Heights is not, as she suggests, the result of recently planning superblocks or segregating urban functions. What is more, one solitary walk through Harlem should have made Mrs. Jacobs revise her notions of the benefits of high density, pedestrian-filled streets, crosslines of circulation, and a mixture of primary economic activities on every residence block, for all these 'ideal' conditions are fulfilled in Harlem—without achieving the favorable results she expects of her prescription.

Mrs. Jacobs gives the show away on the first page, in introducing her new principles of town planning. "I shall mainly be writing about common ordinary things: for instance, what kinds of city streets are safe and what kinds are not; why some city parks are marvellous and others are vice traps and death traps," Mrs. Jacobs says. This sentence reveals an overruling fear of living in the big city she so openly adores, and, as all New Yorkers know, she has considerable reason for fear. Her underlying animus fosters some of her most sensitive interpretations of the quality of life in a genuine neighborhood, but it also fosters a series of amateurish planning proposals that will not stand up under the most forbearing examination.

From her point of view, one of the chief mischiefs of contemporary planning is that it reduces the number of streets by creating superblocks reserved almost exclusively for pedestrian movement, free from through wheeled traffic, with the space once pre-empted by unnecessary paved streets turned into open areas for play or provided with benches and plantations for the sedentary enjoyment of adults. Such a separation of automobile and pedestrian walks runs counter to her private directives for a safe and animated neighborhood; namely, to multiply the number of cross streets, to greatly widen the sidewalks, to reduce all other open spaces, and to place many types of shops and services on streets now devoted solely to residences. The street is her patent substitute for the more adequate meeting places which traditional cities have always boasted.

What is behind Mrs. Jacobs' idea of assigning exclusively to the street the mixed functions and diverse activities of a well-balanced neighborhood unit? The answer, I repeat, is simple: her ideal city is mainly an organization for the prevention of crime. To her, the best way to overcome criminal violence is such a mixture of economic and social activities at every hour of the day that the streets will never be empty of pedestrians, and that each shopkeeper, each householder, compelled to find both his main occupations and his recreations on the street, will serve as watchman and policeman, each knowing who is to be trusted and who not, who is defiant of the law and who upholds it, who can be taken in for a cup of coffee and who must be kept at bay.

This is indeed an 'original' theory of the city, and a new order of city planning. It comes pretty close to saying that if the planners had kept blocks as small and irregular as they are in many old quarters of Manhattan below Fourteenth

Street, and had made universal the mixture of shops and tenement houses that long characterized the main avenues, the blight and corrosion and violence that have now spread over the whole city could have been avoided. By concentrating upon the street and upon such neighborhood activities as the street promotes, Mrs. Jacobs holds, we shall go a long way toward producing a metropolis that shall be at once 'fantastically dynamic'—the adjective is hers—and humanly safe. But if this remedy were a sound one, eighteenth-century London, which met all of Mrs. Jacobs' planning prescriptions, would not have been the nest of violence and delinquency it actually was.

In judging Mrs. Jacobs' interpretations and her planning prescriptions I speak as a born and bred New Yorker, who in his time has walked over almost every street in Manhattan, and who has lived in every kind of neighborhood and in every type of housing, from a private row house on the West Side to an Old Law dumbbell railroad flat, from a grim walkup apartment off Washington Square to the thirtieth floor of an East Side hotel, from a block of row houses with no shops on Hicks Street in Brooklyn Heights to a two-room flat over a lunchroom in the same general neighborhood, with the odor of stale fat filtering through the windows, and with a tailor, a laundry, a florist, grocery stores, and restaurants—Mrs. Jacobs' favorite constellation for "urban liveliness"—immediately at hand. Like a majority of my fellow citizens, I am still unregenerate enough to prefer the quiet flat with a back garden and a handsome church beyond it on Hicks Street to all the dingy 'liveliness' of Clinton Street as it was back in the twenties. Finally, for ten years I lived in Sunnyside Gardens, the kind of well-planned neighborhood Mrs. Jacobs despises: modestly conceived for people with low incomes, but composed of one-, two-, and three-family houses and flats, with private gardens and public open spaces, plus playgrounds, meeting rooms, and an infants' school. Not utopia, but better than any existing New York neighborhood, even Mrs. Jacobs' backwater in Greenwich Village.

As one who has spent more than fifty years in New York, speaking to a native of Scranton who has not, I must remind Mrs. Jacobs that many parts of the city she denounces because they do not conform to her peculiar standards—and therefore, she reasons, are a prey to violence—were for over the better part of a century both economically quite sound and humanly secure. In the urban range of my boyhood, there were occasional rowdy gangs even half a century ago—we always ran for cover when the West Ninety-eighth Street gang invaded our street—but their more lethal activities were confined largely to their own little ghettos and nearby territory, like Hell's Kitchen or the Gas House District. With the policeman on his beat, a woman could go home alone at any hour of the night on a purely residential street without apprehension. (She could even, astonishingly, trust the policeman.) As for the great parks that Mrs. Jacobs fears as an invitation to crime, and disparages as a recreation space on the strange ground that no one any longer can safely use them, she treats as a chronic ailment a state that would have seemed incredible as late as 1935. Until the Age of Extermination widened the area of violence, one could walk the eight hundred acres of Central Park at any time of the day without fear of molestation.

Certainly it was not any mistake of Frederick Law Olmsted's in laying out Riverside Drive, Morningside Park, and St. Nicholas Park that has made these large parks unusable shambles today. What is responsible for their present emptiness is something Mrs. Jacobs disregards—the increasing pathology of the whole mode of life in the great metropolis, a pathology that is directly proportionate to its overgrowth, its purposeless materialism, its congestion, and its insensate disorder—the very conditions she vehemently upholds as marks of urban vitality. That sinister state manifests itself not merely in the statistics of crime and mental disorder but in the enormous sums spent on narcotics, sedatives, stimulants, hypnotics, and tranquillizers to keep the population of our "great" cities from coming to terms with the vacuous desperation of their daily lives and with the even more vacuous horrors that their more lunatic rulers and scientific advisers seem to regard as a reasonable terminus for the human race. Lacking any sense of an intelligible purpose or a desirable goal, the inhabitants of our "great American cities" are simply 'Waiting for Godot.'

Mrs. Jacobs is at her best in dealing with small, intimate urban areas. She understands that the very life of a neighborhood depends upon the maintenance of the human scale, for it fosters relations between visible people sharing a common environment, who meet face to face without intermediaries, who are aware of their personal identity and their common interests even though they may not exchange a word. This sense of belonging rests, however, not on a metropolitan dynamism but on continuity and stability, the special virtues of the village. These virtues remain conspicuous features of Greenwich Village, the area in New York Mrs. Jacobs favors as a model of healthy urban activity. By the beginning of the nineteenth century this part of the city, the old Ninth Ward, was so well defined, so individualized, that the City Planning Commissioners of 1811 did not dare to make it conform to the gridiron pattern they imposed with geometric rigor on the rest of the city.

The larger part of this homogeneous area consisted of two- and three-story red brick houses with white porticoes, some of the best of which, those on Varick and King Streets, were destroyed to make way for the Seventh Avenue extension. For long, a loyal population clung to these quarters partly because—as an old friend of mine who lived there remembers—though the residents of the oldest houses had to draw their supply of water from a common pump in the back yard, they were far cheaper than more up-to-date accommodations. This historic enclave, a weedy backwater left behind in the tide of urban growth, would have lost most of the very features Mrs. Jacobs admires, including its short streets, if it had been sufficiently 'dynamic.' The Village's two special characteristics, indeed, make mock of her 'new' principles—its original low density of population and its well-defined architectural character, which graciously set it off from the up-and-coming brownstone-front city that leaped beyond it. In short, old Greenwich Village was almost as much a coherent, concrete entity, with definite boundary lines, as a planned neighborhood unit in a British New Town.

The contradiction between Mrs. Jacobs' perceptions of the intimate values of neighborhood life and her unqualified adoration of metropolitan bigness and activism remains unreconciled, largely because she rejects the principles of urban design that would unite these complementary qualities. Her ultimate criteria of sound metropolitan planning are dynamism, density, and diversity, but she never allows herself to contemplate the unfortunate last term in the present series—disintegration. Yet her concern for local habits and conventions points her in the right direction for overcoming this ultimate disintegration: the recognition of the neighborhood as a vital urban entity, with an inner balance and an inner life whose stability and continuity are necessary for rebuilding the kind of community that the metropolis, in all its cataclysmic economic voracity—"cataclysmic" is Mrs. Jacobs' happy epithet—has destroyed.

She recognizes that a city is more than buildings, but she fails to perceive that a neighborhood is more than its streets and street activities. The new street system she proposes, with twice the number of intersecting north-and-south streets, would do nothing to give visible reality to the social functions of a neighborhood—those performed by school, church, market, clinic, park, library, tavern, eating house, theater. Mrs. Jacobs has no use for the orderly distribution of these activities or the handsome design of their necessary structures; she prefers the hit-and-miss distribution of the present city. No wonder she opposes the admirable work of Clarence Stein and Henry Wright. These pioneer planners have repeatedly demonstrated—in Sunnyside Gardens, on Long Island; in Radburn, New Jersey; in Chatham Village, Pittsburgh—how much superior a well-planned, visibly homogeneous neighborhood can be to the sort of random community she advocates.

In the multi-dimensional order of the city Mrs. Jacobs favors, beauty does not have a place. Yet it is the beauty of great urban cathedrals and palaces, the order of great monastic structures or the university precincts of Oxford and Cambridge, the serenity and spaciousness of the great squares of Paris, London, Rome, Edinburgh, that have preserved intact the urban cores of truly great cities over many centuries. Meanwhile, the sordid dynamism of the dingier parts of these same cities has constantly proved uneconomic, inefficient, and self-destructive.

Instead of asking what are the best possible urban patterns today for renovating our disordered cities, Mrs. Jacobs asks only under what conditions can existing slums and blighted areas preserve their congenial humane features without any serious improvements in their physical structure or their mode of life. Her simple formula does not suggest that her eyes have ever been hurt by ugliness, sordor, confusion, or her ears offended by the roar of trucks smashing through a once quiet residential neighborhood, or her nose assaulted by the chronic odors of ill-ventilated, unsunned housing at the slum standards of congestion that alone meet her ideal standards for residential density. If people are housed in sufficiently congested quarters—provided only that the buildings are not set within superblocks—and if there is a sufficiently haphazard mixture of functions and activities, her social and esthetic demands are both satisfied. She has exposed these convictions in a flat statement: "A city cannot be a work of art." The citizens of Florence, Siena, Venice, and Turin will please take note! But of course Mrs. Jacobs would have her own smug answer to this: if these places are beautiful they are not and never were cities.

What has happened is that Mrs. Jacobs has jumped from the quite defensible position that good physical structures and handsome design are not everything in city planning to the callow notion that they do not matter at all. That beauty, order, spaciousness, clarity of purpose may be worth having for their direct effect on the human spirit even if they do not promote dynamism, increase the turnover of goods, or reduce criminal violence seems not to occur to Mrs. Jacobs. This is esthetic philistinism with a vengeance.

Mrs. Jacobs' most original proposal, then, as a theorist of metropolitan development, is to turn its chronic symptom of disorganization—excessive congestion—into a remedy, by deliberately enlarging the scope of the disease. It is her belief, unshaken by irrefutable counter-evidence, that congestion and disorder are the normal, indeed the most desirable, conditions of life in cities. But it is now a well-established fact in biology that overcrowded quarters produce conditions of stress even in animals, a state marked by anxiety and hostility. Elbow room is a general condition for even animal health. Since her obstinate belief in high population density underlies Mrs. Jacobs' entire argument, it gratuitously vitiates even her valid contributions.*

Yet despite blind spots and omissions, this book at times offers valuable insights into the complex activities of the

* See Edward T. Hall, 'The Hidden Dimension.' New York: Doubleday & Company, Inc., 1966.

city—especially those urban functions that flourish precisely because of all the interchanges that take place, by chance no less than by plan, most frequently in cities that have reached a certain order of bigness and complexity. Mrs. Jacobs recognizes how much of value they will leave behind, unlike the big corporations and research laboratories that are stampeding into suburbia, in exchange for temporary access to a golf course, a private airfield, or a few domestic acres. She also recognizes, by observation and experience, the communal nucleus of the city—the spontaneous 'primary' association of families and neighbors, upon which all the later complexities of urban life are based. And though she dislikes the notion of a planned 'neighborhood unit,' she chooses for her normal neighborhood the size that Clarence Perry, in his studies for the Regional Plan of New York back in the twenties, hit upon as roughly the proper size for such a unit—about five thousand people. "We shall have something solid to chew on," she observes, "if we think of city neighborhoods as mundane organs of self-government. Our failures with city neighborhoods are, ultimately, failures in localized self-government. And our successes are successes at localized self-government. I am using self-government in its broadest sense, meaning both the informal and formal self-management of society." Excellent. But as against Mrs. Jacobs many of us hold that such activities would be furthered by visible structures and that a planned architectural neighborhood unity will give firmness to its common functions, as it does in the classic example of Venice.

Venice was one of the few cities that, from the Middle Ages onward, were deliberately planned and practically organized on the neighborhood principle, each parish with the little *campo* at the center—occupied by a café, and shops, and fountain—and its guildhall and its church, a building that might boast as fine a Tintoretto as the Ducal Palace. There is still plenty of variety and domestic vitality in such neighborhoods despite their long decay, but they do not follow Mrs. Jacobs' formula of shops and factories strewn all over the quarter. Her overvaluation of the street as a social rendezvous leads to her naïve remedy for combatting random violence. And her prescription ("eyes on the street") is a result of wishful thinking. Since when has the idea of shopkeepers as substitute policemen kept even themselves from being held up and knifed? And what makes Mrs. Jacobs think that policemen are immune to murderous attack?

But about the long-term remoralization of this demoralized metropolitan community, she is emphatically right: the stabilities of the family and the neighborhood are the basic sources of all higher forms of morality, and when they are lacking, the whole edifice of civilization is threatened. When no one cares for anyone else, because we have all become mere computer digits or Social Security numbers, the elaborate fabric of urban life breaks down. Out of this rejection and isolation and emptiness comes, probably, the boiling hostility of both juvenile and adult delinquent.

Mrs. Jacobs' concern for the smallest unit of urban life is, then, pertinent and well directed. Unhappily, the main tendency of the metropolitan economy Mrs. Jacobs zealously supports is to turn all business over to big commercial enterprises, increasingly automatic in operation and automatically increasing in size. The huge, impersonal supermarket is symbolically the ultimate goal of unregulated metropolitan expansion. Mrs. Jacobs wishes to fight new forms of economic organization that are wiping out choice and variety. But the notion of achieving this by multiplying the number of short streets and increasing the population of marginal small business enterprises absurdly ignores the larger forces that must be controlled and humanized. The dominant economic institutions in our cities deliberately work to curtail freedom and reduce autonomy. There is no dividing line between the dynamic forces Mrs. Jacobs favors and the cataclysmic forces she opposes, for they have the same origin—an obsessive concern for power and profit, and an indifference to more humane interests.

In passing from that now barely recognizable unit of urban life, the neighborhood, to the larger problems of the city, Mrs. Jacobs again approaches but never reaches a desirable goal. She has had enough political experience to recognize that the city, by its very size, has got out of hand, particularly out of the hands of its own citizens, and that its hugeness causes it to be misplanned and maladministered. Because they lack any integral organs for formulating policies or making decisions, or even contesting the proposals of the Mayor, the City Planning Commissioners, the Borough Presidents, or Mr. Moses, the political pressure exerted by local areas is feeble and sporadic, and achieved only with great effort through *ad-hoc* organizations. The result has been a docile conformity by our governing agencies to other more powerful financial influences, unconcerned with the common good.

Mrs. Jacobs realizes that if public officials are to be made more responsive to public opinion and to be prevented from making wanton changes in neighborhoods to favor lending institutions, big contractors, and rich tenants instead of the old residents, politics must be organized on a local basis. So, too, her proposed new neighborhood organ of government, like the English borough and unlike the purely formal area of an Assembly District, must have some coherence and integrity as an economic and social unit. Functions that were once pushed to the periphery of the city, or packed into specialized enclaves, like the Seventh Avenue garment district, should be distributed over wider areas in these local-government units. For smaller metropolises like Pittsburgh, she suggests that thirty thousand would be the right population for such units, while for cities as big as Chicago and New York, she chooses a hundred thousand, and she recognizes that to form these boroughs into active municipal entities industry and business must be established in these sub-centers. (See 'The Roaring Traffic's Boom,' in 'The New Yorker' of April 16, 1953, for a similar proposal.)

I take a certain mischievous delight in pointing out that the thirty thousand she has hit on for a self-governing 'district' is precisely the figure Leonardo da Vinci, the first advocate of New Towns, suggested to the Duke of Milan when he proposed to overcome the congestion and sordor of that city of three hundred thousand people by designing ten component cities of thirty thousand, and that thirty thousand is the number Ebenezer Howard—the arch-villain in Mrs. Jacobs' private urban melodrama—tentatively chose for his original Garden City. Nor do I think less of her proposals because the great Leonardo and the wise Howard got there before Mrs. Jacobs. But the recent Royal Commission in Great Britain on the government of London, which included such a masterly interpreter of urban government as Professor William Robson, concluded that a hundred thousand to two hundred and fifty thousand was the desirable population for the boroughs of Metropolitan London. If Mrs. Jacobs errs in laying down the ideal number for a borough, she errs in favor of the smaller unit. I salute her as a reluctant ally of old Ebenezer Howard.

Mrs. Jacobs innocently believes that complexity and diversity are impossible without the kind of intense congestion that has in fact been emptying out the big city, hurling masses of people into the vast, curdled Milky Ways of suburbia. In the desire to enjoy amenities impossible at even a quarter of the density of population she considers desirable, millions of people are giving up the delights and stimulations of genuine city life. It is millions of quite ordinary people who cherish such suburban desires, not a few fanatical haters of the city, sunk in bucolic dreams. Now, it is this massive century-old drift to suburbia, not the building of super-blocks or garden cities, that is mainly responsible for the dilapidation and the near-death of big cities. How could Mrs. Jacobs ignore this staring historic fact?

This movement toward the rural periphery in search of things that were the proud possession of every premechanized city has been helped by the most active enemies of the city—the overbudgeted highway programs that have riddled metropolitan areas with their gaping expressways and transformed civic cores into parking lots. Those who leave the city wish to escape its snarling violence and its sickening perversions of life, its traffic in narcotics and its gangster-organized lewdness, which break into the lives even of children. Not least, the suburban exiles seek to find at least nightly surcease from constant bureaucratic regimentation: Punch the time clock! Watch your step! Curb your dog! Do not spit! No parking! Get in line for a ticket! Move on! Keep off the grass! Follow the green line! Wait for the next train! Buy now, pay later! Don't buck the system! Take what you get! The refugees who leave the metropolis may not keep even the fleeting illusion of freedom and security and a normal family life for long: all too soon rising land values and high rents bring high-rise housing, asphalted parking lots, and asphyxiating traffic jams. But their reaction is evidence of their own spontaneous vitality and a quickened desire for autonomy, which most of the rest of their existence as members of a gigantic, overcongested, necessarily impersonal hive defeats. Strangely, the city that so insistently drives its population into the suburbs is the very same city that Mrs. Jacobs quaintly describes as "vital." She forgets that in organisms there is no tissue quite so 'vital' or 'dynamic' as cancer growths.

But if 'The Death and Life of Great American Cities,' taken as a critique of modern city planning, is a mingling of sense and sentimentality, of mature judgments and schoolgirl howlers, how does it stand as an interpretation of the larger issues of urban development and urban renewal, which the title itself so boldly points to? Here again Mrs. Jacobs heads her argument in the right direction, toward matters that have been insufficiently appreciated or misinterpreted. No one has surpassed her in understanding the reasons for the great metropolis' complexity and the effect of this complexity, with its divisions of labor, its differentiations of occupations and interests, its valuable racial, national, and cultural variety, upon its daily activities. She recognizes that one cannot handle such a multi-dimensional social organization as one might handle a simple machine, designed for a single function. "A growing number of people have begun, gradually," she notes, "to think of cities as problems in organized complexity—organisms that are replete with unexamined, but obviously intricately interconnected, and surely understandable, relationships."

That is an admirable observation, but the author has forgotten the most essential characteristic of all organic growth—to maintain diversity and balance the organism must not exceed the norm of its species. Any ecological association eventually reaches the 'climax stage,' beyond which growth without deterioration is not possible.

Despite Mrs. Jacobs' recognition of organic complexity in the abstract, she has a very inadequate appreciation of the ecological setting of cities and neighborhoods; she brusquely turns her back to all but the segregated local environment. Yet the overgrowth of our big cities has destroyed those special environmental qualities that made their setting desirable and fostered their growth in the first place. The obvious result of the large-scale metropolitan congestion she advocates she flatly ignores—the poisoning of the human system with carbon monoxide and the two hundred known cancer-producing substances usually in the air, the muffling of the vital ultraviolet rays by smog, the befouling of streams and oceanside (once used for fishing and bathing) with human and industrial waste. This is something worse than an over-sight; it is willful blindness.

Mrs. Jacobs approvingly quotes Dr. Karl Menninger's observation that the best remedies for delinquency are "plentiful contacts with other people, work, including even drudgery, and violent play." But the kind of congested conglomeration she advocates would provide no room for violent play, and no sufficient opportunity to find relief from the monotonous and depressing regimentation of the big city. From the days of Ur onward, city dwellers have always had the countryside close at hand. There their homicidal impulses could be exorcised by digging and delving, or by shooting at destructive animals, and there their need for spontaneous muscular exercise could be satisfied by swimming and boating and climbing rather than by knives, brass knuckles, and rumbles. (Emerson long ago prescribed a pasture and a wood lot as the best cure for juvenile village mischief; they didn't call it 'juvenile delinquency' in his day.)

When they have reached a point long ago overpassed by New York, Chicago, London, Tokyo, and Moscow, big cities are under the necessity to expand their operations to a more capacious container—the region. The forces that have formed our cities in the past are now almost automatically, by their insensate dynamism, wrecking them and threatening to destroy whole countries and continents. Against this background, the problem of policing public thoroughfares against violence is minor; violence and vice are symptoms of those far graver forms of disorder that Mrs. Jacobs rules out of consideration because they challenge her rosily sentimental picture of the 'great American city.'

To blame the conditions in the congested, overgrown metropolis of today on the monumental scale and human hollowness of its urban renewal projects is preposterous, for this draws attention from the grim, enveloping realities that our whole metropolitan civilization confronts. The prevailing economic and technological forces in the big city have broken away from the ecological pattern, as well as from the moral inhibitions and the social codes and the religious ideals that once, however imperfectly, kept them under some sort of control, and reduced their destructive potentialities.

Just as there is no limit to the power assigned to those who build nuclear weapons and rockets, who plan space shots and lunatic-cool mass exterminations, so there is no limit to those who multiply motor roads for the sake of selling more motorcars and gasoline and road-building machinery, who push on the market every variety of drug, narcotic, chemical, and biotic agent, without regard to their ultimate effect on the landscape or upon any form of organic life. Under this 'cataclysmic' eruption of power, with its lack of any goal but its own expansion, as Henry Adams presciently predicted half a century ago, "law disappears as a priori principle and gives place to force: morality becomes police: disintegration overcomes integration." The present metropolitan explosion is both the symbol and agent of this uncontrolled power.

Failing to appraise the larger sources of urban disintegration, or to trace the connection between our major adult and our minor juvenile forms of delinquency, Mrs. Jacobs mistakenly regards those who may have a better grasp of the situation as enemies of metropolitan life. Now, under more normal circumstances, the special virtue of the great city was that it did, in fact, tend to keep any one idea or institution or group from becoming dominant. Today, military power, scientific power, technical power, financial power, and, in fact, 'cataclysmic' power in every manifestation operate most successfully, on their own terms, by wiping out diversity and doing away with every mode of organic growth, ecological partnership, and autonomous activity.

'Silent Spring' came to the big city long before it visited the countryside. No planning proposal now makes sense unless it is conceived in terms of truly human purposes—self-chosen, self-limited, and self-directed. The command of this unlimited, automatically expanding power is, again as Henry Adams wisely pointed out half a century ago, the central problem of our civilization. For Mrs. Jacobs to imagine that the horrifying human by-products of the city's disordered life can be eliminated by a few tricks of planning is as foolish as for her to imagine that a too generous supply of open spaces and superblocks fostered these symptoms.

If our urban civilization is to escape progressive dissolution, we shall have to rebuild it from the ground up. Certainly we shall have to do far more than alter street plans, humanize housing projects, or give wider geographic distribution to economic activities. Since such a general transformation will affect every aspect of life, urban politics and planning must of course play an active and significant part. But it is the formative, stabilizing, coherent, order-making forces, not the overdynamic ones, that now need special encouragement.

One cannot control destructive automatisms at the top unless one begins with the smallest units and restores life and initiative to them—to the person as a responsible human being, to the neighborhood as the primary organ not merely of social life but of moral behavior, and finally to the city, as an organic embodiment of the common life, in ecological balance with other cities, big and little, within the larger region in which they lie. A quick, purely local answer to these problems is no better than applying a homemade poultice for the cure of a cancer. And that, I am afraid, is what the more 'original' Jacobsean proposals in 'The Death and Life of Great American Cities' come to.

*The New Yorker*, December 1, 1962.

# 14

# A Brief History
of Urban Frustration*

Though it is a privilege to appear before this committee to explore subjects of such vital importance as those you have under review, Senator Ribicoff will bear witness that it is not a privilege I sought for. On the contrary, I have undertaken this task with great reluctance, since the conclusions I have come to as a student of urbanism, regionalism, and technology in the course of a half century's study do not lend themselves easily to a summary statement, still less to a series of pat recommendations.

What has brought me here, despite this reluctance, is merely a sense of duty as an American citizen, one who has actively promoted regional development and urban renewal, and yet is sufficiently detached from the responsibilities of office and the restrictive discipline of specialized research to be free to bring before you certain fundamental issues that as yet have scarcely been opened up, much less defined, discussed, and debated.

Do not, I beg, misread my occupational qualifications. By profession I am a writer—not an architect, an engineer, or a city planner; and though I have been a professor of

* Statement for the Ribicoff Committee on governmental expenditures, presented at a public hearing in Washington, D.C., April 21, 1967.

city and regional planning at the University of Pennsylvania, I have no wish to appear before you as an urban specialist, an 'expert,' an authority. But please do not read any false humility into this statement. All the colossal mistakes that have been made during the last quarter century in urban renewal, highway building, transportation, land use, and recreation have been made by highly qualified experts and specialists—and as regards planning I should blush to be found in their company.

While I have prudently reminded you of my limitations, I nevertheless have one genuine qualification, unfortunately still a rare one, that of a generalist, equally at home in many different areas of life and thought. My speciality is that of bringing the scattered specialisms together, to form an over-all pattern that the expert, precisely because of his over-concentration on one small section of existence, fatally over-looks or deliberately ignores. Emerson described his ideal of the American scholar as "man thinking"; and it is only in so far as I have been a scholar in this sense, dedicated to seeing life steadily and seeing it whole, that I venture to appear before you.

I shall not waste time listing any other qualifications I may have: for what they are worth, you will find them in any Who's Who or biographical dictionary. But I must lay the ground for the constructive criticism I shall eventually make by briefly summarizing the experience that has led me to my present views.

While still at college, in fact, when only eighteen, I came under the influence of the Scots thinker Professor Patrick Geddes, who shares with Ebenezer Howard, Raymond Un-win, and our own Frederick Law Olmsted, Sr., the distinction not merely of reviving the art of town planning, but also of awakening fresh interest in the nature and function of cities. Though there are now scores of books and college courses available on every aspect of urbanism, half a century ago you could almost count them on the fingers of one hand.

As a disciple of Geddes, I learned to study cities and regions at first hand, living in them, working in them, not least, surveying every part of them on foot: not only my native city, New York, but many others, large and small, Philadelphia, Pittsburgh, Boston, London, Edinburgh, Honolulu, Berkeley, Geneva—not to speak of smaller places like Palo Alto, Middletown, Hanover, and the Dutchess County hamlet of a dozen houses where I find the seclusion necessary for the writing of my books.

More than five-sevenths of my life has been spent in cities, mostly in great metropolises; and when in 'The Culture of Cities' in 1938 I painted a picture of the prospective disintegration of Megalopolis, my experience and my historic researches enabled me to anticipate by thirty years the conditions that you are now belatedly trying to cope with, for the formidable disorders I described in detail were already visible elsewhere, in London and Paris in the eighteenth century, and had become chronic in every congested urban center for the whole last century. No small part of this ugly urban barbarization has been due to sheer physical congestion: a diagnosis now partly confirmed by scientific experiments with rats—for when they are placed in equally congested quarters, they exhibit the same symptoms of stress, alienation, hostility, sexual perversion, parental incompetence, and rabid violence that we now find in Megalopolis.

My interest in cities brought me, as early as 1923, into close relations with a group of men whose human vision and practical judgment, had they been heeded in any large way, could have transformed American housing and planning. If their basic proposals had been carried further, we might have averted the grim conditions you now face.

In the early twenties this group incorporated itself into the Regional Planning Association of America, a small body, with never over twenty members, not to be confused with a different later group, with a more conventional metropolitan approach, indeed a diametrically opposite one, the Regional Plan Association of New York. Such fresh, humanly significant ideas as came into planning and housing during the twenties and thirties were in no small measure the work of these two groups.*

In urban planning, the two leaders of my own group were Clarence Stein and Henry Wright. They pioneered in the planning of a highly successful housing project for mixed-income families, Sunnyside Gardens in Long Island City. And out of that experiment, with the help of a socially responsible realtor, Alexander Bing, grew an even more important experiment, the proposed New Town of Radburn, New Jersey. Though Radburn's career as a new town was abruptly cut short by the depression, it made a contribution in design that has had a world-wide influence.

Radburn was conceived originally as an experimental model under private enterprise for a series of New Towns; and some of its principles were, in fact, partly embodied in the abortive Greenbelt Towns which never became real towns, built by the federal government between 1935 and 1940. During the next twenty-five years Clarence Stein and I kept alive here, almost singlehanded, the fundamental ideas of the New Towns movement. We held that further increase of population in already congested centers should be met, not by intensifying the congestion in high-rise buildings, not by adding endless acres and square miles of suburbs, with ever-longer and more time-wasting journeys to work, but by building new, planned communities on a better model; many-sided, balanced, self-maintaining: in a word, to use your Chairman's term, 'competent.' We conceived that these communities, fully equipped for industry, business,

* See Roy Lubove, 'Community Planning in the 1920's: The Contribution of the Regional Planning Association of America.' Pittsburgh: University of Pittsburgh Press, 1964.

social life, and culture, would be linked together functionally with the central metropolis in a new kind of open urban pattern. This pattern would preserve the countryside for farming and recreation, and bring together the neighborhood, the city, and the metropolis in a new constellation, which we called the Regional City.*

Not merely was I an intellectual associate of Stein and Wright in these activities, but I was equally a close colleague of Benton MacKaye, another member of our group: he who is best known to you, perhaps, as the shrewd Yankee whose activities as forester, conservationist, and geotect led to his projecting the Appalachian Trail. Unlike most bold dreamers, he has lived to see his dream completely realized within his own lifetime through the voluntary cooperation of local groups, without any government aid whatever.

Like myself, MacKaye had served as investigator for the New York State Housing and Regional Planning Commission, of which Stein was Chairman and Henry Wright Planning Adviser. The hearings and reports of that commission played a decisive part in the whole movement for government action, state and federal, to build and subsidize adequate housing for the lower-income groups; and so laid the foundations for the large-scale federal program that was begun during the depression and expanded after the Second World War.

The final report of Stein's commission, with its Regional Plan for the whole state, was so far-sighted and far-reaching that, some forty years later, it still served as the basis for a similar project by Governor Rockefeller's Office of Regional Development—though, unfortunately, he has not seen fit to follow it up.

In 1925 MacKaye and I edited the Regional Planning number of the 'Survey Graphic': the first time in which the ideas of regionalism and regional planning were set forth

* See Clarence S. Stein, 'Toward New Towns for America.' Cambridge: Massachusetts Institute of Technology, 1966 (paperback).

and treated as the essential key to anything fit to be called sound urban or metropolitan development. That number demonstrated the approaching strangulation of life in the great cities, dying because of that cancerous overgrowth and congestion which many highly esteemed experts mistakenly confuse with economic dynamism and social vitality. But we also showed the importance of the electricity grid, the radio, and the motor highway in making possible a more balanced population pattern, distributed over a much wider area than the congested metropolis, preserving the essential resources of the countryside, in a permanent green matrix, instead of wiping out every natural advantage by affluent suburban and slummy sub-suburban expansion and sprawl.

One more point, and this biographic preface is done. Though MacKaye had laid down the main outlines for an effective regional approach to metropolitan problems, in his 1928 book, 'The New Exploration'—a classic introduction republished in 1962 as a University of Illinois paperback—he added a new and important project in 1931: his plan for the Townless Highway. His article on this subject, which appeared in 'Harper's,' was the very first one in which all the main elements of a new type of motor highway, which we now call the throughway or expressway, were put together. In the Appalachian Trail and the Townless Highway this spiritual descendant of Thoreau effectually visualized the backbone of a better environment and proved how much more practical he was than the 'practical' specialists, who keep so closely to their familiar mole-runs that they remain blind and baffled even when, by accident, they come above ground to the light.

Now why, you must be asking yourselves, have I used up your time in rehearsing these past efforts at planning? Not, certainly, to claim priority over those who are advancing many of these same ideas now, as if for the first time: such a claim would be too picayune for words. And certainly not to boast of our successes, though when the Tennessee Valley project was first put forward by President Roosevelt—whom, when Governor, we had chosen as chief speaker for our Regional Planning Conference at the University of Virginia in 1931—we momentarily exulted in the thought that our ten years of preparatory thinking and experimenting had not been in vain.

No: my reason for telling you these things is due to the realization that every advance we projected or succeeded in establishing eventually came to grief: sometimes, like the Regional Plan for the State of New York, by stupid indifference and neglect; but even more, I regret to say, by being taken up on a national scale, with all the force, the authority, and the budgetary resources supplied by the federal government. In coming to life, our ideas were done to death: caricatured or permanently disfigured by forces—technological, bureaucratic, financial, above all, financial—that we had failed sufficiently to reckon with.

Certainly, no group worked harder than we did to establish governmental responsibility, state and federal, for producing and subsidizing good housing for the lower-income groups. But what was the result? Federal housing had hardly gotten under way before the financial-bureaucratic process and the bulldozer mind had wiped out our new concepts for a better urban community, and produced those nightmares of urban anonymity and human desolation that dominate the skyline today: those high-rise housing developments in whose design only financial and mechanical calculations have played a part.

Everything that Jane Jacobs has said in condemnation of these sterile, indeed, humanly hostile, projects is true. But, I hasten to add, they would not be any better if, on her pet formula, the designers had multiplied the number of streets and lined them with shops, and thus produced even more stifling and strangulating forms of congestion. The rapes, the robberies, the destructive delinquencies, the ever-threatening violence, for which she naïvely believes she has found a simple planning antidote, would still be there, since these are symptoms, not just of bad planning, or even of poverty, but of a radically deficient and depleted mode of life, a life from which both the most destitute slum dwellers and the most affluent suburbanites equally, though in different ways, suffer. There is no planning cure for this machine-centered existence which produces only psychotic stresses, meaningless 'happenings,' and murderous fantasies of revenge.

On the basis of this wholesale reversal of our good intentions I must ask you: Is there any reason to suppose that a massive new attempt by the federal government to wipe out the existing slums—however we may define them—will succeed any better than our earlier efforts unless we change both our methods and our objectives?

Is there any plausible reason for expecting any better results from wholesale government intervention, under our present auspices, no matter how much money you are prepared to spend? If you embark on such a program without asking far more fundamental questions about the reasons for our past failures, and if you fail to set up more human goals than those which our expanding economy now pursues, you will be throwing public money down the drain.

And worse: in the course of doing this, you will bring about even more villainous conditions than those which you are trying to correct; for you will wipe out on a greater scale than ever what is left of neighborly life, social cooperation, and human identity in our already depressed and congested urban areas. If you want to know about the human reactions to this, read Studs Terkel's recent eye-opening book, 'Division Street.' Let me respectfully suggest that unless we challenge the current American way of life, all we can soberly expect is more and more of worse and worse.

Or take another failure: what happened to MacKaye's conception of the Townless Highway. When he put forward this proposal, he sought to apply to the motorway efficient transportation principles, like that of an independent right of way, with access only at wide intervals, that had long been incorporated in the railroad line. He did not for a moment anticipate that, in the working out of this system with extravagant federal subsidies, the highway engineers would repeat all the dismal planning errors committed originally by the railroad engineers—such as gouging through the center of the city and pre-empting its most valuable urban land for six-lane highways and parking lots and garages.

Unfortunately, the highway engineers took over every feature of MacKaye's plan except the most important one: that it should be 'townless,' that is, that it should bypass every urban center, small or big. Indeed, with all the insolence of an overcoddled public authority, not merely have they become specialists in despoiling beautiful landscapes and violating land dedicated to national and local parks, but they actively welcome further urban congestion and blight as the best possible justification for still more highway, bridge, and tunnel building. When the city does not create sufficient congestion, these authorities bring it about themselves, as the Port of New York Authority proposes with its hundred-and-ten-story buildings for the World Trade Center.

As a result, these incontinent erections and congestions are steadily breaking down variety and continuity in urban life, wiping out the human contacts, obstructing the social opportunities, undermining further the intimate face-to-face cooperations that the city exists to promote.

There is no use in your voting huge sums for housing and so-called Urban Renewal while a large part of the funds you have allotted to highway building are still being misused for wholesale urban destruction.

I have only touched, necessarily in a sketchy way, on the

dismaying results that followed from carrying out, through federal agencies and federal funds, some of the very policies that the Regional Planning Association and its various active members not merely advocated but participated in. But what of our other contributions—those that were only half carried out, or not carried out at all?

There I have to expose another kind of failure, equally serious. In the nineteen-thirties the ideas of regional planning seemed about to bear very promising fruit: not only in the founding of the T.V.A., with its combination of electrification, improved soil management and farming, and general regional rehabilitation, but also in the founding of the National Resources Planning Board, later the National Resources Committee, which encouraged each state to prepare regional plans, based on more sufficient knowledge, for the better development of its own resources. From the beginning compartmentalized habits of thinking kept regional planning entirely separate from urban planning—which is an absurdity. But if the planning boards had not been disbanded, the very necessities of economic and social life would have eventually brought them together.

Unfortunately, your predecessors in the Congress developed an almost pathological fear of planning, and hated the very word; though no great enterprise of any kind, as A. T. & T. or General Electric or Du Pont would tell you, can be carried on without long-term planning of the most detailed sort, carefully coordinated, and constantly corrected in the light of new conditions and fresh appraisals—what is now, in the jargon of the computer specialists, called feedback.

The result of this rejection of planning was not, of course, that we have done away with planning: the result is, rather, that our country has been the victim of the worst kind of planning possible, that in which each governmental bureau or division, each industry or business, thinks only of its own needs and aims, and tries to seize, for its own narrow purposes, the largest share of the budget, the biggest staff, the greatest amount of power—or, in business, the greatest possible financial return. At the Highway Conference held by the Connecticut General Insurance Company in 1957, it turned out that the federal head of housing and the federal head of highway building had never met, still less exchanged views, until that occasion, though neither could possibly do his work intelligently without reference to the other.

If the surveys and inventories of resources undertaken by the Regional Planning Boards in many states had been continued over the last quarter century, you would not only have an adequate local basis for highway planning, which has been done, so far, with such callous indifference to respecting local needs and establishing a better regional pattern, but you would likewise have a good notion—as you do not in the least have now—of where the new housing, the new neighborhoods, the new towns should be built. I fear that you may be taking for granted the notion that the foul, crowded slums of the past should be replaced by more orderly, more sanitary housing, at equally congested densities, on the same sites. That assumption needs critical reconsideration. It is far from obvious.

Had the state planning agencies supplied the necessary feedback, they might have kept our successive housing authorities from making the errors about the location and density of housing that already have been made—or the worse ones you may now be tempted to make on an even larger scale. If active regional planning boards had been created and maintained, our country would have produced a large corps of trained minds, architects, planners, geotects, regional surveyors, who would now be able to do the job without too much direction from Washington, because they would have accumulated an immense amount of detailed first-hand knowledge of the basic natural and human resources. That knowledge cannot be derived solely from statistics, is not transferable to computers, and is not achievable by any crash programs for education.

May I suggest, then, that if you are not to do far more damage than good in establishing a new housing policy, you must first prepare to rebuild the effective organs for regional planning and regional government, on a state and interstate basis. This will also mean assembling, in the eight or ten major regions of the country, the federal agencies that will, at various points, participate in this program. The Regional Development Council of America, a group that after 1945 continued the older Regional Plan Association, proposed such a permanent decentralization of related federal activities in 1950: but Mr. Stein could get no one in Washington to take this proposal seriously.

Surely it is time that there was a general realization of the fact that we must deliberately contrive a new urban pattern; one which will more effectively mobilize the immense resources of our great metropolises without accepting the intolerable congestion that has driven increasing numbers of people to seek—at whatever sacrifice of time and social opportunity—at least a temporary breathing space in less congested suburban areas. The new form of the city must be conceived on a regional scale: not subordinated to a single dominant center, but as a network of cities of different forms and sizes, set in the midst of publicly protected open spaces permanently dedicated to agriculture and recreation. In such a regional scheme the metropolis would be only '*primus inter pares*,' the first among equals.

This is the organic type of city that the technology of our time—the electric grid, the telephone, the radio, television, fast transportation, information storage and transmission—has made possible. A handful of planners, notably Christopher

Tunnard, has seen the implications of this new scale in urban planning: but most of our planning authorities still remain, like a worn-out, scratched phonograph record, with their needle stuck in the old metropolitan groove. Many people, since the publication of Jean Gottmann's monumental survey, have tried to take comfort in the thought that the present disordered and disintegrating urban mass, which Gottmann has popularized as 'Megalopolis,' is in fact the modern form of the city, new, dynamic, and inevitable, whether we like it or not.

That is a slushy idea, worthy only of a Marshall McLuhan or a Timothy Leary. You might say of this sprawling megalopolitan nonentity, the anti-city, in McLuhan's terminology, that *the mess is the message.* And the more massive the mess, the more muddled the message.

Now, I have had to explain to myself why the ideas we have put forward during the last half century often proved politically and financially acceptable, but only at the price of being sterilized, dehumanized, and degraded. But the full explanation dawned on me only recently in the course of an extensive historical analysis I have been making, in a book dealing with the basic assumptions and goals that have governed all large-scale technology, since the Pyramid Age in Egypt some five thousand years ago.

From the earliest stages of civilization on, as I read the evidence, the most striking advances in mass technology have been the outcome of centralized organizations, deliberately expanding power in every form—mechanical power, political power, military power, financial power, and, not least, the scientific power of accurate analysis and prediction—to achieve control over both the natural environment and the human community. The astounding mechanical success of these high-powered technologies is due to their method of systematically breaking down ecological complexities by deliberately eliminating the recalcitrant human factor. I have called this ancient form of mechanized organization the Megamachine. Wherever it operates, it magnifies authoritarian power and minimizes human initiative, self-direction, and self-government.

Obviously I cannot, at this hearing, present a just appraisal of the many genuine goods produced by these power systems; nor can I offer a detailed explanation of their sinister countertendency to produce an unbalanced, deliberately wasteful, inherently destructive, and increasingly totalitarian economy, seemingly modern, but in fact based on ancient bureaucratic and military models. Even the book I have written, 'The Myth of the Machine,' only opens up the subject, and I have still to trace the story through the last four centuries.

But the main point to observe is that there is a deep-seated antagonism between a mechanistic, power-centered economy and the far older organic, life-centered economy; for a life economy seeks continuity, variety, orderly and purposeful growth. Such an economy is cut to the human scale: so that every organism, every community, every human being, shall have the variety of goods and experiences necessary for the fulfillment of his own individual life-course, from birth to death. The mark of a life economy is its observance of organic limits: it seeks not the greatest possible quantity of any particular good, but the right quantity, of the right quality, at the right place and the right time for the right purpose. Too much of any one thing is as fatal to living organisms as too little.

In contrast, a power economy is designed for the continuous and compulsive expansion of a limited number of goods—those specially adapted to quantity production and remote control. Apart from enlarging the province of mechanization and automation itself, the chief goal of this system is to produce the greatest amount of power, prestige, or profit for the distant controllers of the megamachine. Though these modern power systems produce a maximum output of highly specialized products—motorcars, refrigerators, washing machines, rockets, nuclear bombs—they cannot, on their own terms, do justice to the far more complex and varied needs of human life, for these needs cannot be mechanized and automated, still less controlled and suppressed, without killing something essential to the life of the organism or to the self-respect of the human personality.

For the last century, we Americans have been systematically indoctrinated in the virtues of mass production and have accepted, with unction, the plethora of goods offered, in which even those in need of public relief now seek to participate. But we have been carefully trained to look only at the plus side of the equation, and to close our eyes to the appalling defects and failures that issue from the very success of the megamachine.

No sound public policy in housing and urban renewal can be formulated till we have reckoned with these liabilities. The overproduction of motorcars has not only wrecked our once-efficient and well-balanced transportation system, and turned our big cities into hollow shells, exploding with violence: but it has polluted the air with lethal carbon monoxide, and even, with the use of lead in gasoline, dangerously poisoned our water and food. The chemical industry, in its undisciplined effort to sell a maximum amount of its products, has poisoned our soils and our foods with DDT, Malathion, and other deadly compounds, while heedlessly befouling our water supply with detergents.

So, too, with the pharmaceutical industry, the rockets industry, the television industry, the pornography and narcotics industries: all have become immensely dynamic and profitable enterprises, automatically expanding, and by their compulsive expansion callously disregarding human health, safety, and welfare, while wiping out every trace of organic variety and human choice. As a result, the forces of life, if they break out at all, now must do so in the negative form of violence, crime, and psychotic disturbances. What we have unthinkingly accepted as brilliant technical progress too often results in biological or social regression.

The point I am now making challenges, I regret to say, not only some of the published views of your Chairman, but possibly the views of the rest of this committee. You accept, I take it, the current American faith in the necessity for an expanding, machine-centered economy, as if this were one of the great laws of nature, or if not, then America's happiest contribution to human prosperity and freedom. I wish you were right.

But do you seriously believe that a housing industry based, as Senator Ribicoff has put it, on "the technology of Megalopolis" will be any more regardful of human needs and human satisfactions, or any more eager to overcome the distortions and perversions of a power-obsessed, money-oriented economy? If so, you are ignoring the very factors that have betrayed and ruined so many of our previous well-intentioned efforts at urban improvement. This expanding economy, for all its suffocating abundance of machine-made goods and gadgets, has resulted in a dismally contracted life, lived for the most part confined to a car or a television set: a life so empty of vivid first-hand experiences and so lacking in tangible goods and spiritual values that it might as well be lived in a space capsule, travelling from nowhere to nowhere at supersonic speeds.

Space capsules—yes, stationary space capsules—that is what most of our new buildings are, and our prefabricated foods taste increasingly like those supplied in tubes to astronauts; while in our urban-planning schools I have encountered ominous designs for whole cities to be placed underground, or under water, so that their inhabitants may live and die without ever coming into contact with the living environment, that rich and varied environment which has been essential to the human race, for organic health, psychological stability, and cultural growth, for at least five hundred thousand years.

And in boasting of the fact that automation will soon be able
to do away with all serious and humanly rewarding work,
manual or mental, we are threatening to remove perhaps the
most essential historic invention for preserving mental balance, and furthering the arts of life. These are all danger
signals. Is it not time to give them heed?

Now your Chairman, in his able speech last January, attempted to bring together what seems to me, if I may speak
frankly, two altogether incompatible, in fact downright an-
tagonistic, proposals: on one hand, for restoring neighborhoods as the basic human environment, on the other, for applying to housing what he called, quite properly, "the technology of Megalopolis." Senator Ribicoff wisely recognized
the need to respect the small unit, the neighborhood, in order
to promote those qualities we associate, at least as an ideal,
with the small town—meaning, I take it, a place where everyone has an identifiable face and is a recognizable and responsible person—not just a Social Security number, a draft card
number, or a combination of digits on a computer.

As to neighborhoods, I am entirely on his side. I have not
spent part of my life in a small country community, and another part in a planned neighborhood unit, Sunnyside Gardens, Long Island, without learning to appreciate these intimate small-town virtues. And I believe the greatest defect
of the United States Constitution was its original failure,
despite the example of the New England Township and the
Town Meeting, to make this democratic local unit the basic
cell of our whole system of government. For democracy, in
any active sense, begins and ends in communities small enough
for their members to meet face to face. Without such units,
capable of independent and autonomous action, even the best-
contrived central governments, state or federal, become party-
oriented, indifferent to criticism, resentful of correction, and
in the end, all too often, high-handed and dictatorial.

But if your purpose is to do urban planning and renewal on the basis of neighborhoods and balanced urban communities, you would, I submit, be deceiving yourselves if you imagined that a vast contribution by the federal government—fifty billion dollars over ten years has been suggested—could possibly achieve the happy results you hope for. Such a massive expenditure succeeded, we all know, in producing the atom bomb; and it has been applied with equal success to producing rockets, space satellites, supersonic jets, and similar instruments of physical conquest or destruction.

But note: this method can be applied only to those structures or machine assemblages that can be designed without the faintest regard for the human factor, and without any feedback from the human reaction. This patently leaves out the neighborhood and the city. Unless human needs and human interactions and human responses are the first consideration, the city, in any valid human sense, cannot be said to exist, for, as Sophocles long ago said, "The City is people."

Accordingly, I beg you to look a little more closely at what such a huge supply of capital, with such large prospective profits, would do. Not merely would it skyrocket already inflated land values, so that a disproportionate amount would go to the property owner and real-estate speculator. But worse: it would invite even greater megamachines to invade the building industry. With fifty billion dollars as bait, a new kind of Aerospace Industry would move in, with all its typical paraphernalia of scientific research and engineering design. At that moment your plans for creating humanly satisfactory neighborhoods would go up in smoke. 'General Space Housing, Incorporated' will solve your housing problem, swiftly and efficiently, though not painlessly, by following their own typical method, derived from the ancient Pyramid Builders: eliminate the human factor by enforcing mechanical conformity and imposing automatic obedience. With the aid of their systems analyzers and computers, these high-powered organizations would design housing units even more prison-like in character than those we now have.

Once started, such a scientifically ordered housing industry, commanding virtually unlimited capital at national expense, and providing, as in the Pentagon's favored industries, indecently large salaries and exorbitant profits for private investors, would be geared for further expansion. And it would achieve this expansion, not only by designing units, prefabricated for early obsolescence, but likewise by wiping out, as dangerous rivals, those parts of the rural or urban environment that were built on a more human plan. In the name of 'urban renewal' this method would complete the urban devastation and destruction that you now seek to repair. That is not a pretty prospect. But it is a realistic interpretation of what a fifty-billion-dollar program, designed to use existing power-systems and feed an expanding economy, would do.

I have exhausted the time allotted to me, and have, I fear, more than exhausted your patience; though I have only nibbled at the edges of this difficult subject. So my final words must be brief, and, I regret, mostly words of negation and caution. Go slow! Experiment with small measures and small units, until you have time to prepare better plans and to organize new public agencies to carry out those plans. Whatever you do in extending the policies followed in the past will almost surely meet with the same embarrassments and the same failures. Remember that you cannot overcome the metropolitan congestion of the last century, or the cataclysmic disintegration of urban life during the last thirty years, by instituting a crash program. You are much more likely to produce more lethal congestion, more rapid disintegration—all ending in a greater social cataclysm. The time for action on a massive scale has not yet come. But the time for fresh thinking on this whole subject is long overdue.

# Postscript:
# The Choices Ahead

The foregoing statement before the Ribicoff Committee attracted far wider attention and brought forth more approving comment than I had dared to expect—thanks partly, perhaps, to brief extracts on television. But at many points that statement, though too long for a committee meeting, called for further amplification; so I shall now take the parliamentary privilege of 'extending my remarks.' And first I must add a few relevant highlights to the historical account I presented.

Ever since the eighteen-thirties the effects of bad urban planning and bad housing in accentuating all the miseries of inhuman economic exploitation have been recognized. But the attempts to cope with these evils, even in the provision of elementary sanitary facilities, were feeble, superficial, halting, maddeningly slow; and this was especially true in the more congested urban centers, whose very congestion raised land values, and made the vilest slum tenements far more profitable to their landlords than decent houses for the middle classes.

In 1925, when the Regional Planning number of the 'Survey Graphic' was published, only a few people realized that there was something fundamentally wrong with the quality of life in our 'great' and growing American cities, and that far bolder measures than any so far taken were necessary, if these cities were to remain socially well-balanced and attractive places to work and live in. What then seemed to many people healthy evidences of buzzing social activity and economic dynamism were too often, like kiting land values and congested streets, symptoms of social malfunction or organic defects in planning. Most of the evils now so portentously evident in urban communities today were already visible half a century ago—chronic poverty, blighted areas, filthy slums, gangsterism, race riots, police corruption and brutality (the 'third degree'), and a persistent deficiency in medical, social, and educational services.

But the chief proof that something was radically at fault with the whole pattern of life in our metropolitan centers is that those who could afford to leave the city were deserting it —indeed, they had begun to desert long before, seeking in the residential suburb, with its pleasant gardens, its nearby woods and fields, its quiet and safe residential quarters, its neighborly social life, qualities that were steadily disappearing in the more affluent metropolises. And instead of taking this desertion as an instruction to rehabilitate the central city, the leaders of urban society took it as an invitation to invest profitably in multiplying the means of escape, first by railroads, subways, and trolleys, then by motorcars, bridges, tunnels. Automatic congestion was counterbalanced by an equally automatic decongestion and dispersal; and between them, the notion of the city as a socially concentrated, varied, and stimulating and rewarding human environment vanished.

As living conditions worsened in the overcrowded central districts, the area of suburban dispersal widened, until the overflow of one metropolis mingled with the overflow of another metropolis to form the disorganized mass of formless, low-grade urban tissue that is now nicknamed Megalopolis. Like the suburban flight itself, this megalopolitan conglomeration has been treated, often by urban sociologists who should know better, as a recent phenomenon brought about by equally recent technological developments. But Patrick Geddes identified a similar random massing of sub-urban populations more than half a century ago on the British coal fields, and called it, with nicer accuracy, a conurbation—though it turns out that anti-city would be a still better name for it. Observers who now regard this urbanoid massing as the new form of the city, or praise it as a more complex, though unplannable and uncontrollable, substitute for the city, demonstrate that they have never grasped what the historic functions and purposes of the city actually are.

The ultimate mode of this physical dispersal was presciently foretold by H. G. Wells at the beginning of this century in his 'Anticipations of the Reaction of Mechanical and Scientific Progress upon Human Life': but he had, unfortunately, no premonition of the kind of social disintegration that it would bring about. These results are taking form under our eyes, with the result that the residential quarters of our 'great American cities' now tend to separate out into two kinds of ghetto: an upper-class ghetto of high-rise apartments designed, with or without governmental assistance, as status symbols for the super-affluent, and another, lower-class ghetto, scarcely distinguishable from the first on the exterior, for the lowest-income groups. The latter is the home of the new urban proletariat, mainly Negro and Puerto Rican, seeking to escape even worse conditions in San Juan or the Deep South. Those who do not qualify for either ghetto now swell the mass migration to suburbia.

When one translates into concrete terms the current talk about the increasing urbanization of the United States today, one must understand that sociologists are speaking loosely of people who are, in fact, dis-urbanized, who no longer live in cities, or enjoy, except as visitors or part-time occupants, the concentrated social advantages of the city: the face-to-face meetings, the cultural mixtures, the human challenges. For the growing majority of the non-agricultural population of the United States now lives for better or worse in suburbia: indeed, even many rural areas, where farming is still practiced, are in social content suburban. Meanwhile those who hold fast as residents in the big urban centers—or even in small towns that harbor resentful racial minorities—do so at the peril of their lives. No Berlin walls separate the Gilded Ghetto from the tarnished, oxidized ghettos that spread around them—except in ominously prophetic enclosures like Stuyvesant Town.* But even daylight is not a safeguard against robbery, rape, and murder, as any metropolitan taxi driver will testify.

Yet again we are facing an old situation, which has only been aggravated by the invasion of this new proletariat. The molten human forces that have erupted in a lava flow of violence in our American cities during the last decade have, as in a volcano, manifested themselves earlier in repeated seethings and rumblings. The possibility of such outbreaks of violence was clearly foreseen by Ralph Waldo Emerson more than a century ago. In a passage whose explanatory context the editor of Emerson's 'Journals' unfortunately deleted, he observed: "It is a great step from the thought to the expression of the thought in action. . . . If the wishes of the lowest classes that suffer in these long streets should execute themselves, who can doubt that the city would topple in ruins." Those wishes have now made themselves known from Newark to Detroit, from Boston to Los Angeles.

Even in earlier periods when the repressive forces of law and order seem to have been sufficiently self-confident and ruthless to check any outbreak, the possibility of mass violence lurked under the surface: indeed, one of Louis XIV's acknowledged reasons for building his palace in suburban Versailles was to escape any possible attack by a hostile Paris mob.

* See Chapter Thirteen in 'From the Ground Up, written in 1948. New York: Harcourt, Brace & World, Inc., 1956.

Catherine Bauer (Wurster), in her pioneer work on 'Modern Housing,' went so far as to suggest that the various efforts to improve the housing of the British working classes in the second part of the nineteenth century were due in part to fear of urban uprisings, a fear awakened by Chartist and Trades Union demonstrations.

Both the grievances and the remedies, then, have a long history: but the grievances were grudgingly acknowledged and half-heartedly corrected, and the remedies were, alas! in part the result of a faulty diagnosis. So the threat of further terror and violence remains—indeed, has been magnified in this generation by the widespread acceptance of methods of terror and violence, in so-called democracies as well as in openly totalitarian regimes, as a 'normal' practice of our civilization, along with bureaucratic regimentation and military compulsion.

Meanwhile, during the last three decades, the racial composition of American cities has changed. Into the great vacuum produced by the suburban exodus has rushed a new army of 'internal immigrants.' Faced with this influx of two depressed minorities, ill-educated, impoverished, usually untrained for work except in agriculture, tens of thousands unable to speak English, American municipalities experienced, in even more acute form, the same difficulties that mass migration from Europe had caused between 1870 and 1920. Though the United States Congress had belatedly sought to ease these difficulties by limiting the number of foreign immigrants admitted in any one year, no attempt was made to direct this internal migration, or limit it to proportions that could be absorbed and assimilated in any one community— still less to spread it over many communities by providing jobs, housing, schools.

The problems raised by these newcomers would have been difficult to handle even if the municipalities concerned had not themselves already been hopelessly in arrears in providing out of their own budgets the necessary schools and hospitals, to say nothing of new housing, for the population already established. Even if state and federal funds had been available in sufficient amounts to provide both housing and rent subsidies—and under the terms of our Cold War economy they were not available—the very volume of this sudden influx would have condemned most of the newcomers to the same verminous, insanitary, congested quarters that, in cities like New York and Boston, they were forced to occupy.

With respect to basic deficiencies—lack of light, air, space, privacy, sanitary services, schools—the grievances of the minorities, both new migrants and those long-established, were well justified. But the slowness of municipal authorities in coming to terms with these grievances only reflected an earlier unreadiness to take any measures for improving the city that did not win the approval of real-estate operators, banks, and insurance companies. What was different between this situation and that which had existed in the eighteen-nineties is that the new immigrants had higher expectations and made new demands.

The reader will perhaps have noted that the foregoing essays and papers, though recent, make no attempt, except in the Jacobs review, to diagnose these negative aspects of modern city development: the rising rate of crime, delinquency, drug addiction, and random violence, or less recordable evidences of psychic deterioration. Though Thomas Jefferson's fears for the physical and moral health of his country if its predominantly rural culture became urbanized and industrialized have long been justified by irrefutable statistical evidence, they are still too often treated by historians as a pathetic bucolic prejudice. Yet the mere increase in urbanization has in fact automatically increased the incidence of pathological social phenomena, as compared with still rural areas. Today's manifestations of hatred, fear, despair, and malevolent violence among the depressed racial and cultural minor-

ities only exhibit in more virulent form the normal path-
ologies of everyday urban life.

The reason for my silence was neither ignorance nor indifference: I had already dealt with these evidences of urban
disintegration in three earlier books. As a student of cities, I
knew that all these pathogenic factors had been present in
American cities for the last hundred years, along with the inhuman physical congestion and the economic exploitation that
have helped to incubate them. Indeed, the entire 'cities movement'—urban sanitation, community centers, parks and playgrounds, municipal health services, publicly aided housing for
the lower-income groups—was in large part a response to these
degrading conditions. There is nothing new in the present
urban situation except the startled public realization that
these evils are still with us, on a vaster scale, in a more difficult and desperate form, than ever before.

So far from underrating the human costs of metropolitan
congestion and disorganization as merely surface blemishes
on the otherwise healthy face of urban life, I had persistently
pointed out that they could not be treated by purely tempo-
rizing local remedies, since they were symptomatic of deeper
organic defects in our civilization. Until now, this point of
view has been dismissed as 'unrealistic' or 'pessimistic,' even
'apocalyptic,' by those planners, administrators, and social service workers who sought only to achieve such piecemeal
urban improvements as were acceptable and feasible without
any critical assessment and renovation of current institutions.

This refusal to look any deeper into the causes of urban deterioration, at a time when the vast surplus of energy, wealth,
and knowledge available should have produced a marked improvement of urban life, came out clearly in a common reaction to my book 'The Culture of Cities,' when it was published in 1938. This study of city development was, on the
whole, sufficiently hopeful and constructive to be well received. But one section was singled out by certain critics as

a dark subjective fantasy, inapplicable to contemporary urban culture. The offending section, 'A Brief Outline of Hell,' was one in which I had summed up the current disintegration of urban life and the probable fate of the city, *if these tendencies continued.* This summary was the restatement of a diagram devised by my old master, Patrick Geddes.

In this diagram Geddes traced the city's evolution through an upward curve, beginning with the polis and reaching a climax in the metropolis, or mother city: then through a downward curve, from megalopolis, handicapped by its own overgrowth, to parasitopolis and patholopolis, till it reached a terminal point: Necropolis, the city of the dead. Those who were eager to discredit Geddes' historic scheme apparently never read to the end of my chapter, where I dealt with 'Possibilities of Renewal' and 'Signs of Salvage.' For had they done so they could not so easily have charged me with holding that Geddes' purely theoretic terminal stage of megalopolitan overgrowth was either necessary or inevitable, still less irreparable.

On the contrary, I had pointed out that cities, not being biological organisms, have often shown signs of senile decrepitude at an early stage, or had undergone processes of renewal at a late moment of their existence, and thus got a new lease on life. And, so far from denying the value of large urban concentrations, I had said that as many as thirty great metropolitan centers might prove necessary to serve as a medium for world intercourse, and as containers of world culture. But the fact that I was aware of the pathological conditions undermining urban life caused many critics to regard me, by some quaint logic of their own, as a sworn enemy of the city.

At the end of 'The Culture of Cities' I had written, with a confidence that had somehow survived the First World War and the economic depression of the thirties: "Already, in the architecture and layout of the new community, one

sees the knowledge and discipline that the machine has provided turned to more vital conquests, more human consum-
mations. Already, in imagination and plan, we have tran-
scended the sinister limitations of the existing metropolitan
environment. We have much to unbuild, and much more to
build: but the foundations are ready. . . ."

The rhetoric now sounds hollow, yet what it suggested
seemed possible, even at that late moment. But the Second
World War blasted these naïve hopes. At the end of that war,
instead of laying the foundations for a cooperative civilization,
the citizens of the United States put themselves by passive
consent in the hands of a "military-scientific-industrial élite,"
to use President Eisenhower's accurate characterization. By
imposing a permanent state of war this 'élite' constructed a
vast megamachine, extravagantly supporting and inflating
with public funds an assemblage of private corporate megamachines, operating on the same principles, pursuing the
same ends.

This new strategy, based on fantasies of absolute power
and total control, placed the mass production of extermina-
tion-weapons above human welfare, and so laid the foundations, not for a life economy, but for an anti-life economy,
every part of which is elaborately oriented, as in the Egypt
of the Pyramid Age, toward death. Witness a regime that
spends fifty-seven per cent of its budget every year for military purposes, and has only six per cent available for education, health, and other social services.

But if my hopes for effective urban renovation in America
were soon buried, my grimmest apprehensions about the
urban future came true more swiftly than I could have anticipated. Only two years after 'The Culture of Cities' came
out, the central area of one city after another in Europe was
reduced to rubble by aerial bombardments: first, Warsaw and
Rotterdam, then London and Berlin, then minor cities in an
ever-spreading carnage. Not surprisingly, the harried sur-

vivors of this destruction and massacre, as first instituted by the Nazis, did not find my analysis unduly pessimistic: Necropolis lay all around them. Though my work may have had little visible influence in the United States, the Nazi Luftwaffe and its later Allied Air Force imitators had at least given authority to my most ominous predictions, though the invisible moral debacle proved worse—and more permanent—than the visible physical destruction.

Since all my thought about the city had been toward laying the social foundations for urban rebuilding on a regional scale in both old cities and new communities, by stimulating the regenerative and constructive processes already active in our civilization, those who had followed my work were not unprepared for this challenge. This explains why in Europe 'The Culture of Cities' had a far-reaching influence out of proportion, perhaps, to its immediate usefulness; for it was not merely eagerly studied and discussed in England, even while the bombs were dropping, but was used, I have been told, in the Underground architectural schools set up by planners in Poland, the Netherlands, and Greece, to teach the rising generation of planners a new conception of urban development. This situation, at once so menacing and yet so promising, was an incentive to further thinking on my own part.

In 1945, accordingly, in a critique of Abercrombie and Forshaw's plan for Greater London, I outlined specifically the further steps that should be taken—apart from the needed building of New Towns—to prevent the further congestion of London, and to make possible its rebuilding on a more human scale.* One of these steps was the local decentralization of governmental and business offices into the constituent Boroughs of London, in order to lessen the daily commuter traffic to Central London and restore the metropolis itself as

* See 'City Development: Studies in Disintegration and Renewal.' New York: Harcourt, Brace & World, Inc., 1945.

a place of residence, with amenities equal or superior to those of any suburb, and with greater facilities for human association, unpenalized by time-wasting, energy-depleting travel.

These specific proposals—the building of a series of New Towns, with the removal of suitable industries and bureaux from congested areas to relatively empty ones, the planning of neighborhoods to facilitate family life and autonomous communal activity, the creation of regional authorities to direct the work of urban development over a wider area—were, in fact, all carried on vigorously in Britain after 1947, with the exception of the last item; and even this necessary extension of urban authority, from the metropolis to the region, is now under active discussion. Whatever further initiatives and modifications may be needed, these measures have all proved practical; and in the case of the most disputed and disparaged proposal, that for a large-scale building of New Towns to provide both industrial and social advantages that no congested metropolis can offer, these towns have proved immensely successful—so successful, in fact, that canny speculators even attempted a 'take-over' of the oldest New Town, Letchworth, lured by the prospective increase in values. However modest my own contributions have been to this program, they at least antedated the postwar legislation and building.

But I have an arresting objective reason rather than a personal one for dwelling on these details. And this is to point out that despite Britain's immense constructive achievements in housing and planning and the industrial replenishment of underdeveloped areas, the same general disintegration and demoralization that has been going on in other parts of Western civilization has gone on there. This can no longer be attributed to postwar exhaustion. Three centuries of brutal exploitation, enslavement, destruction, and extermination have left their mark on civilized society. In England now, no less than in the United States, the same marks of urban disintegration have nevertheless appeared in massive quantities

—police corruption, marital promiscuity, random reproduction, overt racial and class antagonism, narcotic addiction, cultivated sadism, defiant criminality. The cult of anti-life, symbolically prefigured in much of the *avant-garde* art and music and drama of our time, is now spreading actively into every part of megalopolitan routine. Patholopolis and Parasitopolis, in fact, are fast establishing themselves as normal forms of the city, or, rather, as negative heavens: ideal environments for the psychotic, the criminal, the feckless, and the demoralized. The terminal stage in city development would seem nearer than ever.

Now, in all societies, the upbuilding and the breaking-down processes go on side by side, as they do in living organisms. As long as the constructive processes are dominant the organism survives, and to the extent that it has a margin of free energy and maintains its powers of self-direction and self-replication, the organism may flourish. What makes the present situation so singular and so threatening, is that the extra energies available, when not claimed by the production of lethal weapons and space rockets, are absorbed by the centralized bureaucratic and technological processes that are scattering the specialized parts of the city over the landscape. These individual urban groups and communities no longer have effective control over their own destinies. As a result, if anything goes wrong locally, the defective part, so to say, can no longer be repaired on the spot, but must be 'sent back to the factory.'

These facts have convinced me, and I think should convince any unbiassed observer, that the underlying causes for the recurrent outbreaks of violence among the disturbed minorities are not to be found solely in the sordid physical conditions of the cities themselves. While the recent demonstrations and revolts are partly accountable as a long-delayed reaction to poverty, slum housing, unemployment, social discrimination, police animosity, and segregation, the cities that have taken the most vigorous measures to deal with these evils, like Detroit and New Haven, have proved no more immune to attack than those that have been inert and indifferent. So, though the continued effort to turn the city into a comely, life-fulfilling environment is still one of the great collective tasks of our day, it is not a panacea. Such efforts will enhance the goodness of the city's goods; but they will not abate the evil of its real evils, since the latter are not under local control, nor have they only a local origin.

Those who now impatiently demand, or confidently prescribe, a heavy national investment in good housing or a 'model cities program,' as an antidote for demonstrative mass violence or as a curb to juvenile delinquency and adult criminality have not looked carefully enough at the evidence. If juvenile delinquency, for example, were mainly the result of poverty and alienation, why should it break out equally in spacious upper-class, white American suburbs? Certainly the common denominator here is not a bad physical environment. To ask the legislator or the planner to apply such immediate remedial measures to restore order is to ask for quackery. It is not just the city but the whole body politic that demands our attention. The advertiser's mirage of the Affluent Society may tease and torment the depressed minorities that are denied a full share of this affluence, but the reality itself appals the overfed, overstimulated, overcoddled young who are bored by its smooth lubricity.

These outbreaks are but local incidents in the vast eruptions and lava flows of collective violence that mark the last half century as the most violent age in history, with a record of wholesale destruction and merciless extermination that makes the most savage conquests of the Assyrians, the Tartars, and the Aztecs seem the work of diffident amateurs. What has been happening in our cities can be neither understood nor controlled except in the light of this larger example of insensate destruction. The progressive technology that the

Victorian exponents of industrialism looked upon as a certain means of assuring peace and plenty has been increasingly corrupted by its commitment to organized nihilism and aggression. Its greatest achievements—nuclear bombs, computers, radar, rockets, supersonic planes—are all by-products of war. Constant indoctrination in violence is the main office of our ubiquitous agents of mass communication and mass education. To believe that a single organ of the body politic, the city, can be cured of this disease while the same deadly cells flow through the entire bloodstream is to betray an ignorance of elementary physiology.

One thing should at least be obvious by now. Neither the past diagnoses of urban defects nor the positive regimens offered for urban health have proved competent or effective. So, though the kind of constructive planning I have advocated in these chapters is still viable, and indeed more urgent now than ever, it would be foolish to put forth these proposals as a means of averting future gang rumbles, 'race riots,' or Negro–Puerto Rican revolts. That situation has another dimension.

The need to make a fresh start on a more human basis is imperative, as many of the younger generation—at least those who have not 'dropped out'—plainly realize. But this fresh start must be made at many different points, and what is done in one area must, from the beginning, be coordinated with many similar efforts to restore effective human initiative and human goals. Perhaps the surest way of abating urban violence in the United States would be to set a striking national example of moral continence by the voluntary withdrawal of American forces from Vietnam. This could be more effective in reversing the currents of violence than even the dedication of the vast sums of money and energy wasted in military adventures to the imaginative replenishment of American life. But it might take a whole generation before even such an act of national self-discipline and moral atonement would make a positive contribution to comity and order.

At all events, to suppose that a fresh start can be made merely by pouring millions of dollars into the same public housing and urban renewal projects that have already proved so futile would be to nourish further illusions. This is like prescribing massive doses of penicillin to a patient in the terminal stages of a chronic disease—though, at an earlier moment, diet and surgery might have cured him. No quick miraculous recovery can now be hoped for; or, rather, the one conceivable miracle that might yet occur is that a sufficient number of people should recognize that every part of our life must be overhauled, including "the technology of Megalopolis" and the supporting ideology of an affluent society under an ever-expanding economy.

This larger theme is not one that I can handle even sketchily in a postscript. Many contemporary thinkers have at least made a beginning in diagnosing our present situation, from Spengler, Toynbee, and Schweitzer onward; and I have made an extensive contribution in a series of books, most recently in 'The City in History' and 'The Myth of the Machine.' In this final comment I shall only pose some of the difficult immediate problems that neither the dissident minorities, justifiably outraged and impatient, nor the once blindly complacent majority have so far been willing to face.

Let me return to the immediate issues before the Ribicoff Committee, indeed, before the whole country. My statement, necessarily a brief one, was open at one point to a serious misinterpretation; namely, that I seemed to be opposed to any large-scale expenditures by the national government on housing and urban renewal. I was able to clear this up in the subsequent discussion. *Eventually far vaster sums than are now being proposed will be needed: at least the equivalent of our present vast annual military expenditure.* When I said "Go Slow" I meant "Do not hastily pour tens of billions into any national program until the mistakes that had been made during the last quarter century have been analyzed and corrected, until new procedures and new plans have been worked out, until new agencies on a regional basis are created—indeed, until the whole program is completely rewritten, and more humane minds in architecture, planning, and administration are installed as leaders." Such leaders must be capable of both learning from and patiently teaching those groups for whom these projects are intended. Technological and architectural exhibitionists, more interested in abstract models and structures than in concrete human realities, have no place in such a program.

In short, "Go Slow" only meant: "Go slow in repeating and multiplying the present deadly stereotypes of urban renewal." This was all the more necessary because the best places to make a fresh start might be, not in the existing congested centers, but in other smaller centers, as I indicated in my earlier appreciation of the Regional Plan for the State of New York.

What made me specially apprehensive that we might, in desperation, be on the point of committing more crippling errors than in the past was Senator Ribicoff's published suggestion that a more humane type of housing, based on the neighborhood, could be done quickly and efficiently by calling upon "the technology of Megalopolis," for this was the very technology whose ruthless dynamism had already done so much to break down the coherent structure of the historic city. This technology is based upon accommodating human requirements to the demands of automation, mass production, maximum financial profit, and remote control: it would dismiss any human needs, desires, appetites, and sentiments that do not conform to its system of production as rigorously as it would dismiss an astronaut's normal freedoms in the design of a space capsule.

In a small way, as I pointed out, "the technology of Megalopolis" had already exhibited its characteristic absence of human dimensions in our current urban renewal projects. These projects were designed to satisfy the needs of the real-estate operator, the building contractor, the municipal administrator, the governmental bureaucracy—but without any respect for the traditions, the desires, or the hopes of the displaced slum dwellers, only a small part of whose numbers, even when qualified, have in fact consented to occupy the new buildings.

On this radical failure, the evidence was already at hand: in the new quarters sunshine, fresh air, modern plumbing, modest rents had cancelled out old physical defects: but this had not satisfied more basic human desires, eased anxieties, torments, resentments, or fostered self-respect, self-control, and autonomous action. Such residual autonomy as could be recaptured came mainly through vice and crime.

Sterile and humanly inadequate though current public housing has been, its failure to do justice to human needs would be nothing to what "the technology of Megalopolis" would achieve, under the aegis of such typical corporations as I satirically nicknamed 'General Space Housing, Incorporated.' The coming generation of architects, already conditioned to the neatly programmed world of computers, insulated from ecological realities, organic and human, has far worse designs in store. The draughting boards in architectural schools are nowadays full of anti-urban designs for nonliving: projects for heaping fifty thousand people, or even a million, into a single structure, now in the air, now submerged in water, now under a geodesic dome: highly ingenious structures, each as original as a space capsule, and as unfitted for permanent human habitation.

The one factor left out of these designs is precisely the factor that would reveal what is wrong with these go-go structures: the faintest concern for what kind of houses, neighborhoods, and cities people actually want to live in. There is no single answer to this problem, because even durable wants change socially and esthetically from generation to generation. But the one answer that is no answer at all is to ignore these wants in order to come up with a uniform solution that completely satisfies the criteria of systems analysis, mass production, and automation. To reduce the human factors to those a computer can handle is to eliminate the better half of life. The current catch phrase 'instant cities' is a perfect example of these sterile anti-historic conceptions put forward by under-dimensioned minds.

Whenever a poll has been taken to find out what kind of housing people really want, it turns out that an overwhelming majority vote for the single-family house. In a sense, the results of such polls have been anticipated in the wholesale exodus to the suburb; but even in a country like France, where city people have long been addicted to flats, an overwhelming majority in a recent poll—eighty per cent—voted for the single-family house.* Though the financial success of a series of Levittowns confirms the wisdom of heeding this demand, the needless esthetic dreariness and social monotony of these particular suburban enclaves—pace Herbert Gans!—show that even more humane intentions in mass production succumb to the limitations of the method itself.

To suppose that the abstract intelligence that proved so brilliant in developing nuclear reactors and supersonic planes will be equally successful in finding technological solutions that could be applied wholesale to the rebuilding of our cities is to misconceive the nature of the whole problem. There is little prospect of overcoming the errors that have been made,

* See the three volumes entitled 'Les Pavillonaires.' Paris: Centre de Recherche d'Urbanisme, 1966.

first in building and extending our cities, and now in repairing and reconstructing their more outmoded or outlived structures, unless we put the human condition first. This means that we must be ready, before legislating or planning, to revise the obsolete premises, financial, political, architectural, and technological—not least, technological—upon which our constructive efforts have so far been based. The kind of thinking needed is too important to be left to experts and specialists. In this situation we are all amateurs, for our life experience is more important than any technical expertise. Hence a solitary walk through an urban slum may provide more valuable insight than millions of Foundation dollars spent for statistically impeccable research.

The shudder of apprehension that followed the recent outbreaks of mass violence in many once-orderly American cities has perhaps produced a body of citizens at last willing to face and to cope with the cumulative anti-social realities. Since the ameliorative measures so far followed have proved ineffective, there is room for a more comprehensive view of the urban situation. and for more far-reaching constructive proposals, based on deeper insight into our whole civilization. We are faced not only with the task of physical renovation, hygienic or esthetic: we have the burden of offering a valid alternative to a kind of existence that the neglected and the deprived are no longer reconciled to, because they suspect that something better is possible, indeed, almost within their reach, but arbitrarily withheld from them. On these essential human concerns, as I remarked to the Ribicoff Committee on this matter, Studs Terkel's 'Division Street' or Oscar Lewis' 'La Vida' have more to teach us than our multiplying Institutes for Urban Research.

Now I have no special competence to analyze the immediate social factors that have brought on the current eruptions of violence which make the task of urban improvement so pressing. Here I must trust the abundant testimony of those who have been in close daily contact with the minority groups concerned. But I know enough of the history of modern metropolises, like my own city of New York, to realize that poor sanitation, congested, bug-ridden, rat-infested dwellings, and desperate poverty are not in themselves sufficient to promote more than comparatively minor hoodlumism and gangsterism, since all these conditions had been chronic for almost a century among a diversity of white immigrant populations without provoking comparable riots.

To go deeper into this immediate situation we must, I suggest, distinguish between three aspects, only one of which is open to immediate rectification. We must first separate out the problems that are soluble with the means we have at hand: this includes such immediate measures as vermin control, improved garbage collection, cheap public transportation, new schools and hospitals and health clinics. Second, those that require a new approach, new agencies, new methods, whose assemblage will require time, even though the earliest possible action is urgent. And finally, there are those that require a reorientation in the purposes and ultimate ideals of our whole civilization—solutions that hinge on a change of mind, as far-reaching as that which characterized the change from the medieval religious mind to the modern scientific mind. Ultimately, the success of the first two changes will hinge upon this larger—and, necessarily, later—transformation. So, far from looking to a scientifically oriented technology to solve our problems, we must realize that this highly sophisticated dehumanized technology itself now produces some of our most vexatious problems, including the unemployment of the unskilled.

Let me touch on the hardest aspect first, for though the goal indicated is remote, a beginning should be made at once. In the most general terms, this basic problem is the control of power, quantification, automatism, aimless dynamism. That problem has become acute in our age, because scientific technology has colossally magnified the amount of energy that advanced industrial societies command. But even more, it has become difficult because in our overreliance upon purely intellectual enlightenment we have allowed earlier systems of moral, political, and social control to break down, and have transferred systematic discipline and order to the very corporate organizations that must be brought once more under human direction, if they are to pursue human ends.

Once the traditional system of moral restraints and personal inhibitions has dissolved in any society, as completely as has happened during the last half century throughout the Western world, the warfare of each against all, which Thomas Hobbes falsely pictured as the original state of primitive man, becomes more than a theoretic possibility: it has, in fact, become a demonstrable reality. And unfortunately, the very institution that Hobbes relied upon to put down this internecine strife, the Leviathan state, is now the chief offender in flouting law and order, in extending the sphere of violence and magnifying all the possibilities of destruction and extermination. In effect, the policeman is the chief criminal, and his bad example has proved infectious.

There is not a single human problem posed in our cities, as between White Power and Black Power, that was not prefigured in the last three centuries of conquest, colonization, enslavement, exploitation, and extermination; and there is not a difficulty faced by the United Nations, seeking to achieve a balance between tribalism and universalism, between nationalism and cosmopolitanism, that will not have to be worked out in the smallest neighborhood.

The forces that have violated the elemental moralities and that now threaten all life on this planet will not be easily or quickly brought under control. But in so far as command of these menacing forces means imposing salutary inhibitions, restraints, prudences, it is open to every sane, responsible person to make a beginning in his own life. Only those who have lost respect for the principle of autonomy may either 'go with' the forces of disintegration or express their disillusioned dissent merely by 'dropping out.'

With regard to the immediate urban situation, one must qualify the boldest measures by a realization that they must overcome a massive inertia: indeed, they must go against the dominant forces in our civilization, even those forces in science and technology which, if we eventually emerge from this Age of Violence, may be at last put to more admirable human uses. But our first duty here is to recognize the symptoms of decay, and not to cooperate further with the forces of disintegration. If the Romans had learned that lesson, at the moment when they boasted of their unchallengeable power and affluence under the Pax Romana, they might not so soon have lost their grip.

Unfortunately, even some of the urban problems that would seem to be immediately soluble, once we accepted the high price of a solution, are not quite so simple as reformers have hitherto believed. To begin with, consider desegregation. The mass migration of Negroes and Puerto Ricans into Northern communities has turned once-diffused minorities into concentrated metropolitan enclaves that will soon, if present tendencies continue, constitute a hapless proletarian majority. No open housing or school busing can overcome the isolation and resultant self-segregation that sheer numbers have produced. Before any urban renewal program can be instituted for the benefit of given racial or cultural groups, the first question that must be answered, by the minorities themselves, is whether they are willing to move out of their present neighborhoods, even if this means scattering widely in a mixed community, and losing some of their present identity and cohesion.

If they choose to remain in numbers where they are, they commit themselves to continued segregation: not merely to segregation but also to congestion, and, along with congestion, to insufficient recreation areas and overcrowded health and hospital services, too. But if they choose to move far enough away to invite the provision for good housing, new industrial or agricultural opportunities, and stable neighborhood facilities, they will become a part of New Towns, suburbs, or growing rural communities; and they will, like any other newcomers, perhaps need a generation before they are fully integrated, no matter how faithfully their legal status as citizens is secured.

This decision cannot be made in local City Halls, still less in Washington; for only those concerned have the right to make it, after the way has been sufficiently opened by experimental planning and building to make a genuine choice possible. Yet no intelligent program of urban renewal can be framed until this alternative has been built into the program itself. Only one thing can be predicted: if the immigration to big cities and the metropolitan birth rate continues at the past high levels, there will be no alternative to organizing dispersal and relocation, both regionally and nationally, into smaller communities. Fortunately, a rational program for re-settlement—what was called in the Preface 'the Fourth Migration'—is still an open option, more open now than ever, because so many industries and business organizations have been, during the last two decades, sporadically moving away from the metropolis.

But the underlying human factors are still too delicate and uncertain to admit quick decisions. The policy of dispersal now quietly favored by educated middle-class Negroes in professions and businesses, thanks partly to Morris Milgrim's initiative in providing open suburban housing, would leave the metropolitan ghettos without leadership; and so, worse off socially than before. Dispersal would also have the effect of undermining the sub-culture that has developed in Harlem and other major metropolitan centers: yet this sub-culture, through its expression in music, the dance, and the theater, is one of the chief sources of the Negro's and the Puerto Rican's individuality and self-respect. (Certainly, something was lost to the once-thriving Yiddish sub-culture by its voluntary removal to improved living quarters away from the Lower East Side.) By now there is an activist Negro minority—how large is anyone's guess—that would resist such assimilation. Neither choice is clear and easy: so both must be kept open.

But if the slums and the blighted areas where the minorities now live were to be rehabilitated for the existing overcrowded population, this would mean continuing to build superslums, whether on the open high-rise pattern favored by municipal authorities, or the dense housing on crowded lots, without provisions for sunlight, open air, or visual amenity, favored by Jane Jacobs, in which streets would remain the chief play areas, though filled, as now, with dangerous traffic. Neither the frying pan nor the fire is attractive; for housing designed at three hundred to four hundred people to the acre—to say nothing of the greater number some favor—is not conducive to health, neighborly cooperation, or adequate child care. The slum dwellers' justifiable resentment against arbitrary uprooting and his unwillingness to return to the kind of inhuman high-rise apartments offered has now been fully demonstrated; and to go on building in this fashion would be foolish.

The core of any adequate neighborhood housing program should be, above all, the provision for the health, security, education, and adult care of young children; and except perhaps in health, all high-rise projects are, by their very scale and impersonality, an alien and even hostile environment for the young, since, apart from organized playground games, it leaves the majority of children such little scope for their own activities. In these new quarters, even the mildest outbreak of juvenile adventure or wanton mischief becomes all too quickly labelled as juvenile delinquency—on which terms, Robert

Frost once confessed to me, he probably would have spent his own boyhood in San Francisco in a reformatory.

Lacking both normal parental disciplines and normal outlets for defiance of adults, something worse now takes place. One of the most sinister features of the recent urban riots has been the presence of roaming bands of children, armed with bottles and stones, taunting and defying the police, smashing windows and looting stores. But this was only an intensification of the window-breakings, knifings, and murders that have for the past twenty years characterized "the spirit of youth in the city streets."

As I pointed out earlier, juvenile delinquency is not confined to a depressed minority living in slums: it is also an upper- or middle-class white, suburban phenomenon. But in both cases it seems to point to two underlying conditions: an idle, empty, purposeless existence, and a total breakdown of parental guidance and communal discipline. In both groups we find, among the younger adults, that marital promiscuity and parental irresponsibility have undermined the basic unit of all stable societies—the family. The fact that, according to current estimates, in the Negro metropolitan community half the children cannot identify their fathers, not merely deprives them of the supervision and example of the male parent, but probably also undermines their own sense of personal loyalty and identity.

This family disintegration can only in part be attributed to bad housing. Unfortunately, it has been worsened by what was, by intention, a humane achievement in legislation: the provision of welfare relief to mothers solely responsible for their children's support. This legislation turns out, in the case of husbandless mothers, too often to be a subsidy to sexual irresponsibility and an invitation to chronic idleness. The demoralizing effects of this remedy come out in the disturbing, if perhaps apocryphal, story of the little girl brought up under such conditions who, when asked what work she intended to do when she grew up, replied that she wanted to draw. Inquiry revealed that what she wanted to 'draw' was not pictures, but a welfare check, as her mother did.

Obviously, the high rate of unemployment among Negroes and Puerto Ricans, and the lower wages and poorer conditions offered needier groups, both colored and white, discourages stable marriages, and perhaps vitiates male parental feeling as well. But to think of correcting this condition solely by rent subsidies, that is, in effect, more welfare checks, or by better physical housing, is to overlook the equal need for active responsive cooperation by those concerned. Promiscuity cannot be legally suppressed: but marital stability and parental prudence could be honorably rewarded, not only by year-round employment, but by family wages to the fathers of families, as in France; financed in the United States as Social Security is financed—with bonuses that would cease after the third child. This lies outside the scope of urban renewal; but no adequate renewal program will be possible until the restoration of the basic family constellation is taken as one of the essential goals of adequate housing.

On this matter, if one can safely accept a recent report, the example of Hong Kong is pertinent, for it would seem to show that moral factors count for more than purely physical ones, as soon as a certain minimum standard of sanitation has been achieved. In that oppressively congested metropolis, high-rise housing has been provided for the lowest-income groups at much higher densities than any housing authority has dared to establish in America. About the best that can be said for these quarters is that they are ratproof, fireproof, sanitary. Since the parents and the older children must work, the very young are habitually locked in their flats all day. On the surface, these grim conditions would seem to intensify all the domestic difficulties and juvenile disturbances that characterize high-rise housing for lower-income groups in America.

But however far from ideal the conditions for family life

are in the municipal tenements of Hong Kong, they are partly redeemed, it would seem, by two factors not present in contemporary American communities: one is that the Chinese cult of the family still prevails, with the young conditioned to respect their elders and accept their authority, while the parents shoulder their responsibility; and the other is that, under bitter pressure of necessity, every member of the family, old and young, has daily work to do. Thus the young are demoralized neither by the breakdown of the family nor by the absence of active duties and serious tasks; nor yet are their parents haunted by such dreams of effortless affluence as would make their present poverty harder to bear. Even Hong Kong's sweatshop labor seems less demoralizing than total idleness. To protect the young from overidleness has now become as important as it was once to protect them from overwork. To this end both child labor legislation and trade union regulations need to be judiciously overhauled.

One would have reservations about this Hong Kong report, but for the fact that it is confirmed by earlier American experience. Much the same conditions for stability prevailed in American cities among the older immigrant groups; for they were held together by Old World village loyalties, by family closeness, by religious precept and ritual: such hopes as they cherished for a better future were based upon their own foresight, thrift, and self-education. The physical conditions of life in the nineteenth-century slums were often as bad as those in Harlem today and much worse than those in Watts: but there were strong moral counterweights that have now been lost through the more general dissolution of human values.

I have said enough to indicate that neither public housing, slum clearance, nor neighborhood rehabilitation, even when done along more human lines than those now in evidence in urban renewal areas, will suffice by themselves to overcome the internal disorders of the city. Those disorders are symptoms of a wider moral breakdown in our whole civilization; and though good planning, like pure water, is essential to urban health, it is not any more than water a prescription for curing disease. Anything worthy to be called urban renewal today must recapture in concrete form many of the values that our affluent, remote-controlled, electronically massaged society has lost. And there is no urban program that one might offer to minority groups that is not just as imperatively applicable to the rest of society. In that sense, there is no Negro problem and no Puerto Rican problem: there is only a human problem.

On this subject we should do well to heed Dr. C. G. Jung's observations about his own life. In his autobiography, 'Memories, Dreams, Reflections,' Jung recalled a difficult period when he was in a psychotic state, at the mercy of his unconscious. What kept him from going completely to pieces was his consciousness that he was an identifiable person, with a family to support, that he was a member of a respected profession, living in a particular house, in an equally familiar and recognizable city, where he had daily duties to perform. By clinging to these reassuring evidences of stability, he was able to resist the internal forces of disintegration.

All of these vital conditions for social continuity and personal integrity have been breaking down in both the central metropolis and its outlying areas; and they have most completely broken down among the lowest-income groups. This unfortunate minority lacks regular work and the self-respect that comes from performing such work: their immediate neighborhood and city have undergone and are still undergoing abrupt structural changes, for both bad and good, that erase their familiar social patterns and destroy their sense of belonging, so that their own selves become so much scattered debris in the larger demolition process. Neither family nor property nor vocational respect nor an earned income nor an identifiable home helps the segregated or displaced minority to resist further internal disintegration.

In analyzing the conditions that saved him from disruption, Jung demonstrated the unique advantage of the historic city over the unstable, incoherent, haphazardly dispersed Megalopolis. In that act, he put his finger likewise on the essential requisites for overcoming the forces that have been disintegrating and dehumanizing both our cities and our civilization.